# THE RELATIONSHIP BETWEEN LIBERALISM AND CONSERVATISM

*To my mother and the memory of my father.*

# The Relationship between Liberalism and Conservatism

## Parasitic, competitive or symbiotic?

ANN BOUSFIELD
*University of Luton*

Routledge
Taylor & Francis Group
LONDON AND NEW YORK

First published 1999 by Ashgate Publishing

Reissued 2018 by Routledge
2 Park Square, Milton Park, Abingdon, Oxon, OX14 4RN
52 Vanderbilt Avenue, New York, NY 10017

*Routledge is an imprint of the Taylor & Francis Group, an informa business*



Publisher's Note
The publisher has gone to great lengths to ensure the quality of this reprint but points out that some imperfections in the original copies may be apparent.



A Library of Congress record exists under LC control number: 99072662

ISBN 13: 978-1-138-35540-8 (hbk)
ISBN 13: 978-1-138-35403-6 (pbk)
ISBN 13: 978-0-429-42766-4 (ebk)

# Contents

# Acknowledgements

This book originated as my PhD thesis. Such a work cannot be completed successfully by any individual without dedicated support from others. I have been especially fortunate in this respect. Without the unstinting efforts of my two supervisors, Dr. Bob Brecher of Brighton University and Ms. Susan Khin Zaw of the Open University, this book would never have been completed. They not only provided me challenging and supportive academic advice; they also proved to be valued and loyal friends during particularly difficult personal circumstances. I would like to take this opportunity to offer them my heartfelt thanks.

I would also like to thank my friends and colleagues at the Department of Politics and Public Policy at the University of Luton for their encouragement and support.

# 1 Introduction

Much current debate within liberalism has arisen from the division of liberal allegiance between 'deontological' liberalism (represented by Rawls, Nozick, Dworkin and Hayek) and 'communitarian' liberalism (represented by Sandel, Taylor and Rorty). In particular, controversy has raged over different interpretations and theoretical justifications of the characteristically liberal claim to *neutrality* between competing conceptions of the good. This book, in contrast, will argue that liberalism is not in fact neutral between different conceptions of the good. On the contrary, liberal 'neutrality' actually depends on a conception of the good that is based on a specifically liberal understanding of what human beings are, and hence of what their flourishing consists in. This book will examine the possibility that the political problems facing liberalism are no more than the symptom of liberalism's failure to establish that its conception of the good is indeed neutral, arguing that the bid to establish liberalism's neutrality between competing conceptions of the good ultimately undermines any effort to establish a workable normative foundation for liberalism.

Developments in the thought of John Rawls, the leading liberal philosopher of the late 20th century, indicate the seriousness of these problems. In response to critiques, such as those of Walzer and Sandel,[1] Rawls has shifted his position, most notably in *Political Liberalism*,[2] to one where the neutrality claim is specifically limited to rational procedures and the claim of liberalism to universal applicability on the basis of its supposed value-neutrality is dropped. In one sense dropping universalism means that the liberal claim to neutrality does not need to be comprehensive, a point Rawls in effect concedes in *Political Liberalism*:

> [P]olitical liberalism assumes that, for political purposes, a plurality of reasonable yet incompatible comprehensive doctrines is the normal result of the exercise of human reason within the framework of the free institutions of a constitutional democratic regime. Political liberalism also supposes that a reasonable comprehensive doctrine does not reject the essentials of a democratic regime. Of course, a society may also

[1] Michael Walzer, 'Philosophy and Democracy', *Political Theory*, 9, 1981, pp379-99, and *Spheres of Justice* (Blackwell, Oxford, 1983); Michael Sandel, 'The Procedural Republic and the Unencumbered Self', *Political Theory*, 12 (February 1984), pp81-96.

[2] John Rawls, *Political Liberalism* (Columbia University Press, New York, 1993).

> contain unreasonable and irrational, and even mad, comprehensive doctrines. In their case the problem is to contain them so that they do not undermine the unity and justice of society.[3]

Rawls here is granting that within a liberal polity, ethical agreement about the foundations of a liberal society is improbable, and radical disagreement possible. But instead of invoking liberal neutrality towards the politics of illiberal minorities, he suggests such illiberal minorities should be contained in order to prevent them undermining liberal values. This cannot be a neutral position. In effect Rawls, in *Political Liberalism*, recommends the type of prescriptions advocated by Richard Bellamy, who seeks to develop a form of liberalism stripped of ethical pretensions.[4] However the problem of liberal non-neutrality extends far more widely than Rawls and Bellamy: it is endemic throughout the history of liberalism, as this book will show. Moreover, liberalism is not only not neutral about forms of the good life, the point conceded by Rawls in *Political Liberalism*: in the end it resorts to conservative justifications of the liberal order. For example, again in *Political Liberalism*, Rawls recognises the limits placed on political philosophy by historical conditions and by political practice:

> I also hold that the most appropriate design of a constitution is not a question to be settled by considerations of political philosophy alone, but depends on understanding the scope and limits of political and social institutions and how they can be made to work effectively. These things depend on history and how institutions are arranged.[5]

Far from calling on liberalism's usual preference of reason over tradition, Rawls here seems to suggest that cautious pragmatism is a better guide to constitutional design than bold applications of theory - a typically conservative position.

The argument of this book may be outlined as follows. Liberalism takes itself to be neutral regarding conceptions of the good. Thus, liberals claim (most famously in the case of Rawls) that the 'right is prior to the good'.[6] Moreover, because of the neutrality with regard to the good implied by the right being prior to the good, liberalism typically maintains that it is both genuinely autonomy-respecting as to ethics, and universally applicable as to politics. But these claims are not valid; liberalism's own purported neutrality

---

[3] ibid., ppxviii-xix.

[4] Richard Bellamy, *Liberalism and Modern Society* (Polity Press, Cambridge, 1992).

[5] John Rawls, *Political Liberalism*, pp408-9.

[6] John Rawls, *A Theory of Justice* (Oxford University Press, Oxford, 1973), pp30-1.

is itself (part of) a specific historically-conditioned conception of the good. For the individual human being at the heart of liberalism is indeed a *liberal* individual, that is, a specifically liberal conception of individuality; similarly, the autonomy of these individuals that liberalism claims to respect is *liberal* autonomy. But these conceptions, which form the essential content of liberal theory, incorporate substantive values, which can be shown to be a product of specific historical circumstances. This has profound implications for liberal theory, producing tensions within it, some of which have been recognised to some extent by some liberals. But none - not even Rorty who has explicitly disavowed foundational Enlightenment liberalism[7] - have fully developed the implications of liberalism's inconsistencies. The most important of these implications is that liberalism, to the extent that it can be justified at all, can be justified, only on conservative grounds. For the result of liberalism's ambivalence about neutrality is that in the end, all liberals can do by way of justification is assert the primacy of liberal values, not on the basis of a coherent rational foundation, but on the basis that liberals have found much to enjoy and value in them, that they are their own values, that because of this they are the foundation a way of life that liberals are determined to protect, and that, finally, experience shows them to be the least repressive form of political arrangements so far discovered. Such a justification suggests that liberalism has closer historical and conceptual links with conservatism than has traditionally been supposed. A justification of liberal values which properly acknowledged this would, first, take seriously the culturally specific nature of liberalism and recognise the limitations for meta-theory that that imposes; and second, recognise that cultural and historical specificity compels liberals to distinguish certain values ahead of others, in other words compels them to relinquish any claim to neutrality between competing conceptions of the good.

This is an extremely contentious argument, of course, and not least if we examine the history of liberalism. After all, that liberalism depends on a conservative axiology is contrary to what most liberals believe liberalism to be. Liberalism originated from ideas that emerged in the scientific revolution and the Enlightenment in the 17th and 18th centuries. It was predicated on the belief that, by the use of reason, people could be emancipated from the shackles of religious and political superstition. Liberalism as it originated was the antithesis of tradition and superstition. All established institutions and procedures were to be considered in the light of reason, to discover whether they promoted the human good or human liberty. Within liberalism,

[7] Richard Rorty, *Contingency, Irony and Solidarity* (Cambridge University Press, Cambridge, 1989), see pxv.

as it came to be formulated, there could be no presumption in favour of an institution because it had existed for centuries; the only defence of such institutions was that they could be justified by reason. It was, at least in intention, profoundly anti-conservative. But that intention could not be realised.

Since liberalism's emergence as a self-conscious philosophy it has been founded on a particular view of how people are, from which claims about the social and political obligations of individuals are derived. In this liberalism's philosophical strategy is no different from that of any other political philosophy, or indeed from certain religious creeds. Where liberalism differed radically from what had gone before was in its claim that as a view of man, and as a political doctrine, it claimed to be both universal, in the sense that it applied to all men at all times, and more importantly was grounded not in faith or prejudice, but was developed by reason from claims about the real nature of man and society. The basis of the liberal view of man (*sic*) is that he has rights by virtue of his essential human nature. I shall argue that the rights that liberals claim individuals should have are not prior to the political practices of liberal societies; rather they are products of those practices. In effect, liberal individuals themselves and the rights that they claim are not universal to all times and places as liberals argue, but are abstracted from their context in existing liberal societies.

Kenneth Minogue percipiently describes the liberal view:

> [T]he liberal conception of man has all the beauties of a child's mecccano set; from the basic device of man as a desiring creature, any kind of human being, from a Leonardo da Vinci to a Lizzie Borden, can be constructed ... For a desire being a vague and ambiguous conception, permits of endless modifications. The movement from the desired to the desirable launches an ethics of improvement in terms of which any moral term can be reinterpreted ... But if one strips off from this abstract figure [the liberal 'individual'] each of the components ... what then remains? Only the creature who was born free and yet everywhere is in chains, a faceless and characterless abstraction, a set of dangling desires with nothing to dangle from... Such an abstract figure could not possibly choose between different objects of desire.[8]

What Minogue is pointing to here is the central weakness of the liberal conception. It is all too easy to see in Minogue's 'abstract figure' of a 'set of dangling desires with nothing to dangle from', the disembodied,

[8] Kenneth Minogue, *The Liberal Mind* (Methuen, London, 1963), pp52-3.

unencumbered selves in Rawls's original position[9] whose good can be understood only in terms of getting as much of what they want as is possible and fair. This attenuated conception of human nature cannot independently support the substantive ethics and axiology which in fact underlie liberalism's claims to neutrality. It is a flaw that goes to the heart of liberalism and it cannot be remedied within a liberal paradigm.

Let me reiterate that familiar paradigm. Liberty is something whose value we can acknowledge whatever our views on how it should be exercised, just as we can recognise the value of money irrespective of what we want to purchase. Take for example two people who disagree fundamentally and in every particular about how life is to be spent, an ascetic and a hedonist. Each has his or her own conception of the good life, in the light of which he or she regards the other as at best profoundly mistaken. Each will thus regard the necessity of living a life in the preferred manner of the other as an evil. Consequently, they will regard their freedom to pursue their own conception of the good as of supreme value. This argument works whatever an individual's conception of the good is, provided the individuals in question are rational and believe that the satisfaction of their own wants constitutes a moral imperative of itself. 'My good', whatever it may be and provided it does not harm others, requires me to accept 'your good' whatever it may be, provided it does not harm others. Everyone, no matter what else they disagree on, provided they are rational, can agree on this - which is why John Rawls, for example, regards liberty as a primary good.[10] So, because liberals believe that liberty is a necessary condition for all individuals to pursue what they see is good, they claim that it is - and what is more that it ought to be - neutral between competing conceptions of the good. Neutrality is of fundamental importance to liberalism because it is only by political arrangements being neutral between competing conceptions of the good that the state protects the liberty of individuals. Once the state begins to favour one version of the good ahead of another it becomes coercive of individuals who do not adhere to that version of the good; and so, to that extent, it deprives them of their liberty. As Jeffrey Reiman succinctly puts it:

> ... liberalism contends that living one's own life according to one's own rational judgements is a condition of living a good life; that promotion

[9] John Rawls, *Theory of Justice*, Chapter 3.
[10] ibid., p396.

of the ability to so live is a moral ideal that all societies should foster and the right of individuals to so live (as far as this is compatible with all individuals being able to do so) is a right that all human beings have a duty to respect.[11]

As is commonly argued, neutrality between the competing conceptions of the good of individuals presents liberalism with two related problems, however. First, if liberalism is to be wholly neutral between competing conceptions of the good it can offer no moral reason for preferring liberal values ahead of any other. The second problem for liberalism is related to the first. If man is fundamentally a desiring animal then either liberalism must be completely neutral between any wants that individuals have, as long as they do not harm others, or (and this is where the neutrality of liberalism breaks down) it must offer a hierarchy of wants, some of which are perceived by liberals as being more valuable or acceptable than others. Only liberalisms with explicit developmental dimensions, like those of Mill, Hobhouse or Green, consciously offer a ranking of wants: for example, Mill's notion of the higher and lower pleasures. Where all liberals depart from their neutrality, whether they advocate a developmental view of the individual or not, is in how they deal with challenges to the liberal order from within or without, in particular the rejection of liberal individualist values for collective social values, whether such rejection stems from traditional religious or nationalist groups. Hence, the real challenge to liberal neutrality comes not from a hierarchical ranking of wants *per se*, but from the survival, and indeed flourishing, both within and outside liberal states, of illiberal groups. Under these circumstances, despite protestations to the contrary, liberals invariably rank those wants commensurable with liberalism ahead of those that are incommensurable.

My purpose is to examine the ideas of key thinkers from the discrete traditions of liberalism - Mill, Hayek, Hobhouse, Green and contemporary advocates of a liberal good such as Richard Rorty and William Galston - in order to show, first, that the criticism of these traditions in terms of their not being neutral in respect of the good, despite their professed adhesion to such neutrality, is justified; and second that such criticism does not go far enough for it is not only not neutral, it is conservative. Here the work of John Stuart Mill is crucial, both as the exemplar of liberalism and as a figure who straddles two of the three traditions. Moreover, Mill is important because, despite his position as the leading figure in the liberal pantheon, the tensions

[11] Jeffrey Reiman, *Critical Moral Liberalism* (Rowman & Littlefield Publishers Inc., Lanham, Maryland, USA, 1997), px.

and contradictions within liberalism, which I will explore, are clearly apparent in his thought, we see them, for instance, in Mill's incipient historicism and the developmental nature of the individuality he espouses. Hayek by contrast attempts to restate classical liberalism by placing it upon empirically secure foundations. His claim to neutrality is therefore fundamentally an empirical one. Liberalism is neutral because it reflects the world as it is, not how we would like it to be. For this reason, as well as his economic libertarianism, I believe Hayek is a more representative figure of the libertarian strand in contemporary liberalism than, say, Robert Nozick whose adoption of neo-Lockean theory places him firmly in the classical liberal camp. Finally, some consideration will be given to the (allegedly) explicitly liberal conceptions of the good present in the ideas of thinkers who attempt to provide liberalism with a moral foundation; this is a strand of liberal thought which began with the social liberalism of Hobhouse and Green and is represented in contemporary liberal discourse, and in this book, by William Galston, Jeffrey Reiman and Tibor Machan. Also included in this group is the anomalous figure of Richard Rorty who attempts to discover a moral dimension to liberalism while rejecting the search for rationalist normative foundations. This last group is crucial because its members attempt to discover liberal solutions to precisely the same problems created by liberalism's lack of convincing moral foundations that are being considered here. It is therefore vital to the argument being presented in this book to show that such attempts are ineffective, and that they do indeed degenerate into conservative justifications of liberalism.

Finally, I shall deal with Rawls only in outline for there is already a wealth of literature about his neutrality, or lack of it. Moreover, the direction he has recently pursued, especially in *Political Liberalism*[12] brings him very close indeed to the position of Rorty who I discuss in chapter 5; and the relationship between communitarian minded objections to his 'unencumbered individual' and my argument as regards conservatism is also something I shall return to in chapter 5. But a brief consideration here of the deontological liberal position, as exemplified by Rawls, will illustrate the nature of the tensions within liberal theory which I wish to explore in this book. Deontological liberalism attempts to solve the problem of moral pluralism in contemporary society. It attempts to find ways in which the state can treat individuals with equal respect and not seek to impose one particular conception of the good on them. This is not a new claim within the liberal tradition. The claim to neutrality goes back at least as far as Mill's 'harm

[12] John Rawls, *Political Liberalism*.

principle' as it was formulated in *On Liberty*.[13] Liberals should allow every individual, or group of individuals, to pursue their own conception of the good provided they do not harm others because liberalism itself has no conception of the good. Rather, it exists to promote the good freely chosen by individuals. In order to achieve this end, liberals do not claim that their 'good' is neutrality, rather they claim they have no 'good' at all. Rawls, at least in a *Theory of Justice*,[14] attempts to demonstrate this absence of a liberal good by means of a thought experiment. He begins his argument with the assumption that an individual's good consists in getting as much of what they want as is reasonably possible. To get what we want we need freedom, resources and power. Rawls places all individuals behind a 'veil of ignorance' where individuals do not know what their material or social position will be within society; and no one is aware of their physical or mental capacities.[15] Rawls argues that behind such a 'veil of ignorance' it is possible to define a set of primary goods which are wanted by any person, whatever their own conception of the good might be. Rawls uses a device called a 'thin' theory of the good[16] to explain the issue. All rational persons have 'thick' or developed theories of the good, and these are often incommensurable. That is to say, people have a plan of life, an idea of what they would like to be or what they would like to achieve in life, and of their own nature, personality and purposes. However, this does not mean that individuals cannot agree on a 'thin' theory of the good, which will consist of that range of primary goods which are required by any rational person in order to pursue their own developed or 'thick' theory of the good: 'primary goods ... are things, which it is supposed a rational man wants whatever else he wants. Regardless of what an individual's rational plans are in detail, it is assumed that there are various things that he would prefer more of rather than less.'[17]

Rawls contends that while conceptions of the good differ radically, they do not do so in terms of the necessary conditions for framing and executing a person's plan of life. In this sense Rawls suggests that individuals can arrive at a definition of basic goods to be distributed in society which is *neutral* in respect of specific human purposes because it is the same for all such purposes. For Rawls these goods must include rights and liberties,

[13] John Stuart Mill, *On Liberty* (Penguin, Harmondsworth, 1974), p68.
[14] John Rawls, *A Theory of Justice*, Rawls's position has changed considerably over the years. Since the publication of *Political Liberalism* he has adopted a more historicist position with respect to liberalism. However, despite reinterpretations, *A Theory of Justice* remains the definitive exposition of deontological liberalism.
[15] ibid., pp136-42.
[16] ibid., pp395-99.
[17] ibid., p92.

opportunities and powers, income and wealth and a sense of self-respect. Rights and liberties are necessary conditions for pursuing a conception of the good, because without various sorts of freedoms guaranteed by constitutional rights individuals will not be in a position to pursue their own conception of the good in society; without material resources individuals will not be able to implement their plans of life; and without a sense of self-respect an individual's plan of life will be meaningless and their conception of the good will not seem important.

But the problem with Rawls's argument, and indeed the arguments of other deontological liberals, is that his 'thin' theory of the good *cannot* be neutral because it depends on a notion of the self that is itself derived from liberal theory; and which is the substantive basis of that 'thin' theory of the good. Referring to the principles of justice, Rawls says:

> [T]he argument for the two principles of justice does not assume that the parties have particular ends, but only that they desire certain primary goods. These are things that it is rational to want whatever else one wants. Thus given human nature, wanting them is part of being rational.[18]

In Rawls's view then, our 'thin' good consists in being in a position to get as much of what we want as is possible. Justice consists in distributing these 'thin' goods impartially or neutrally: Rawls's liberal theory of justice depends on neutrality between competing individuals. But all this depends on a conception of the individual as a self to whom getting what one wants is the only good.

I shall be arguing, further, that, where there is a conflict between wants which do not contravene liberal values and wants which do contravene liberal values liberals inevitably choose the liberal; and that these values turn out to be barely, if at all, distinguishable, from conservative ones. To put it schematically: what grounds do liberals offer for this preference? Compare Mill's prohibition of the right of individuals to sell themselves into slavery[19] with William Galston's restrictions on the limits of diversity within liberal states.[20] Mill rejects the right of individuals to sell themselves into slavery because the reason for not interfering with a person's conscious actions - except where he or she might harm others - is out of consideration for the

[18] ibid., p253.
[19] Mill, *On Liberty*, pp172-3.
[20] William Galston, 'Value Pluralism and Political Liberalism', Report from the Institute for Philosophy and Public Policy, Volume 16, No. 2, Spring 1996. http://www.puaf.umd.edu/ippp/galston.htm 30/11/97.

individual's liberty. The very act of choosing is evidence that what an individual chooses is desirable. However, if an individual sells him - or herself as a slave he or she relinquishes their liberty for all time. The individual thus negates the very justification for not interfering in an individual's self-regarding actions. The individual is no longer free and instead is in a position where there is no longer a presumption in his or her favour of allowing the individual to choose their self-regarding acts. Individuals cannot be allowed to choose to become slaves because by choosing in this way they deny the reason for allowing individuals liberty in the first place.

> By selling himself for a slave, he [an individual] abdicates his liberty; he forgoes any future use of it beyond that single act. He therefore defeats, in his own case, the very purpose which is the justification of allowing him to dispose of himself. He is no longer free, but is thenceforth in a position which has no longer the presumption in its favour that would be afforded by his voluntarily remaining in it. The principle of freedom cannot require that he should be free not to be free. It is not freedom to be allowed to alienate his freedom.[21]

Galston offers a parallel argument in defence of diversity. Diversity ought to be prized in liberal states because it does not overly disadvantage individuals or groups that are committed to tradition and faith. However, diversity is permitted only provided that such groups do not impose their vision of the good on those around them, because to allow them so to do would contradict the reason why they were allowed to pursue a traditional or faith-based lifestyle in the first place. Neither Mill nor Galston remain neutral between liberal and non-liberal lifestyles. That, of course, need not be objectionable *per se*: after all, why should it be? Surely no political theory can - or should - be neutral between what does and what does not conform to its values. But the problem for liberalism is, I shall argue, that this not only undermines liberalism's idea of itself as not reliant on any particular notions of the good - a not uncommon criticism - but that it leads it to fall back on what is in fact a conservative axiology. In the remainder of this introduction I shall outline the sort of case made later in detail about my chosen liberals in order to make clear at the outset how my overall argument builds on certain established, even if not always accepted, critiques of liberalism, and how it moves from these to offer the much more radical analysis that liberalism must finally rest on conservative values.

[21] Mill, *On Liberty*, p173.

For Mill, all wants have value provided they do not harm others because it is only through choosing which wants to pursue that individuals develop a character. Although all wants have value, however, those that most directly lead to development as a rational being are the most valuable. Mill insists that individuals cannot be coerced against their will into either pursuing wants or desisting from pursuing wants unless such activity results in harm to others; despite himself having very explicit ideas about which wants are good and which are not, Mill insists that it is wrong to force people to behave well. Inasmuch as Mill ranks wants in terms of their value, his neutrality breaks down, as in the case with his argument that a person 'who pursues animal pleasures at the expense of those of feeling and intellect must expect to be lowered in the opinion of others'.[22] First, Mill denies that state or society has any right to coerce individuals other than to prevent harm to others, but then he identifies behaviour which, although it should be permitted, is wrong, and which other individuals should condemn. Strict neutrality concerning competing conceptions of the good, however, would preclude the latter. Furthermore, it is the political and social traditions of Mill's society, the basis of Mill's 'character', which in fact serve to fill the logical space that such neutrality leaves.

Mill's objective, of course, is to find ways to encourage individuals *voluntarily* to want the type of things that will lead them ultimately to develop a fine character; and it is this voluntarism that allegedly makes liberalism different from conservatism. Values are to be chosen, not blindly accepted. Moreover, they are to be chosen on the basis of the free play of the individual's reason and not on account of their being considered by others to be the best, or the best available. For liberals 'the best' is whatever individuals take to be the best: since the content of 'the best' is the subject of *any* political philosophy, that, after all, is what distinguishes liberalism from its rivals, and from conservative philosophy in particular.

Now, Mill admits that not all people at all times are capable of self-improvement; hence his praise in *On Liberty* for comparatively enlightened rulers such as Akbar and Charlemagne.[23] Mill's thought, as will be explained in Chapter 2, contains an explicit historicist dimension. Coercion is justified if people have not reached a stage where they are capable of being improved by rational discussion. Mill's doctrine, therefore, is relevant only to individuals within those societies who have reached the stage of intellectual and moral development where rational discussion can be engaged in. There is, after all, a right view to take of what is good, and only some people are

[22] ibid., p144.
[23] ibid., p69.

capable of taking it. Furthermore, Mill's liberty, like the individuals who are capable of being improved by it, is also the product of particular histories. Thus Mill is in fact attempting to derive universal values, those of autonomy and rationality, from the development of a discrete and complex political tradition. Mill is unable to establish either an empirical or an *a priori* foundation for his contention that true human happiness rests in the individuality which comes from autonomy and rationality. Moreover, because he argues that the reason why no one must interfere with the self-regarding actions of individuals is that liberty is the means to these desirable ends, Mill is unable offer empirical or *a priori* foundations for the neutrality he espouses in the 'harm principle'.

Thus, individuality, rationality and autonomy are desirable because *competent* judges desire them, and not because *just anyone* desires them. Mill departs from classical liberalism to the extent that he wishes individuals *voluntarily* to want things that are good (and good because individuals of character and judgement want them), rather than maintaining only that things are good whatever they are because they are wanted.[24] While the latter clearly is his position - 'the sole evidence it is possible to produce that anything is desirable, is that people do actually desire it'[25] - it is not the whole of his position, since the evidence constituted by some people's desires counts for more than that constituted by others' desires. Mill has after all something of a substantial conception of the good.

In *Considerations on Representative Government*, for example, Mill makes it plain that he regards representative government the best form of government:

> [T]here is no difficulty in showing that the ideally best form of government is that in which the sovereignty, or supreme controlling power in the last resort, is vested in the entire aggregate of the community; every citizen not only having a voice in the exercise of that ultimate sovereignty, but being, at least occasionally, called on to take an actual part in the government, by the personal discharge of some

---

[24] The classical liberal formulation of this derives from Hobbes.

'But whatsoever is the object of a man's appetite or desire, that it is which he for his part calleth *good*: and the object of his hate and aversion, *evil*; and of his contempt *vile* and *inconsiderable*. For these words of good, evil, and contemptible, are ever used with relation to the person that useth them: there being nothing simply and absolutely so;' - Thomas Hobbes, *Leviathan* (Blackwell, Oxford, 1957), p32.

[25] John Stuart Mill, *Utilitarianism*, in *Utilitarianism, On Liberty and Considerations on Representative Government* (Everyman, London, 1984), p36.

public function, local or general.[26]

Mill goes on to explain that, apart from certain local conditions which will eventually disappear, representative government is a form of government that should be regarded as proper to any society which had reached a certain level of civilisation.[27] Mill is confident, unlike a conservative such as Oakeshott, that such government is to be understood 'as an approximation to some ideal manner of government', whereas for Oakeshott, or any other conservative, it is 'simply what emerged in Western Europe where the impact of the aspirations of individuality upon medieval institutions was greatest'.[28] Mill clearly regards a certain type of government as preferable to others, *whether desired or not*. And that is not a neutral position with regard to what is good for people.

Hayek's effort is, in a sense, more ambitious than Mill's because of his attempts to show that what he describes as the 'Great Society', the liberal order, is not only the sole form of political arrangement that allows individuals to live freely, but is also, inevitably, the order that allows material prosperity for the greatest number of people. Significantly, it is Hayek's 'Great Society', that by favouring the dissemination of knowledge, allows individuals to live together and co-operate without agreement on a substantive notion of the good:

> [T]he Great Society arose through the discovery that men can live together in peace and mutually benefiting each other without agreeing on the particular aims they severally pursue. The discovery that by substituting abstract rules of conduct for obligatory concrete ends made it possible to extend the order of peace beyond the small groups pursuing the same ends, because it enabled each individual to gain from the skill and knowledge of others whom he need not even know and whose aims could be wholly different from his own.[29]

The empirical foundations of human rationality far from constituting a problem, are what make possible such living together, for they allow for people not agreeing on substantive ends. But Hayek's insistence on the empirical basis of human rationality leads him to have a distinctly

---

[26] John Stuart Mill, *Considerations on Representative Government*, in *Utilitarianism, On Liberty and Considerations on Representative Government*, p223.
[27] ibid., p234.
[28] Michael Oakeshott, 'The Masses in Representative Democracy', in A. Hunold (ed) *Freedom and Serfdom: An Anthology of Western Thought* (Reidel, Dordrecht, Holland, 1961), p156.
[29] Hayek, *Law, Legislation and Liberty*, Vol. I-III (Routledge & Kegan Paul, London, 1982), Vol. II, p109.

conservative prejudice in favour of established rules and traditions within liberal states. In particular, he praises the system of common law as it emerged in Britain, the British white settlement colonies and the USA for its purposeless nature:

> [T]he important insight to which an understanding of the process of evolution of law [by custom and precedent] leads is that the rules which will emerge from it will of necessity possess certain attributes which laws designed by a ruler may but need not possess, and are likely to possess only if they are modelled after the kind of rules which spring from the articulation of previously existing practices. ... The [common] law will consist of purpose-independent rules which govern the conduct of individuals towards each other, are intended to apply to an unknown number of further instances, and by defining a protected domain of each, enable an order of actions to form itself where individuals can make feasible plans. It is usual to refer to these rules as abstract rules of just conduct ... The contention that a law based on precedent is more rather than less abstract than one expressed in verbal rules is so contrary to a view widely held, perhaps more among continental rather than Anglo-Saxon lawyers, that it needs fuller justification. The central point can probably not be better expressed than in a famous statement by the great eighteenth-century judge Lord Mansfield, who stressed that the common law 'does not consist of particular cases, but of general principles, which are illustrated and explained by those cases'. What this means is that it is part of the technique of the common law judge that from the precedents which guide him he must be able to derive rules of universal significance which can be applied to new cases.[30]

Hayek is arguing two points here: on the one hand he is suggesting that laws which evolve through the common law are not designed to achieve specific social purposes, and hence are neutral between competing conceptions of the good; and on the other that the empirically-based common law tradition as it emerged in Britain, her colonies and former colonies is more favourable to the establishment of what he describes as the 'Great Society' than the theoretically-based continental tradition of Roman Law or the *Code Napoléon*.

However, as I shall demonstrate in chapter 3, Hayek's epistemological and psychological claims are not wholly successful; and he has therefore to fall back on another claim, the claim that liberty is of value in itself. But that

[30] ibid., Vol. I, pp85-6.

too is also unsuccessful, as we shall see. What, then, is left to Hayek? In effect, if not by direct intent, the analysis he offers of the nature and role of 'law' and 'the precedents which guide' judges takes exactly the same form as Oakeshott's avowedly conservative understanding of the provenance of the 'Rights of Man'. A brief comparison is instructive: Oakeshott sees liberalism, as it emerged in, first, the thought of Locke and as it figured in the American and French Revolutions, as an 'abridgement' of the English political tradition:

> [O]n August 4, 1789, for the complex and bankrupt social and political system of France was substituted the Rights of Man. Reading this document we come to the conclusion that somebody has done some thinking. Here, displayed in a few sentences, is a political ideology: a system of rights and duties, a scheme of ends - justice, freedom, equality, security, property, and the rest - ready and waiting to be put into practice for the first time. 'For the first time?' Not a bit of it. This ideology no more existed in advance of political practice than a cookery book exists in advance of knowing how to cook. Certainly it was the product of somebody's reflection, but it was not the product of reflection in advance of political activity. For here, in fact, are disclosed, abstracted and abridged, the common law rights of Englishmen, the gift not of independent premeditation or divine munificence, but of centuries of the day-to-day attending to the arrangements of an historic society. Or consider Locke's *Second Treatise of Civil Government*, read in America and in France in the eighteenth century as a statement of abstract principles to be put into practice, regarded there as a preface to political activity. But so far from being a preface, it has all the marks of a postscript, and its power to guide derived from its roots in actual political experience. Here, set down in abstract terms, is a brief conspectus of the manner in which Englishmen were accustomed to go about the business of attending to their arrangements - a brilliant abridgement of the political habits of Englishmen.[31]

What matters for both Oakeshott and Hayek is the general and abstract nature of law and its independence from specific social purposes. Both agree, although in different ways that this is embodied in what might be described as the Anglo-Saxon tradition of Britain and her former white settlement colonies, including the USA. The advantage of the common-law

[31] Michael Oakeshott, *Rationalism in Politics and Other Essays* (Methuen, London, 1962), pp120-1.

is that though it is based on precedent - 'attending to the arrangements of an historic society' - it allows judges to derive universal and abstract precedents. By citing Mansfield, Hayek recognises that these universal precedents emerge from practice within existing states. But it is practice according to a tradition of political behaviour that emerges, not from meditation in advance of political practice, but from political practice itself. The 'Great Society' turns out to be a conservative society. Furthermore, the point concerns not simply his view of English common law: it has quite general applications. For if Hayek's epistemology and psychology are correct, and traditions are fundamental to ensuring liberty, then those traditions will be undermined by his view of 'progress'. 'Progress', therefore, has to be understood purely in those ways that the traditions concerned would recognise as such. Thus he takes it for granted that the basic ideas of nineteenth century liberalism did not constitute just another ideology but were grounded in reality: only on that - empirically inaccurate - basis can they be thought properly to guide policy in modern society. The ideas of classical liberalism are true, in effect, because classical liberalism takes them to be so. Again is this not exactly what might - quite properly - be expected of a conservative political philosophy? As a recent author puts it, 'Hayek believed as firmly in scientific liberalism as any Marxist in scientific socialism'.[32] But such a belief remains both (a) a *liberal* one and (b) one which is no different in form from Oakeshott's *conservative* belief that 'the political habits of Englishmen',[33] do - and should - determine what is to be done, even if, of course, Hayek is not explicit about this. But then it is only the lack of such explicitness that finally differentiates liberal from conservative thought in this regard.

More generally, Hayek's conception of the human mind as governed by meta-conscious rules which escape conscious scrutiny has clearly conservative implications. We can never know our own minds sufficiently to be able to govern them, since our explicit knowledge is simply the tip of the iceberg of a vast fund of tacit knowledge. Thus, for Hayek, the rationalist ideal of the government of the mind by itself is delusive. Even more of a delusion is the ideal of a society of minds, which governs itself in the light of conscious reason. This is the foundation of Hayek's critique of constructivism in all its forms, be they socialist or otherwise. For Hayek all the projects of 'constructivist rationalism', from Mill's developmental idea of the individual through the various species of Marxism, seek to achieve the impossible because to succeed they need to convert tacit to explicit knowledge and to govern social life by doctrine. But only tacit knowledge

[32] Andrew Gamble, *Hayek: The Iron Cage of Liberty* (Polity, Cambridge, 1996), p9.

[33] See footnote 31 above.

can engender government and some tacit knowledge is lost in attempts to convert it into explicit knowledge.[34] For if we cannot know our own mind, and if knowledge embodied in practices is partially lost when we attempt to articulate it, then theory is inescapably limited by the incapability of human beings to understand their own minds and articulate their own knowledge. The political implications of this epistemology and philosophy of mind is a form of the classically conservative contention of the primacy of practice over theory.

If I am right, then, it should be no surprise that liberalism should transform itself into unreasoning conservatism when threatened - for its most fundamental justification (whether or not successful) is a conservative one. Consider for example the attitude of what might described as the liberal literary establishment to the Salman Rushdie affair:

> [W]hen their [British Muslims'] noisy but peaceful protests [about the publication of Rushdie's *Satanic Verses*] got nowhere, a small group of them burned a copy of it. Rather than stimulate a reasoned discussion of their grievance, the book-burning incident led to a torrent of denunciation. Muslim's were called 'barbarians', uncivilized', 'fanatics', 'fundamentalists' and compared to the Nazis. Many a writer, some of impeccable liberal credentials, openly wondered how Britain could 'civilize' them and protect their innocent progeny against their parents' 'medieval fundamentalism'.[35]

On the one hand the attitude of liberals to the challenge of Islam is conservative in that it seeks to maintain the established order from internal threats whether real or imagined. On the other hand, however, the retention of liberalism's claims to be universally applicable leads to a marked lack of tolerance in cases where a group, such as those British Muslims who believed that Rushdie's book was deeply insulting to them and their religion, apparently contravene liberal values whilst seeking redress for their grievances. It is hardly surprising, then, that such cases should prove paradoxical for liberals.[36]

---

[34] Hayek outlines this argument most fully in Chapter 5 of *The Fatal Conceit: The Errors Socialism* (Routledge & Kegan Paul, London, 1988).

[35] Bhikhu Parekh, 'The Rushdie Affair: A Research Agenda for Political Philosophy', in Kymlicka (ed) *The Rights of Minority Cultures* (Oxford University Press, Oxford, 1995), p308.

[36] This is a problem with liberal theory which has recently given much cause for concern. Will Kymlicka diagnoses the problem thus:

> [T]he problem is not that traditional human rights doctrines give us the wrong answer to these questions. It is rather that they often give us no answer at all. The right to free

> speech does not tell us what an appropriate language policy is; the right to vote does not tell us how political boundaries should be drawn, or how powers should be distributed between levels of government; the right to mobility does not tell us what an appropriate immigration and naturalization policy is. These questions have been left to the usual process of majoritarian decision-making within each state. The result…has been to render cultural minorities vulnerable to significant injustice at the hands of the majority, and to exacerbate ethnocultural conflict. - Kymlicka, *Multicultural Citizenship* (Clarendon Press, Oxford, 1995), p5.

Kymlicka is surely right in this diagnosis: where he is mistaken is in assuming that solutions to these problems can be found within the liberal democratic paradigm. The problems such rights face arise directly from Kymlicka's own formulation of minority rights. The rights in question are:

- self-government rights (the delegation of powers to national minorities, often through some form of federalism);
- polyethnic rights (financial support and legal protection for certain practices associated with particular ethnic or religious groups); and
- special representation rights (guaranteed seats for ethnic or national groups within the central institutions of the larger state). - p7.

The conceptual framework of these rights is unexceptionable. The problems that arise for liberals come when these rights are put to substantive use. In each of the three cases noted by Kymlicka it is easy to imagine that groups might seek to use minority rights to maintain their community in an illiberal way. In the case of self-government for national minorities, discriminatory taxation might be used to discourage immigration, property ownership might be restricted to members of the self-governing national minority and laws could be passed to ensure conformity with their values. Polyethnic rights to financial support and legal protection for practices associated with particular ethnic or religious groups could be used to protect and pay for a family's right to have their daughter circumcised, or possibly to establish schools that would ensure that young women were educated in such a way that they accepted domination by a patriarchal religious community. The guaranteed seats that ensure special representation rights for ethnic or national groups within the central institutions of the larger state could be used by élites from traditionalist, or faith-based minority communities to win concessions from the majority to retain control over their own communities, or possibly prevent the reconciliation of another minority group with the wider society. Of course no liberal would accept such results. Kymlicka is no exception and he insists on the limitation of minority rights. - pp152-3.

Kymlicka makes the point that his conception of minority rights is impeccably liberal: however, liberals tend not to have problems dealing with the rights of those minorities who are either quietist or who accept the legitimacy, or even the authority of liberal states. The problems liberals have are with militant religious or nationalist groups who would neither respect the legitimacy of liberal states, nor would brook any compromise with them. Kymlicka does not get to grips with this crucial difficulty; instead he falls back on an argument that states that the only diversity that is permitted is that which is commensurable with liberalism. Thus individuals have the final say on whether or not internal restrictions to maintain communities are acceptable to them or not, and no consideration is given to the cultures who argue that religious or social solidarity is more important than individual rights. Moreover, Kymlicka, while he accepts a *modus vivendi* with illiberal minorities within liberal states, he clearly believes that their mode of political or social organisation is inferior to that of liberalism, so that incentives and encouragement should be provided for such groups to abandon their illiberal ways.

I am arguing, then, two things, first that liberalism's view of itself is fundamentally mistaken inasmuch as its neutrality is not what it appears to be: specifically, it is not in fact a neutrality at all, but a set of views and assumptions predicated upon a far from neutral conception of the individual, such that the 'autonomy' which is its anchor, while offering an apparently value-neutral basis for liberalism's political proposals, in fact does no such thing: second that not only is liberalism not neutral regarding the good, but turns out to rely on traditional conservative understandings of it. It is important to be clear exactly what these related criticisms do and do not amount to.

One possible objection to the alleged neutrality of liberal 'autonomy' might be this. If 'autonomy' turned out, as a matter of fact, not to guarantee that individuals' wants were maximally satisfied, then - since the good for individual human beings is getting as much of what they want as is possible subject to their not preventing others from doing the same - it would turn out not to be a fundamental value at all. 'Autonomy', then, is both instrumental and, therefore, partial. For inasmuch as its value is contingent upon facilitating individuals in getting what they want, it consists in a substantive and contingent content and not a neutral one. But such an objection misses the point. For the liberal connection between 'autonomy' and want-satisfaction is logical rather than empirical. That is to say that its efficiency in allowing people to get what they want can never be a contingent matter and thus cannot be (merely) instrumental. For 'autonomy' and want-satisfaction are understood in terms of each other. 'Autonomy' just consists in getting what you want since, as Berlin has it, it is a 'freedom from' and not a 'freedom to'. [37] And this is what neutrality amounts to: it merely, so to speak, puts a fence around whatever one's own substantive 'goods' happen to be, rather than proposing or insisting upon any particular such goods. However, that is not the end of the story.

The proper objection to the alleged value-neutrality of liberal 'autonomy' is this: the value placed upon getting what you want is not universal and thus cannot support 'thick value-neutrality', because the conception of the individual and the individual's relation to his or her desires assumes a particular, historically and culturally specific, 'individual'. To put it

---

Kymlicka is advocating precisely the same teleological approach to liberalism as Mill but on a group, rather than an individual basis. Obvious examples of illiberal practices such as direct harm to others are to be prohibited; illiberal practices that do not directly harm individuals are to be eradicated by persuasion and encouragement. The encouragement of diversity is no more than a mask for liberals to declare the primacy of liberal values.

[37] Isaiah Berlin, 'Two Concepts of Liberty', in *Four Essays on Liberty* (Oxford University Press, 1969), pp121-22.

schematically: liberalism's 'individual' is just that, the individual as conceived and understood within the liberal tradition - it is neither free-standing nor universal any more than are the 'sense-data' of empiricist epistemology.[38] And consequently it is not substantively value-neutral either.

Although this is a comparatively well-known problem for liberals;[39] it is curious that liberals have traditionally paid little attention to it, with the notable exception of John Stuart Mill in his attempt to show that it is not the case that individuals should be allowed to sell themselves into slavery. This is a crucial example because it demonstrates that, even if only implicitly, liberalism cannot but operate with a substantive and not a neutral conception of the good. For Mill's tortuous and curiously Kantian argument is at best an *ad hoc* measure which in fact fails to disguise the fact. The only exception that Mill allows to the supremacy of the individual over his own mind and body, let us recall, is when someone might choose to sell themselves into slavery. In order to escape from the dilemma posed by such a case Mill declares that 'by selling himself for a slave' the individual 'abdicates his liberty... [and]... therefore defeats, in his own case, the very purpose which is the justification of allowing him to dispose of himself'.[40] This appeal to a notion of self-contradiction is a surprisingly Kantian move. It subordinates what a person wants to a form of contingency in action, one which is part practical and part rational. It therefore seems that Mill himself recognises the flaw of using wants as a normative foundation for liberalism and realises that such a normative position must ultimately fail.

What is important for my argument here, however - and this brings us to the accusation of a reliance on a conservative axiology - is not so much this recognition, as the fact that in so recognising, he exposes the precariousness of liberal neutrality regarding the 'individual', a neutrality cashed out in terms of a value-neutral 'autonomy' which turns out not to be value-neutral at all. For while Mill's argument smacks somewhat of desperation, what it shows is that, despite his explicit rejection of 'social rights', he recognises, implicitly in the case of slavery, that certain self-regarding acts of individuals can and do 'harm' the wider society. This can be the only good reason for Mill to reject slavery, even if voluntarily entered into. 'Harm' to

---

[38] For a discussion of the nature of the liberal individual as a 'wanting thing' see Bob Brecher, *Getting What You Want? A Critique of Liberal Morality* (Routledge, London, 1998), Chapter 2.

[39] See for example, Alasdair MacIntyre, *After Virtue* (Duckworth, London, 1985), Chapter 5; T.H. Green, *Prolegomena to Ethics* (Clarendon Press, Oxford, 1899), Introduction; Michael Oakeshott, *Morality and Politics in Modern Europe* (Yale University Press, New Haven and London, 1993), p83-6; and David Selbourne, *The Principle of Duty* (Sinclair-Stevenson, London, 1994), Chapter 3.

[40] Mill, *On Liberty*, p173.

the wider society from voluntary slavery can occur on two levels. Once voluntary slavery is accepted it could become an option for people in desperate circumstances, so that by being accepted it becomes acceptable.[41] Second, and this is more important for my argument, slavery, or indeed any other social practice, will have indirect repercussions throughout the whole of society. A voluntarily undertaken slavery could become institutionalised as a social practice, so undermining the liberal nature of a liberal society. Even if Mill's attempt at a type of Kantian refutation of the right of individuals to sell themselves as slaves were not fundamentally inconsistent with the rest of his thought, and whether or not it is valid, what matters in this respect regarding slavery is that voluntary slavery would alter and undermine the practices and traditions on which liberal values rest. To use Oakeshott's terms the acceptance of voluntary slavery is not intimated by the liberal tradition. We reject voluntary slavery, not because of Kantian self-contradiction, but because it contravenes the values which we enjoy and appreciate within liberal societies.[42] And that is a conservative argument.

My point, then, is this: while liberals explicitly seek to eschew conservative forms of justifying their political philosophy - they eschew, that is to say any substantive conception of the good, insisting instead on a neutrality between whatever conceptions of the good happen to be extant in

---

[41] Compare here Mill's famous move from 'x is desired' to 'x is desirable': even if not (intended as) a syllogistic argument, but only as indicating 'the sole evidence' available, it remains a sociologically accurate description.

[42] For a further exploration of the weaknesses and inconsistencies of Mill's position regarding slavery see Brecher, *Getting What You Want?*, pp150-3. However, both C.L. Ten in *Mill on Liberty* (Clarendon Press, Oxford, 1980), pp117-19; and Jonathan Riley in *Mill on Liberty* (Routledge, London 1998), pp132-5; argue that Mill's argument is not inconsistent because the contract of 'voluntary slavery' must commit the individual in question to servitude in perpetuity. If, however, the slave decides that he or she no longer wishes to be a slave, then the slavery ceases to be voluntary. Riley comments:

> Mill seems correct, then, to insist that a society committed to his liberty doctrine must prohibit any practice of selling oneself into slavery. There cannot be any liberty, by right, to buy and control another's very person. Slavery contracts are by their nature irrevocable. Society cannot recognize them without sacrificing all means of discriminating between voluntary and involuntary servitude, on the part of the seller-slave. Unless prepared to enforce in perpetuity a state of absolute vulnerability, which the once-willing slave may come to regret and now wish to alter, society must refuse to enforce slavery contracts. - p134.

Riley, and Ten for that matter, are surely right about the irrevocability of voluntary slavery contracts, but this is surely true of any non-temporary contract including, for example, one that might involve a small farmer or peasant selling their ancestral land to resolve temporary financial difficulties. The farmer has, just like the voluntary slave, made an irrevocable decision to abrogate independence. This shows that slavery is not the special case that Mill, Riley and Ten take it to be, but the same as any other non-temporary contract. Therefore, the 'in perpetuity' argument must fail.

any particular societies, cultures, communities or sub-groups thereof - they fail in their endeavour. The very notion that the right, as a formal, non-substantive, procedural notion should take precedence over any particular (conception of the) good is one which is itself, ultimately predicated on one such conception of human nature, of, that is to say, its 'individual'. Furthermore, that the 'individual' for all its autonomy and rationality remains the product both of specific conceptions of society and of specific societies. And while conservatives recognise and laud the fact, liberals seek, unsuccessfully to evade or deny it.

# 2 Mill, Neutrality and Inconsistency

In Chapter 1, I set out the key argument to be made in this book: that is, that liberalism is not what it claims to be; and specifically that liberalism is not substantively neutral because, as I shall argue in detail, instead of having no substantial conception of the good, its conception is in fact based on the underlying tradition of thought from which liberalism emerged. The good that liberalism is founded upon - its own view of itself notwithstanding - is not neutral but normative, and in particular it is conservatively normative. In this chapter I shall show how this argument applies to John Stuart Mill, in many ways liberalism's central figure.

Mill's objective, formulated in the 'harm principle' in his celebrated work *On Liberty*, is to assert that the only justification, collectively or individually, to interfere with the freedom of action of another individual is self-protection. Such a position appears unequivocally neutral; but even an admirer of Mill like Hobhouse[1] recognises that within his thought are fundamental inconsistencies - which when analysed undermine its claim to neutrality. Nowhere is this more clearly demonstrated than in Mill's own ambivalent attitude towards the conception of the good that is, at the very least, implicit within his thought. The roots of Mill's ambivalence lie in the dichotomy between his neutralist liberalism, clearly formulated in the 'harm principle', and his utilitarianism. Mill insists that his utilitarianism is logically prior to his liberalism.[2] Utilitarianism, however, is a teleological doctrine which declares that the criteria for judging the moral worth of an action is whether or not it promotes pleasure or inflicts pain. Is it possible then, for Mill to remain neutral between competing conceptions of the good? The heart of the difficulty lies in the very nature of Mill's commitment to neutrality. It is not clear whether Mill is committed to neutrality as an end in itself, or whether it is for him simply a means to his (implicit) conception of the good - in which case his system can hardly be neutral. Mill's position is further complicated by the nature of the utilitarianism he adopts of which there are at least two interpretations. John Gray,[3] for example, sees Mill,

[1] L.T. Hobhouse, *Liberalism*, in J. Meadowcroft (ed) *Hobhouse; Liberalism and other Writings* (Cambridge University Press, Cambridge, 1994), p52.
[2] John Stuart Mill, *On Liberty*, p158.
[3] John Gray, *Mill on Liberty: A Defence*, Second Edition (Routledge, London, 1996).

implicitly at least, as a rule utilitarian. Mill is not always seen in this way, being more often interpreted as an orthodox act utilitarian.[4] This interpretation states that he believes it is never morally right to perform an action when some alternative would produce more happiness. Rule utilitarianism, however, supposes that it may be morally right to perform an action which is in accord with a moral rule, on the grounds that the general practice of the rule does more good than the omission of such a practice or the practice of an alternative rule, even if the specific action concerned does not *itself* lead to a balance of pleasure over pain or happiness over unhappiness. Rule utilitarianism evaluates the moral rightness of an action, not by its actual consequences, but by the hypothetical consequences of what would happen if the rule which the action follows were generally practised.[5] The crucial hypothetical consequence to be sought, and which Mill believes the establishment of liberty will promote, is the development of autonomous rational individuals. For Mill, only such individuals are capable of being truly happy.

If Mill is an indirect utilitarian in this way, as Gray alleges, then his neutrality between the competing conceptions of the good of individuals is adopted as a means of pursuing a higher good, that of the true happiness of individuals. I shall argue in this chapter that this is indeed the case and that Mill's problem is that he cannot offer a foundation for the conception of the good, the idea of the establishment of rational choosing individuals, that is implicit within his thought without resorting to assumptions inherent in the

---

[4] See for example, J.D. Mabbott, 'Interpretations of Mill's Utilitarianism', in P. Foot (ed) *Theories of Ethics* (Oxford University Press, Oxford, 1967), pp137-43.

[5] See, for example, J.O. Urmson, 'The Interpretation of the Moral Philosophy of John Stuart Mill', in P. Foot (ed) *Theories of Ethics*, pp128-36, and J. J. C. Smart & Bernard Williams, *Utilitarianism For & Against* (Cambridge University Press, Cambridge, 1973), pp9-11. Most commentators' concerns centre on the relationship between utility as a standard for moral action and some of Mill's other ideals, for example, liberty. Until recently an exception to this general interpretative rule was John Robson's view. Robson construes Mill's utilitarianism as a 'relativistic' standard of human improvement centred on individual self-development. Robson's interpretation stands out for its stress on the character of Mill's utilitarianism as a general ethic. John Robson, *The Improvement of Mankind: The Social and Political Thought of John Stuart Mill* (The University of Toronto Press, Toronto, 1968), pp117-59. In recent years similar interpretations of Mill's utilitarianism have appeared, for example, Wendy Donner, 'Mill's utilitarianism', in John Skorupski (ed), *The Cambridge Companion to Mill*, (Cambridge University Press, Cambridge, 1998). Donner argues that 'Mill jettisons the Benthamite felicific calculus; he offers in its place a method employing the preferences of self-developed agents'. - p273. Roger Crisp in his *Mill on Utilitarianism* (Routledge, London, 1997), also offers a utilitarian interpretation of Mill based on self-development. He describes it as 'utilitarian generalization' and, although similar in structure to rule utilitarianism, such a system 'requires that we perform no action which is such that, if people were generally to perform it, welfare would not be maximized'. - p116.

intellectual tradition of which he is a part.

## 2.1 'Harm' and neutrality

To demonstrate that Mill does indeed have recourse to a non-neutral substantive conception of the good let us examine the putative neutrality of his 'harm principle'. Mill's objective in *On Liberty* is

> ... to assert one very simple principle, as entitled to govern absolutely the dealings of society with the individual in the way of compulsion and control whether the means used be physical force in the form of legal penalties or the moral coercion of public opinion. That principle is that the sole end for which mankind are warranted individually or collectively in interfering with the liberty of action of any of their number is self-protection. That the only purpose for which power can be rightfully exercised over any member of a civilised community, against his will, is to prevent harm to others. His own good either political or moral, is not a sufficient warrant. He cannot rightfully be compelled to do or forbear because it will make him happier, because, in the opinions of others, to do so would be wise or even right. These are good reasons for remonstrating with him, or reasoning with him, or persuading him, or entreating him, but not for compelling him or visiting him with any evil in case he do otherwise. To justify that, the conduct from which it is desired to deter him must be calculated to produce evil to someone else. The only part of the conduct of anyone for which he is amenable to society is that which concerns others. In the part, which merely concerns himself, his independence is, of right, absolute. Over himself, over his own body and mind, the individual is sovereign.[6]

The 'harm principle' seems unequivocally neutral because it specifies that no one may interfere with an individual pursuing his own conception of the good even if they believe him to be mistaken or foolish: where actions affect only the individual in question no one, whatever their opinions to the contrary has the right to compel an individual to act against their will. From the statement of this principle Mill develops his distinction between self-regarding actions - that is, actions that affect only the individual concerned - and other-regarding acts. Where an act affects only the self, no matter how foolhardy, no matter how dangerous or immoral others may deem it to be,

[6] John Stuart Mill, *On Liberty*, p68.

there should be no force used against the individual to prevent it.

There are, then, three possible separate senses in which individuals can be harmed: first, someone can be physically harmed; second, they can be emotionally harmed; and third, their essential interests as human beings can be harmed. Of these three, only physical harm is straightforward; but Mill cannot restrict his notion to physical harm because that would mean rejecting the 'harm' caused by failure to keep contracts or loss of property resulting from fraud. What then does Mill mean by 'harm'? He recognises that some self-regarding acts can cause moral outrage to others without unequivocally harming them. As examples, Mill cites the moral outrage caused to some members of religious confessions by certain acts, and he accepts as a harm the distress caused by observing others engage in acts believed to morally wrong, perverse, or unacceptable. Note his comments on the effect eating pork has upon Moslems:

> [T]here are few acts which Christians and Europeans regard with more unaffected disgust than Mussulmans regard this particular mode of satisfying hunger. It is, in the first place, an offence against their religion; but this circumstance by no means explains either the degree or the kind of their repugnance; for wine also is forbidden by their religion, and to partake of it is by all Mussulmans accounted wrong, but not disgusting.[7]

Despite the distress it causes, however, Mill rejects any blanket prohibition of eating pork even in a society in which the majority is Moslem:

> [W]ould it be a legitimate exercise of the moral authority of public opinion, and if not, why not? The practice is really revolting to such a public. They also think that it is forbidden and abhorred by the deity. Neither could the prohibition be censured as religious persecution, since nobody's religion makes it a duty to eat pork.[8]

He says of the demands of religious groups like sabbatarians and Moslems to such interference:

> [S]o monstrous a principle [regarding the perpetration of acts that create moral outrage as a type of harm done to those outraged] is far more dangerous than any single interference with liberty; there is no violation of liberty which it would not justify; it acknowledges no right to any

[7] ibid., pp152-3.
[8] ibid., p153.

freedom whatever, except perhaps to that of holding opinions in secret, without ever disclosing them.[9]

As Mill argues (see below) neither the intensity of the distress, nor the number of people who share it affect the conclusion that it is illegitimate for the majority to impose its values on the rest of society. Such a position, however, runs counter to a strict interpretation of utilitarianism. If someone enjoys eating pork, it gives them momentary satisfaction from hunger, but it is unlikely to be a necessary condition of their long-term happiness or well-being in any direct sense of cause and effect; whereas the eating of pork has a directly harmful effect on Moslems as it causes the pain of moral outrage. But the inadvertent creation of such outrage is justified, because to allow public opinion, however strongly and deeply felt, to dictate the conduct of individuals would be to undermine the objective of limiting interference with the self-regarding acts of individuals. Mill says:

> [H]ow will the remaining portion of the community like to have the amusements that shall be permitted to them regulated by the religious and moral sentiments of the stricter Calvinists and Methodists? Would they not, with considerable peremptoriness, desire these intrusively pious members of society to mind their own business? This is precisely what should be said to every government and every public who have the pretension that no person shall enjoy any pleasure which they think wrong.[10]

He deplores the state of affairs in which: 'Wherever the sentiment of the majority is still genuine and intense it is found to have abated little of its claim to be obeyed.'[11] Moral outrage is specifically rejected as a species of harm for two reasons; first because in undertaking acts which cause moral outrage, such as drinking on Sundays or eating pork, individuals do not intentionally calculate evil against sabbatarians and Moslems; and second, because to accept moral outrage as a species of actionable harm would be to accept the right of intense, genuine public opinion to interfere with even the 'self-regarding acts' of individuals.

The third and most complex element of Mill's 'harm' is that done to the essential interests we have as human beings. That this is likely to be what Mill meant fundamentally by 'harm' is apparent when we see why Mill deplores interference in the 'self-regarding' acts of individuals. Mill believes

---

[9] ibid., p158.
[10] ibid., pp154-5.
[11] ibid., p67.

that individuality is a necessary ingredient of human happiness. For Mill, happiness is a condition of successful activity in which individuals express their distinctive natures.[12] It is as one of the dimensions of autonomy, and thereby one of the conditions of individuality, that freedom, as the absence of coercion, is vital as a condition of happiness. The promotion and protection of such freedom, however, requires neutrality. For if state and society are not neutral between competing conceptions of the good, then they must impinge upon the autonomy of persons which is a pre-condition for individuality (and hence their happiness). Therefore, state and society must be neutral between the purposes of competing individuals and voluntary groups provided they do not harm each other. For if a state or society attempts to impose its own collective purpose or conception of the good on individuals, then it must infringe the autonomy of those individuals - because autonomy, if it is to be meaningful, must include the pursuit of goals set according to the individual's own conception of the good. It is a pre-condition for the development of individuality that individuals have different and sometimes competing conceptions of the good. If everyone pursued the same purposes and had the same conception of the good imposed upon them, they would not then be individuals (individuals, that is to say as understood by the liberal tradition). Hence, to harm someone turns out for Mill some how to impugn the essential interests individuals have in autonomy, because without autonomy they cannot be individuals. It is this essential interest in autonomy that is harmed if there is interference in individual self-regarding actions.

At its simplest, harm to these essential interests would include the moral harm done to individuals by, for instance, lying or failing to keep promises. However, as Mill believes that human beings have an essential interest in individuality, he also insists that they have essential interests in freedom of speech, association and religion, freedom from arbitrary arrest and imprisonment, and the security of person and property. Prohibition of these freedoms does not necessarily require physical harm. But restrictions on them would be harmful to any essential interest that we have in autonomy. Equally, harm to those interests might also include harm to the institutions and social conditions that promote autonomy and individuality. And given Mill's statement that every person should bear 'his share of the labours and sacrifices incurred for defending the society or its members from injury and

---

[12] Mill notes in *On Liberty*, 'Where not the person's own character but the traditions or customs of other people are the rule of conduct, there is wanting one of the principal ingredients of human happiness, and quite the chief ingredient of individual and social progress'. - p120.

molestation',[13] he clearly regards the failure to perform public obligations as a species of harm.

Does this mean that, according to Mill, society after all has rights against the individual? What he argues is that although the self-regarding acts of individuals are not to be interfered with by society, society is certainly entitled to disapprove of their actions:

> [A] person who shows rashness, obstinacy, self-conceit - who cannot live within moderate means; who cannot restrain himself from hurtful indulgence; who pursues animal pleasures at the expense of those of feeling and intellect - must expect to be lowered in the opinion of others, and to have a less share of their favourable sentiments.[14]

Furthermore, in dealing with self-regarding conduct that is regarded as socially unacceptable, coercion and selfish indifference are not only the only options open to society:

> [I]t would be a great misunderstanding of this doctrine to suppose that it is one of selfish indifference which pretends that human beings have no business with each others conduct in life, and that they should not concern themselves about the well-doing or well-being of one another, unless their own interest is involved. Instead of any diminution, there is need of a great interest in physical exertion to promote the good of others. But disinterested benevolence can find other instruments to persuade people to their good than whips and scourges.... I am the last person to undervalue the self-regarding virtues; they are only second in importance, if even second, to the social. It is equally the business of education to cultivate both. But even education works by conviction and persuasion as well as by compulsion, and it is by the former only that, when the period of education is passed, the self-regarding virtues should be inculcated. Human beings owe to each other help to distinguish the better from the worse, and encouragement to choose the former and avoid the latter. They should be forever stimulating each other to increased exercise of their higher faculties and increased direction of their feelings towards wise instead of foolish, elevating instead of degrading, objects and contemplations.[15]

Beyond persuasion and exhortation, however, Mill is not prepared to go.

---

[13] ibid., p141.
[14] ibid., p144.
[15] ibid., p142.

To demonstrate his hostility to the idea, Mill invokes the 'social rights' claimed by members of the temperance organisations that demand interference with the self-regarding acts of individuals. Social rights are understood as follows:

> [I]f anything invades my social rights, certainly the traffic in strong drink does. It destroys my primary right of security by constantly creating and stimulating social disorder. It invades my right of equality by deriving a profit from the creation of misery I am taxed to support. It impedes my right to free moral and intellectual development by surrounding my path with dangers and by weakening and demoralizing society, from which I have a right to claim mutual aid and intercourse.[16]

For Mill, such a theory of social rights means 'that it is the absolute social right of every individual that every other individual shall act in every respect exactly as he ought; that whosoever fails thereof in the smallest particle violated my social right and entitles me to demand from the legislature the removal of the grievance'.[17] Yet it appears that nothing would be more certain to undermine the conditions for the development of individuality, and hence the essential interests that an individual has in autonomy, than the excessive use of strong drink. As a section of the community, drinkers - at least while drunk - can hardly be pursuing their rationally chosen goals. Equally, if people are spending a significant portion of their income on alcohol, they are not living moderately and are hardly building up the store of capital that would help make them autonomous and financially secure. Thus on such an interpretation, the ability to buy strong drink can be seen to be harmful to the essential interests individuals have in autonomy and security. Mill, however, regards the doctrine of social rights as pernicious, saying of the temperance campaign's arguments that: '[T]he doctrine ascribes to all mankind a vested interest in each other's moral, intellectual, and even physical perfection, to be defined by each claimant according to his own standard.'[18]

Mill is arguing here against what is a very strong conception of social rights. However, he also believes that public and private condemnation of socially damaging self-regarding acts is not only justified, but also a moral duty. Now, although it is possible, or even probable, that the sale of strong drink causes harm to the wider society, Mill is not prepared to accept its prohibition. On what basis does Mill argue for this limitation of social

---

[16] ibid., pp157-8.
[17] ibid., p158.
[18] ibid., p158.

rights? As a utilitarian Mill cannot resort to using terms like 'natural rights', but nevertheless he does claim that individuals can have positive rights established by law and convention:

> [W]hen we call anything a person's right, we mean that he has a valid claim on society to protect him in the possession of it, either by the force of law, or by that of education and opinion. If he has what we consider to be sufficient claim, on whatever account, to have something guaranteed to him by society, we say that he has a right to it.[19]

Later in the same work, Mill attempts to explain the nature of these essential interests that are to be regarded as rights: '[T]he moral rules which forbid mankind to hurt one another (in which we must never forget to include wrongful interference in each other's freedom) are more vital to human well-being than any maxims, however important, which only point out the best mode of managing some department of human affairs.'[20] Transgression of these moral rules with respect to individuals is what constitutes harm for Mill. They have greater priority than any issue of managing human affairs, even if such management would secure greater autonomy than that offered by Mill's insistence on non-interference in the self-regarding actions of individuals. It is these moralities 'which protect every individual from being harmed by others, *either directly or by being hindered in his freedom of pursuing his own good,* [they] are at once those which he himself has most at heart, and those which he has the strongest interest in publishing by word and deed... *it is these moralities primarily which compose the obligations of justice*'.[21] For Mill, then the good of individuals *as they themselves understand it* is prior to justice. Injustice, then, is anything that contravenes individual's self-defined good:

> [T]he most marked cases of injustice, and those which give the tone to the feeling of repugnance which characterises the sentiment, are wrongful aggression, or wrongful exercise of power over someone; the next are those which consist in wrongfully withholding from him something which is his due; in both cases inflicting on him a positive hurt, either in the form of direct suffering, or of the privation of some good which he had reasonable ground, either of a physical or of a social

[19] John Stuart Mill, *Utilitarianism*, in *Utilitarianism, On Liberty and Considerations on Representative Government*, p55.
[20] ibid., p62.
[21] ibid., emphasis added.

kind, for counting upon.[22]

In so identifying autonomy and security as the essential interests of individuals, Mill must believe they are to be regarded as more important than straightforward utilitarian criteria such as revealed preferences. Indeed, Mill concludes the chapter by saying:

> [J]ustice remains the appropriate name for certain social utilities which are vastly more important, and therefore more absolute and imperative, than any others are as a class... which, therefore, ought to be, as well as naturally are, guarded by a sentiment not only different in degree, but also in kind; distinguished from the milder feeling which attaches to the mere idea of promoting human pleasure or convenience, at once by the more definite nature of its commands, and by the sterner nature of its sanctions.[23]

To reiterate, then, harm for Mill is both direct harm to individuals - such as physical injury or failure to honour contracts - and individuals being prevented from pursuing their own good. The reason why Mill adopts this conception is that he sees the essential interests we have as human beings contravened by any attempt to prevent us from pursuing our own good in our own way. However, this does not necessarily mean that human beings have an infallible sense of what is their own good. As Mill recognises, people can be mistaken; or they can pursue foolish or even wrong personal goods. The reason why this conception of harm calls into question Mill's neutrality is that underlying his neutrality towards individuals pursuing their own good is a conception that suggests this is only the means to attain a higher good, that of the development of rational, choosing individuals possessed of a fine character. And this constitutes a substantive conception of the good. It is, so to say, as if his neutrality regarding people's self-chosen goods remains in place only if those self-chosen goods are of a particular sort; or, politically more accurately, as if his neutrality were applicable only to those people who have as a matter of fact achieved a certain 'character' just as he thought was the case *vis à vis* 'uncivilised' peoples.[24]

Mill's thoughts on rights, harm and essential interests suggest that there is indeed a conception of the good underlying his thought, at least with respect to the well-being of individuals. It is possible that this is the only intrusion of the good into Mill's thought, but if Mill adopts a position of

[22] ibid.
[23] ibid., p67.
[24] See Mill, *On Liberty*, p69. I shall pursue this in more detail, pp42-8 below.

neutrality on most self-regarding acts for the instrumental purpose of human beings achieving individuality, then it is also at least possible that he sees the development of rational choosing individuals as a collective good for the whole of society. This raises two further questions relating to Mill's putative neutrality: first, why should the individual achievement of rationality and an ability to choose be a good; and second, what is the origin of the idea that the development of rational choosing individuals is a good?

## 2.2 *Utilitarianism* vs. *On Liberty*

Let us see how what *Utilitarianism* tells us about Mill's views on these questions compares with what he says in *On Liberty*. In *On Liberty* he is clear that the development of the capacity to enjoy individuality is an historical process. Furthermore it is (therefore) culturally specific too: the development of individuality is not available universally, although as a condition it is universally desirable. Not all people at all times have the capacity to be individuals in the Millian sense. Until then

> [D]espotism is a legitimate mode of government in dealing with barbarians, provided the end be their improvement, and the means justified by actually effecting that end. Liberty, as a principle, has no application to any state of things anterior to the time when mankind have become capable of being improved by free and equal discussion. Until then, there is nothing for them but implicit obedience to an Akbar or a Charlemagne, if they are so fortunate as to find one. *But as soon as mankind have attained the capacity of being guided to their own improvement* by conviction or persuasion ... compulsion, either in the direct form or in that of pains and penalties for non-compliance, *is no longer admissible as a means to their own good* and justifiable only for the security of others.[25]

Mill's thought thus contains an explicit historicist dimension. Despotism is justified if it improves mankind. Liberty is valuable only once people have achieved the capacity to be improved by free and equal discussion. Is the realisation of such a capacity not the instantiation of an implicit conception of the good? In *Utilitarianism,* Mill describes the ultimate end for all human beings as

> ... an existence as exempt as far as possible from pain, and as rich as

[25] ibid., p69, emphasis added.

> possible in enjoyments, both in point of quantity and quality; the test of quality and the rule for measuring it against quantity, being the preference felt by those who in their opportunities of experience, to which must be added their habits of self-consciousness and self-observation, are best furnished with the means of comparison. This being according also to utilitarian opinion, the end of human action, is necessarily also the standard of morality; which may accordingly be defined, the rules and precepts for human conduct, by the observance of which an existence such as has been described might be, to the greatest extent possible secured to all mankind.[26]

This description clearly sees human existence as having a developmental and historical nature. It is not only enjoyment *per se* that is important for what Mill would see as a worthwhile existence, but the quality of that enjoyment, which is determined by what is valued by rational, choosing individuals who have had the opportunity to experience as wide a possible range of human pleasures. As people become more experienced, and as they acquire more knowledge within a developing civilisation, then their values are changed for the better and the content of happiness will also change:

> [L]ife would be very poor thing, very ill provided with sources of happiness, if there were not this provision of nature, by which things originally indifferent, but conducive to, or otherwise associated with, the satisfaction of our primitive desires, become in themselves sources of pleasure more valuable than the primitive pleasures, both in permanency, in the space of human existence that they are capable of covering, and even in intensity.[27]

The autonomy required to make choices is a much 'thicker' conception than that of a simple capacity to choose between pushpin and poetry. For unless the individuals concerned have had the opportunity to experience both - unless that is, they are no longer 'primitive' - their 'autonomy' will not be of the requisite nature.

The autonomous individual is the *end* of the process of human improvement. But ends are normative, and not neutral, even if a particular end, such as Mill's, requires neutrality for its realisation. At the 'meta'-level there is no neutrality, but a specific and concrete conception of the good: the development of the distinctively human capacity for rationally justifiable

---

[26] John Stuart Mill, *Utilitarianism*, p12.

[27] ibid., p39.

choice - poetry over pushpin, for example.

Is this another example of Mill's inconsistency, or is freedom as the capacity to make informed choices consistent with his wider theory, and in particular his ideas about freedom formulated in the 'harm principle'? In *On Liberty*, where Mill is seeking to establish a space for the clear development of individuality, he states that '[T]he sole end for which mankind are warranted individually or collectively in interfering with the liberty of any of their number, is self protection.'[28] Two points can be made that link this conception to the substantive notion of autonomy to which I have alluded, that is the power to pursue one's own conception of the good, rather than simply freedom from interference. First, it is a normative rule of liberty, that is to say, it prescribes an area within which individuals ought to be free (and by freedom, Mill means 'liberty of action', *not* simply freedom from coercion). Second, and related to the first point, although Mill is generally regarded as an advocate of 'negative freedom' - on the grounds that the 'harm principle' is a negative principle defining an area of non-interference - the statement of the principle as outlined above is positive rather than negative. The substantive question of whether Mill is in the end a negative libertarian or not hinges upon the kind of concept of freedom which Mill wishes to see applied within the space delineated by the 'harm principle'. If Mill simply sees that space as one where no one may interfere with the self-regarding actions of another, then Mill is a negative libertarian. In that case he can plausibly be accused of inconsistency, and can be said to be neutral at least between competing individual conceptions of the good. If, on the other hand, Mill wishes to see a positive notion of freedom or autonomy apply in the space delineated by the 'harm principle', then not only is his position consistent but the conditions he seeks to promote rest on a notion of the good clearly drawn from the political traditions of Britain in the nineteenth century, a conception which includes ideas of duty, personal responsibility and a leadership role for élites. The same tradition also includes ideas of self-help, and the ability of individuals to transcend adverse circumstances by their own efforts. However, most significant of all as far as Mill's teleological doctrine is concerned, individuals brought up in that tradition were 'capable of being improved by free and equal discussion'.[29]

A number of interpretations have been offered of Mill's position on this. H.J. McCloskey[30] argues that though Mill starts out with 'doing what one wants' as his 'official' definition of liberty, he quickly develops a much more positive notion. R.B. Friedman maintains that the typical liberal idea of

---

[28] John Stuart Mill, *On Liberty*, p68.

[29] ibid., p69.

[30] H.J. McCloskey, *John Stuart Mill: A Critical Study* (Macmillan, London, 1971), pp104-5.

freedom according to which 'the agent's own desires are taken as given data, and he is understood to be free if no one restrains him from giving effect to them', is accompanied by a positive conception of freedom embodying a moral ideal of unservile self-assertion. Friedman goes on: 'men are thought of as unfree not essentially because of the coercive interference of *other men*, but instead because they "do not desire liberty", and servility is not, on this view, a feature of the relations among men, but rather an attribute of character.'[31] Reasons for scepticism about Mill's adherence to negative freedom are easy to find. One of the major preoccupations in *On Liberty*, set out with admirable clarity in the introductory chapter, is with the rise of democratic conformism. But if freedom is construed simply as a matter of unfrustrated want satisfaction, how can Mill depict conformity as the insidious threat to liberty that he does? The conformist is precisely someone who wants to do only whatever he or she is permitted to do. The core of Mill's position is probably best described by Berlin: 'Mill believes in liberty, that is, the rigid limitation of the right to coerce, because he is sure that men cannot develop and flourish and become fully human unless they are left free from interference by other men within a certain minimum area of their lives, which he regards as - or wishes to make - inviolable.'[32]

Berlin has here identified the essential theme of *On Liberty*, that individuality or self-development cannot be realised without freedom to pursue alternative conceptions of the good, and to do that individuals must have knowledge of such alternatives. Berlin's 'rigid limitation of the right to coerce' refers to the 'harm principle'; freedom in this negative sense is for Mill a necessary condition of individuality. In his *Two Concepts of Liberty*, Berlin, whilst attributing a negative conception of liberty to Mill, goes on to insist that this concept is in fact inadequate for use by genuine liberals:

> [I]f I find that I am able to do little or nothing of what I wish, I need only contract or extinguish my wishes, and I am made free. If the tyrant (or 'hidden persuader') manages to condition his subjects (or customers) into losing their original wishes and embrace ('internalise') the form of life he has invented for them, he will on this definition, have succeeded in liberating them. He will, no doubt, have made them *feel* free....But what he has created is the very antithesis of political freedom.[33]

If this form of negative liberty is what Mill meant by freedom, then the

---

[31] R.B. Friedman, 'A New Exploration of Mill's Essay On Liberty', *Political Studies*, Vol. 14, 1966, pp281-304, p289.
[32] Isaiah Berlin, 'John Stuart Mill and the Ends of Life', in *Four Essays on Liberty*, p190.
[33] Isaiah Berlin, 'Two Concepts of Liberty', in *Four Essays on Liberty*, pp135-40.

'harm principle' could not possibly function as Berlin claims Mill intends. It could not guarantee, or even encourage, the achievement of individuality, because it would inevitably lead to the passive acceptance of social conformity, since constraints could all too easily be perceived as freedoms: the person imprisoned by a tyrant who nonetheless 'feels free', for instance. Such an acceptance would ensure that autonomy could never be achieved, let alone enjoyed, because the acceptance of conformity must limit the range of experience and experiments in living needed if the higher pleasures were first to be identified and later enjoyed. Mill must reject such a concept of freedom because it would mean that anyone whose desires had been ironed into conformity would be just as free as one of Mill's rational choosing individuals.

Mill believes in the individual's right to a sphere of freedom, but as Berlin notes, he is convinced that 'man differs from animals primarily neither as a possessor of reason, nor as an inventor of tools and methods, but as a being capable of choice'.[34] By 'choice', Mill must mean rational and informed choice: for otherwise, again, there would be no difference between choosing pushpin and poetry. The conception of freedom actually at work in *On Liberty* is intelligible only against the particular view of human beings as beings who need autonomy to secure happiness. The effective conception of freedom in *On Liberty* must be freedom as real, or positive, freedom of choice, not freedom as merely unfrustrated want satisfaction. Were it not so Mill would not have spent so much time in that work condemning the conformity induced by social pressure; nor would he have explicitly condemned the conformist tendencies of democracies in his review of Tocqueville's *Democracy in America*,

> ... where the majority is the sole power, and a power issuing its mandates in the form of riots, it inspires a terror which the most arbitrary monarch often fails to excite. The silent sympathy of the majority may support on the scaffold the martyr of one man's tyranny; but if we would imagine the situation of a victim of the majority itself, we must look to the annals of religious persecution for a parallel.[35]

It could of course be argued that real, or positive, freedom of choice is still a fundamentally negative concept of liberty. Someone who enjoys freedom of choice is simply someone faced with a range of uncoerced opportunities and the larger the range, the greater the freedom. This,

---

[34] Isaiah Berlin, 'John Stuart Mill and the Ends of Life', in *Four Essays on Liberty*, p178.

[35] John Stuart Mill, 'M. de Tocqueville on Democracy in America', in G.L. Williams (ed) *John Stuart Mill on Politics and Society* (Fontana, Glasgow, 1976), p215.

however, ignores the complications introduced by the idea that options are available only to beings capable of rational choice. For although it is possible to accommodate this dimension of free agency by simply stipulating that all human beings, except extreme cases such as infants, the certifiably insane, or the mentally subnormal, are to be assumed to enjoy powers of rational judgement and decision, so that the question of freedom remains restricted to visible and external impediments on human actions, this presents a further problem. Again a comparison with Berlin is germane. Berlin is reluctant to incorporate questions of rationality into his concept of freedom as choice because the notion of rationality in general, and the rational will in particular, is linked with the positive variant of liberty which he rejected. Berlin thinks that the positive idea of freedom is underlain by a monist and rationalist conception of the good. According to Berlin, the Hegelian or Platonic idea of freedom consists not in choice but in obedience to the rational will - whereas choice presupposes genuine rivalry between conflicting goods, rational will points to one, and one only course of action, one form of life for the individual. Mill refuses to recognise the validity of social rights for precisely the same reasons; such a doctrine would mean that individuals only have a right to act in their own rational, or in society's, interest. It would follow from this that others might have a right to coerce them on the basis of a more accurate discernment of their own, or society's, one true interest. For Mill, given his critique of social rights in *On Liberty* - and for that matter for Berlin - this would be unacceptable. Furthermore, Mill explicitly denies such a position when he says in that 'the only purpose of which power can be rightfully exercised over any member of a civilised community against his will, is to prevent harm to others. *His own good*, either physical or moral is not a sufficient warrant. He cannot rightfully be compelled to do or forbear... because in the opinion of others it would be wise or even right'.[36]

Mill's position, then, appears to be that whilst freedom is more than the absence of external constraints, the absence of external constraints is its necessary condition. Once people have 'attained the capacity of being guided to their own improvement by conviction or persuasion',[37] then under no circumstances are external constraints to be placed in the path of individuals, even if such constraints would promote the more positive dimension of freedom.

How then can the positive dimension of Mill's conception of liberty be justified? A possible way is through Mill's doctrine of the higher pleasures,

[36] John Stuart Mill, *On Liberty*, p68, emphasis added.

[37] ibid., p69.

and its relationship with his thoughts on freedom of choice. Mill objects to blind conformity to custom, for the sake of custom, because there is an absence of choice: 'to conform to custom merely as custom does not educate or develop any of the qualities which are the distinctive endowments of a human being. The human faculties of perception, judgement, discriminative feeling, mental activity, and even moral preference are exercised only in making a choice.'[38] Our end is to fully achieve our human nature. We cannot do that unless we develop the qualities that are exercised in making informed rational choices between competing conceptions of the good of equal quality. Individuals can then make rational informed choices between poetry and visual art, rather than between pushpin and pornography. Mill believes that individuals who do not, or who are unable to exercise this distinctively human capacity for choice, have lost that which is distinctively human, because that is what marks us out from the rest of nature.[39] Animals cannot have a purpose (even metaphorically) other than survival. Machines cannot have a purpose, but are designed by human beings to serve the purposes of human beings. Once a machine has been built which successfully serves its purpose, copies of it will be just as good as the originals. Humans, however, are different: '[H]uman nature is not a machine to be built after a model, and set to do exactly the work prescribed for it, but a tree, which requires to grow and develop itself on all sides, according to the tendency of the forces which make it a living thing.'[40]

So, even if a template for a perfect human being could be devised, it cannot be that all human beings would be of equal worth even if they were compelled to conform to it:

> [I]t is possible that he [a human being] might be guided in some good path, and kept out of harms way... But what will be his comparative worth as a human being? It really is of importance, not only what men do, but also what manner of men they are that do it. Among the works of man which human life is rightly employed in perfecting and

[38] ibid., p122.

[39] It should be noted, however, that Mill does not place the exercise of autonomous choice in a moral vacuum, but rather squarely within the core of his moral theory, especially relating to the development of character (see pp40-1 below. And as Helen Morales, states in *Perfect Equality: John Stuart Mill on Well-constituted Communities* (Rowman & Littlefield, London, 1996):

> [C]hoice from character is choice that unmistakably reveals the deliberation, reasoning, observation, judgement, feeling and decision of a moral agent. From Mill's perspective, if people are denied the conditions necessary for self-development and are taught to accept that the goodness of certain ways of life lies in its conformity to *a priori* notions of wisdom, propriety or rightness, they will not be in a position to make free choices. - p107.

[40] John Stuart Mill, *On Liberty*, p123.

beautifying, the first in importance is man himself.[41]

'Man himself' is lost in the forced imitation by human beings of ideal models, however worthy. It is considered choice between alternatives which allows the development of truly human potentialities:

> [H]e who allows the world or his own portion of it, choose his plan of life for him has no need of any other faculty than the ape-like one of imitation. He who chooses his plan for himself employs all his faculties. He must use observation to see, reasoning and judgement to foresee, activity to gather materials for decision, discrimination to decide, and when he has decided, firmness and self-control to hold his deliberate decision. And these qualities he requires and exercises exactly in proportion as the part of his conduct which he determines according to his own judgement and feelings is a large one.[42]

People who make choices develop a 'character'; their desires and feelings are the products of their own conscious choices, they will have experienced the consequences of previous choices and will have developed judgement and discrimination with respect to the higher and lower pleasures. But what are the alternatives in question? Mill opposed the type of conformism that developed in democracies in his time because he believed they circumscribed choice. In his review of Tocqueville's *Democracy in America*[43] he is scathing about both the dominance of public opinion where 'speculation becomes possible only within the limits traced by our free and enlightened citizens and our free and enlightened age': and the state of American 'products of the intellect'. This critique sheds light on the nature of the choices to which Mill is referring. Mill says of American works of art that: '[D]istracted by so great a multitude, the public can bestow but a moments attention on each; they will be adapted chiefly for striking at the moment. Deliberate approval, and duration beyond the hour, become more and more difficult of attainment.'[44] He goes on:

> [L]iterature thus becomes not only a trade, but is carried on by the maxims usually adopted by other trades which live by the number, rather than by the quality of their customers; that much pains need not be bestowed on commodities intended for the general market, and that

[41] ibid., p123.
[42] ibid.
[43] John Stuart Mill, 'M. de Tocqueville on Democracy in America', in G.L. Williams (ed) *John Stuart Mill on Politics and Society On Politics and Society*, pp218-19.
[44] ibid., p219.

> which is saved in the workmanship may be more profitably expended in self-advertisement. There will be an immense mass of third- or fourth-rate productions and very few first-rate.[45]

What Mill is arguing here is that what matters is not the range of the choices available but the quality. This positive conception of choice implies that he is using a notion of the good within the space of non-interference delineated by the 'harm principle'. He is convinced that no one who has reached a stage of moral and intellectual development where they can enjoy and appreciate the 'higher pleasures' would be content with the lower.[46] So choice is not just valuable *per se*, as in the choice of choosing whether to get drunk or go to a concert, it is valuable because once people have chosen to pursue the higher pleasure, i.e. going to a concert, they will recognise it is more worthwhile. To develop truly human qualities, and hence individuality, people must freely choose in favour of the higher pleasures, and reject the lower. Why should this be necessary if all Mill seeks is to be *neutral* between competing conceptions of the good? The answer, of course, is that this is not all that Mill seeks; and the reason why he desires people to choose the higher pleasures ahead of the lower will become apparent in the next section.

### 2.3 Pleasure, conformism and the 'good of humanity'

In *On Liberty*, Mill paints a devastating picture of the effects of conformism:

> [I]n our times, from the highest class of society down to the lowest, everyone lives under the eye of a hostile and dreaded censorship. Not only in what concerns others, but in what concerns only themselves, the individual or the family do not ask themselves, what do I prefer? or, what would suit my character and disposition? or, what would allow the

---

[45] ibid., p220.

[46] Helen Morales in *Perfect Equality: John Stuart Mill on Well-constituted Communities* clearly outlines the basis of Mill's argument:

> [H]e [Mill] argued that human beings have higher faculties that require fostering: the intellect, the feelings, the imagination and the moral sentiments. These faculties are sources of pleasures different from sensual pleasures. More importantly, the pleasures that people derive from the development and exercise of the higher faculties have a 'higher value' as pleasures than do sensual pleasure. Mill contended that after experiencing a range of alternatives, people would *prefer* a 'manner of existence' that includes the development and exercise of their higher faculties over one that does not. - p83.

Helen Morales, *Perfect Equality: John Stuart Mill on Well-constituted Communities* (Rowman & Littlefield, London, 1996).

best and highest in me to have fair play and enable it to grow and thrive? They ask themselves, what is suitable to my position? what is usually done by persons my station and circumstances? or (worse still) what is usually done by persons of a station and circumstances superior to mine? I do not mean that they choose between what is customary in preference to what suits their own inclination. It does not occur to them to have any inclination except for what is customary. Thus the mind itself is bound to the yoke: even in what people do for pleasure, conformity is the first thing thought of; they like in crowds; they exercise only among things commonly done; peculiarity of taste, eccentricity of conduct are shunned equally with crimes, until by dint of not following their own nature they have no nature to follow: their human capacities are withered and starved; they become incapable of any strong wishes or native pleasures, and are generally without either opinions or feelings of home growth, or properly their own. Now is this, or is it not, the desirable condition of human nature?[47]

Such conformist individuals are free inasmuch as they are not suffering interference with their self-regarding actions; but they are not free in Mill's more positive sense because they are not using their capacities for true freedom of choice. But what makes choice worthwhile? For Mill, there are two dimensions to a worthwhile choice: on the one hand, the choices that are made; and on the other how the choices are made. The first dimension involves freely choosing the higher pleasures ahead of the lower. Mill believes that, '... no intelligent human being would consent to be a fool, no instructed person would be an ignoramus, no person of feeling and conscience would be selfish and base, even though they should be persuaded that the fool, the dunce, or the rascal is better satisfied with his lot than they are with theirs'.[48] But, what makes a pleasure a higher pleasure? In *Utilitarianism* Mill writes: 'It is quite compatible with the principle of utility to recognise the fact, that some *kinds* of pleasure are more desirable and more valuable than others. It would be absurd that while, in estimating all other things, quality is considered as well as quantity, the estimation of pleasures should be supposed to depend on quantity alone.'[49] Mill then equates the quality of pleasures with their kind:

[W]hat is there to decide whether a particular pleasure is worth purchasing at the cost of a particular pain, except the feelings and

[47] John Stuart Mill, *On Liberty*, pp125-6.
[48] ibid., p9.
[49] John Stuart Mill, *Utilitarianism*, p8.

judgement of the experienced? When, therefore, those feelings and judgement declare the pleasures derived from the higher faculties to be preferable *in kind*, apart from the question of intensity, to those which the animal nature, disjoined from the higher faculties, is susceptible,. they are entitled to be subject to the same regard.[50]

So how can the quality of pleasure be measured? Mill argues as follows:

[I]f I am asked, what I mean by difference of quality in pleasures, or what makes one pleasure more valuable than another, merely as a pleasure, except its being greater in amount, there is but one possible answer. Of two pleasures, if there be one to which all or almost all who have experience of both give a decided preference irrespective of any feeling of moral obligation to prefer it, that is the more desirable pleasure. If one of the two is, by those who are competently acquainted with both, placed so far above the other prefer it, even though knowing it to be attended with a greater amount of discontent, and would not resign it for any quantity of the other pleasure which their nature is capable of, we are justified in ascribing to the preferred enjoyment a superiority in quality, so far outweighing quantity as to render it, in comparison, of small account.[51]

The point, then, is that it is those individuals who have undergone development and self-development that are in the best position to make judgements about the quality of pleasures. Mill bases his argument for this position on the reluctance of those who have undergone development to sink back into a trough of stupidity or ignorance. Despite Mill's believing that beings of higher faculties require more to make them happy, and are capable of more complete suffering, he is certain that they would not wish to exchange their condition for that of someone or something of lesser faculties: '[I]t is better to be a human being dissatisfied than a pig satisfied; better to be Socrates dissatisfied than a fool satisfied. And if the fool or the pig, are of a different opinion, it is because they only know their own side of the question. The other party to the comparison knows both sides.'[52] The difference between the fool and Socrates is an awareness of potential, and an ability to compare. An intelligent, informed being will have developed their capacities to such an extent that they are capable of autonomous choice among higher pleasures, and between higher and lower pleasures. So Mill's

[50] ibid., p11.
[51] ibid., pp8-9.
[52] ibid., p10.

procedure for determining the value of pleasures involves ascertaining the preferences of those who are deemed to be competent judges.

This brings in the second dimension of Mill's conception worthwhile choices. How and why do some people become competent judges? Education plays a vital role here; it is the process by which individuals become sufficiently developed to be able to distinguish between higher and lower pleasures. Development consists in the inculcation of objective standards for judging the value of happiness. These standards teach individuals to distinguish between to and evaluate different pleasurable experiences. Teaching offers models that allow individuals to discover and appreciate what it is about species of pleasure that makes them worth pursuing. It is their development as an individual that influences what a competent judge will find in a higher pleasure. Such personal development can only occur when conditions allow individuals to have experience of choosing amongst a wide range of options. Once they have had that experience Mill believes they will have developed in such a way that they will prefer the higher pleasures ahead of the lower. The picture that emerges of Mill's individual is of a person who is the product of a tradition that encourages experiment, self-help and self-improvement. People brought up within that tradition are capable of self-improvement because they all pursue different, and sometimes competing, conceptions of the good. Some of the goods pursued will be representative of the higher pleasures. Once these have been experienced, Mill believes, individuals will thirst for more. The result of these positive choices will be the establishment of what Mill and other nineteenth century theorists such as Matthew Arnold, Samuel Smiles and John Morley[53] described as a character. A person who has developed such a character is not hidebound by custom; nor is he or she a slave to the baser passions. They are capable of being improved by rational argument and discussion. Moreover, they represent precisely the individuality that Mill sees as his ideal.

In the preceding discussion of the 'harm principle' Mill's negative case for individuality was explained: his doctrine of character offers positive arguments for that ideal. Liberty allows the greatest potential for human progress, hence liberty is claimed to be instrumentally better than any circumstances that inhibit human potential. Yet much of Mill's argument here is aesthetic rather than utilitarian. Mill's critique of Bentham makes this clear: '[M]an is never recognized by him [Bentham] as a being capable of pursuing spiritual perfection as an end; of desiring for its own sake, the

[53] Matthew Arnold, *Culture and Anarchy and other Writings* (Cambridge University Press, Cambridge, 1993); Samuel Smiles, *Character* (London, 1871); John Morley, *On Compromise* (London, 1886).

conformity of his own character to his standard of excellence, without hope of good or fear of evil from other sources than his own inward consciousness.'[54] Mill's justification of the intrinsic value of individuality is difficult to pin down, his most clearly developed attempt to offer such a justification comes in the final chapter of *A System of Logic*.[55] He begins the process by drawing a general distinction between art and science. Science is defined as 'inquiries into the course of nature'.[56] That part of moral philosophy that deals with the natural consequences of actions (including those that relate to human nature) is a science. But that part of it, which deals in ultimate ends, or precepts, lies in the realm of art. The relation between the realm of art and the realm of science can be characterised thus:

> ... the art proposes to itself an end to be attained, defines the end, and hands it over to the science. The science receives it, considers it as a phenomenon or effect to be studied, and having investigated its causes and conditions, sends it back to art with a theorem of the combination of circumstances by which it could be produced. Art then examines these combinations of circumstances, and according as any of them are or are not in human power, pronounces the end attainable or not.[57]

Art, which can be appreciated only through the development of character and judgement, tells individuals what given ends are desirable. The result is the enhancement and progress of humanity as a whole:

> ... by cultivating it [individuality] and calling it forth, within the limits imposed by the rights and interests of others, ... human beings become a noble and beautiful object of contemplation; and as the works partake the character of those who do them, by the same process human life also becomes rich, diversified, and animating, furnishing more abundant aliment to high thoughts and elevating feelings. [58]

Mill *values* individuality because it improves mankind and acts as a motor to progress. It ensures that not only the quality, but also the quantity of happiness is increased. But is this also the reason Mill gives in defence of individuality? On this particular issue Mill is ambivalent. In *Utilitarianism* he insists that: '[Q]uestions of ultimate ends are not amenable to direct

---

[54] John Stuart Mill, Bentham, in *Essays on Ethics, Religion and Society*, J.M. Robson (ed) *Collected Works*, vol. 10 (Toronto University Press, Toronto, 1969), p95.
[55] John Stuart Mill, *A System of Logic*, Eighth Edition (London, 1900).
[56] ibid., p616.
[57] ibid., p617.
[58] John Stuart Mill, *On Liberty*, p127.

proof.'[59]

Of what proofs are ultimate ends susceptible? Mill says that

> ...the sole evidence it is possible to produce that anything is desirable is that people do actually desire it. If the end which the utilitarian doctrine proposes to itself were not, in theory and in practice, acknowledged to be an end, nothing could ever convince any person that it was so. No reason can be given why the general happiness is desirable, except that each person, so far as he believes it to be attainable, desires his own happiness. This, however, being a fact, we have not only all the proof which the case admits of, but all of which it is possible to require, that happiness is a good: that each person's happiness is a good to that person, and the general happiness, therefore, a good to the aggregate of all persons. Happiness has made out its title as *one* of the ends of conduct, and consequently one of the criteria of morality.[60]

Now, let us accept, for the time being, that Mill is the utilitarian he claims to be. He has proved by way of an arguably, but perhaps not necessarily viciously, circular argument that happiness is desirable because individuals desire it.[61] Why, then, does Mill believe that the development and protection of individuality is the key to promoting the greatest happiness for the greatest number? In an apparently contradictory section in *A System of Logic*, Mill first commits himself to the principle of utility: 'I ... declare my conviction, that the general principle to which all rules of practice ought to conform, and the test by which they should be tried, is that of conduciveness to the happiness of mankind, or rather, of all sentient beings: in other words, that the promotion of happiness is the ultimate principle of Teleology.'[62] But he immediately qualifies this statement, which is why he is sometimes taken to be a rule utilitarian:

> I do not mean to assert that the promotion of happiness should be itself the end of all actions or even of all rules of action. It is the justification, and ought to be the controller of all ends, but it is not in itself the sole end. There are many virtuous actions, and even virtuous modes of action, ... by which happiness in the particular instance is sacrificed,

[59] John Stuart Mill, *Utilitarianism*, p4.

[60] ibid., p36.

[61] Mary Warnock in her introduction to *Utilitarianism, On Liberty and Essay on Bentham* argues that Mill's position is not necessarily circular. See, John Stuart Mill, *Utilitarianism, On Liberty and Essay on Bentham*, edited and introduced by Mary Warnock (Fontana, London, 1962), pp26-7.

[62] John Stuart Mill, *A System of Logic*, p621.

> more pain being produced than pleasure. But conduct of which this can be truly asserted admits of justification only because it can be shown that on the whole more happiness will exist in the world if feelings are cultivated which will make people, in certain cases, regardless of happiness.[63]

Mill then goes on to argue that the good of humanity as a whole is best served if human beings take for their ultimate aim the development of what is best in themselves, irrespective of whether this would promote the happiness of the individual, or the happiness of humanity. How then can Mill still claim to be utilitarian when he says the 'cultivation of an ideal nobleness of will and conduct' should be subordinate to the individual or collective pursuit of happiness?[64] The point is that Mill valued excellence of character in the same way as he valued individuality, the pre-condition for developing a character, solely as a condition of happiness. However, this was not simply happiness in the sense of the lower pleasures and absence of pain, but rather the happiness that comes from nobleness of character:

> [T]he character itself should be, to the individual, a paramount end, simply because the existence of this ideal nobleness of character, or of a near approach to it, in any abundance, would go further than all things else towards making human life happy, both in the comparatively humble sense of pleasure and freedom from pain, and in the higher meaning of rendering life, not what it now is almost universally puerile and insignificant, but such as human beings with highly developed faculties can care to have.[65]

It would be hard to argue that Mill was in this respect a utilitarian, even in the most minimal sense, if he was concerned with individuals pursuing fineness of character for its own sake and no other. But Mill clearly believes that the development of fineness of character is likely not only to promote the happiness of the individual concerned, but also the happiness of those around them. Developing a character is a surer way than adopting a felicific calculus of becoming a practically wise agent and promoting the public happiness.

Mill's objectives are, therefore, far from neutral as between different conceptions of human flourishing. His aim is to establish a society where, through education, individuals develop fine, well-rounded characters in

---

63 ibid.

64 ibid.

65 ibid., pp621-2.

which intellectual rigour coexists with imagination, liveliness and prudent judgement. Such qualities are desirable, both because they are grounds for happiness in themselves, and because people who possess such qualities are likely to be more sympathetic to others, and hence promote their happiness.

Where does this leave Mill's neutrality? Mill's adherence to neutrality is based on the idea of lexical priorities.[66] He recognises that individual, self-regarding actions can and do damage the wider development of individuality; but coercion of individuals once they have reached a certain stage of historical development can do more harm to this ultimate goal than any harm done by individual actions. However, this leaves open the possibility of using persuasion and leadership by élites to protect and promote conditions that allow individuality to flourish. This, more than anything else, demonstrates the limits of Mill's commitment to neutrality.

Although self-regarding acts may not be interfered with, if such acts 'are hurtful to others or wanting in due consideration for their welfare, without going to the length of violating any of their constituted rights,' then the individual may be 'justly punished by opinion though not by law'.[67] Mill also makes clear that individuals who pursue 'animal pleasures at the expense of those of feeling and intellect'[68] must expect to be judged unfavourably by their fellows. He believes that it would be doing such a person a favour to warn and persuade them against committing any acts that would result in justifiable public opprobrium. Moreover, individuals who indulged in the lower pleasures at the expense of the higher will be, and indeed should be, subject to the spontaneous penalties of society:

> [W]e have a right, also in various ways, to act upon our unfavourable opinion of anyone, not to the oppression of his individuality, but in the exercise of ours. We are not bound, ...to seek his society; we have a right to avoid it...for we have a right to choose the society most acceptable to us. We have a right, and it may be our duty, to caution others against him if we think his example or conversation likely to have a pernicious effect on those with whom he associates. We may give others a preference over him in optional good offices, except those which tend to his improvement. In these various modes a person may suffer very severe penalties at the hands of others for faults which

[66] There is a parallel here with the interpretation of Mill's utilitarianism offered by Wendy Donner in 'Mill's utilitarianism', in John Skorupski (ed) *The Cambridge Companion to Mill*. She suggests that in Mill's view 'there is a strong and central role for secondary moral principles; but there are also instances where a direct appeal is made to the principle of utility in particular cases'. - p279.

[67] John Stuart Mill, *On Liberty*, p141.

[68] ibid., p144.

directly concern only himself; but he suffers these penalties only in so far as they are the natural, and, as it were, the spontaneous consequences of the faults themselves, not because they are purposely inflicted on him for the sake of punishment.[69]

Mill is saying that if people choose to prefer the lower pleasures over the higher, if they behave in ways which will not lead them to develop 'fineness of character', then they must at best be persuaded of the error of their ways; and at worst, if they still refuse to conform to his ideals, then they may be justifiably shunned by the rest of society. Mill's neutrality, then is not an end in itself, but a means to achieving his goal of rationally choosing individuals, which in turn, is his indirect utilitarian way of achieving the greatest happiness for the greatest number. His neutrality regarding people's choices, pleasures and means of achieving happiness, serves in his view as the most efficient way of furthering his conception of a 'good society' - and that is a far from neutral conception.

That this really is Mill's position is confirmed by his argument on slavery. The act of an individual's selling himself or herself into slavery must be a self-regarding act. It affects the essential interests of no one but the person who has agreed to be a slave. It could, of course, be argued that by doing so the individual concerned was damaging the well-being of the wider society by their act, but so, in Mill's view, were drunkards, gamblers and fornicators, and he insisted that they should not be punished for their actions beyond public censure. The act of selling one's self into slavery though is different because

> [T]he reason for not interfering, unless for the sake of others with a person's voluntary acts is consideration for his liberty. His voluntary choice is evidence that what he so chooses is desirable, or at least endurable, to him, and his own good is on the whole best provided for by allowing him to take his own means of pursuing it. But by selling himself for a slave, he abdicates his liberty; he forgoes any future use of it beyond that single act. He therefore, defeats, in his own case, the very purpose that is the justification of allowing him to dispose of himself. He is no longer free, but is thenceforth in a position which has no longer the presumption in its favour that would be afforded by his voluntarily remaining in it. The principle of freedom cannot require that he should be free not to be free. It is not freedom to be allowed to alienate his

[69] ibid.

freedom.[70]

On the one hand this position is inconsistent, in that it limits the right of individuals to undertake self-regarding acts without interference. But in the light of previous discussions on Mill's relationship with the principle of utility and the higher pleasures, it is remarkably consistent. Freedom, although of some intrinsic value, is fundamentally to be seen as the instrument by which human beings attain individuality. That is how they become rational choosing individuals and possessors of Mill's fine character. The possessors of such characters are not only happy in themselves, but they are more likely to promote happiness amongst their fellow human beings.

This is the conception of the good that is implicit in Mill's thought. His neutrality is not like that of deontological liberals like Rawls, who declare that the 'right is prior to the good'; rather it is neutrality in respect of the means whereby the good is to be achieved. For Mill, the good would seem to be prior to the right, since the latter is a question of the efficiency of the actions concerned in helping to achieve the good. In all cases where choices are made that still allow people to retain freedom, then that is the means to their good, and they are not to be interfered with, other than by persuasion. However, in a case such as making a choice to become a slave, where the choice cuts off any hope of attaining the good, then that act is prohibited.

Mill's system would still remain utilitarian because, as John Gray has argued,[71] he believes that the 'Principle of Utility' should be applied to social systems in their entirety, not only to specific acts or rules. Mill's 'Principle of Utility' is axiological and not practical in force: it is a principle for the evaluation of whole codes of rules or social system, and not one that is invoked directly by legislators or private individuals to settle questions of conduct. Mill's ultimate good is the true happiness that comes from individuality and a fine character.

To conclude, Mill's thought has its own internal coherence. The problem for Mill is in establishing either an empirical or an *a priori* foundation for his contention that true human happiness is to be found in individuality. Mill is adamant that the happiness that comes from individuality and a fine character is worthwhile only because people desire them and having experienced them would not willingly return to a previous condition. On the other hand, people who do not desire these suffer from a lack of development. What, then, comes first? In the end his position is an empirical one: his 'good' is desirable because people desire it. This is surely the antithesis of what liberalism is supposed to be about. The liberal project is

[70] ibid., p173.

[71] John Gray, *Mill on Liberty: A Defence*, Second Edition.

predicated on the idea that it is possible to form a social order in which individuals could emancipate themselves from the contingency and particularity of tradition by appealing to genuinely universal tradition-independent norms.[72] By his insistence that ultimately the only evidence we have that something is desirable is that people desire it, Mill is abandoning the liberal quest for universal foundations because, as he recognises with his concern for the development of democratic conformity in the USA and elsewhere, what people, as a matter of fact, desire is socially conditioned. What Mill does not grasp is that if desires in general, are a product of the social context then so is the particular desire that he wishes to see encouraged, namely the desire for individuality.

Where does this leave the normative foundations of Mill's thought? He wishes to see the maintenance and development of rational choosing individuals. He offers no coherent non-circular defence of the desire of people to become such individuals, other than that they do indeed desire it. In other words, they have a prejudice in favour of the establishment of individuality, because, according to Mill, they believe, or at least those qualified to judge believe, that in true happiness lies in individuality. The only justification of this is that individuality is a quality that at least some - developed - people have been found to enjoy and therefore, Mill believes, we should have a predisposition in its favour. The reason for that predisposition is simply that people have enjoyed the experience of individuality.[73] Mill's normative foundation amounts, then, to this: individuality is good because people enjoy it. However, individuality itself and its enjoyment was not something that appeared out of the blue on the eve of July 14th 1789 or even 5th November 1688: rather it was the development of a long historical process which allowed the development of traditions institutions and attitudes which held that individuality was a good.[74] But it is not just that Mill is not neutral. It is that the defence of something because it has existed, and because people have found much to enjoy in it, is a classical conservative defence of any institution, tradition or mode of life - as Mill recognises in his strictures against conformity. Mill, despite accurately

---

[72] See, Alasdair MacIntyre, *Whose Justice? Which Rationality?* (University of Notre Dame Press, Notre Dame, Indiana), p335.

[73] Despite Mill's alleged élitism, C.L. Ten in *Mill on Liberty*, for example argues that the ideal of individuality is within the reach of all. However, Ten nonetheless recognises that Mill holds that there should be a special role for the élite as: '[H]e [Mill] believes that only a few men are capable of *initiating* new practices. The rest are, however, capable of realising their individualities too because they can choose for themselves among a range of alternatives which they have not initiated.' - p71.

[74] See Oakeshott, 'The Masses in Representative Democracy', in A. Hunold (ed) *Freedom and Serfdom: An Anthology of Western Thought.*

perceiving the historically grounded nature of the liberal tradition does not himself draw the conservative inference that to preserve and encourage individuality, it is necessary to preserve and maintain existing traditions and institutions lest the conditions which allow individuality to flourish be lost. But that is at the cost of consistency; and it is at the cost of consistency the he remains a liberal.

# 3 Hayek's Libertarian Neutrality

Mill straddled the divide between the classical and the new liberalism. While he unquestionably valued the liberal principles of $17^{th}$ and $18^{th}$ century liberal thinkers, he attempted to provide a normative basis for freedom and the rule of law by arguing that proto-liberal values were a necessary, if not sufficient, condition for the voluntaristic development of the ultimate goal of liberalism, the evolution of rational choosing individuals. Hayek, by contrast, claims that his work is an attempt to restate and refine the arguments of the early thinkers of classical liberalism: David Hume, Adam Smith, James Madison, Immanuel Kant and Alexis de Tocqueville.[1] He believes that precisely the developmental element that emerged in liberalism thanks to Mill's emphasis on the evolution of character fundamentally undermined the elements in liberalism that had led to what he described as the 'Great Society'. Hayek attempts to prove two things. First, that the liberal order is 'natural', in the sense that it is unplanned, the product of human actions but not of human design; and second, on the basis of his epistemology and empirical psychology, that the liberal order is the best form of society if human beings are to have satisfying lives. Indeed, Hayek would go further and argue that the only meaningful forms of good life are to be found in liberal societies, where individuals can pursue their own purposes, and not have the purposes of others imposed upon them. Ironically, despite these claims, Hayek is rigorous in his disavowal of any conception of the good. His putative neutrality rests on his claim that the case for liberty rests on value-free empirical foundations, in contrast to Mill, who, as we have seen, argued that the establishment of ultimate moral ends could not be a scientific enterprise.[2]

In this chapter, I shall argue that Hayek's conception of a 'spontaneous order' is not, however, neutral in the sense of being value-free. Furthermore, I shall argue, his epistemology and empirical psychology cannot bear the weight of proof that his theory requires. Hayek's *oeuvre* ranges over several traditional academic disciplines and he participated in some of the key intellectual debates of the $20^{th}$ century; this chapter therefore cannot claim to be a comprehensive account even of his work on liberalism. What it is concerned to do, however, is to demonstrate that underpinning his allegedly

[1] See F. A. Hayek, *Law, Legislation and Liberty*, Vol. I, Chapter 1.

[2] John Stuart Mill, *A System of Logic*, Book VI, Chapter 12.

value-free conceptions of the human mind and the spontaneous order is a tacit conception of the good, and that for all his claims to be scientific and value-free, Hayek's thought ultimately rests on a subjective adherence to the liberal tradition. Only those elements of Hayek's thought directly relevant to achieving this objective will be examined in detail.

Hayek, of course has often been interpreted as a conservative.[3] However, what appears not to have been noticed is the contradictory nature of his empirical and Kantian arguments and the role of that tension in his (conservative) thinking. Moreover, an examination of these tensions demonstrate that Hayek, far from being an aberrant liberal as is usually claimed, is in fact clearly representative of the liberal tradition. Hayek's normative prescriptions depend, either in part or in full, on empirical psychological and epistemological foundations. Whereas Mill believes that tradition and conformity are threats to individuality, Hayek argues that they are - as a matter of fact - its foundation. How does Hayek reach these conclusions? Hayek's thought is both explanatory and prescriptive: he explains the nature of man and society and on the basis of those explanations develops a prescriptive theory which allows him to defend liberty as the foremost value in society.

Hayek's objectives were always clear. His aim, set out in a series of works beginning with *The Road to Serfdom* in 1944 and culminating with the publication of the first volume of his collected works, *The Fatal Conceit: The Errors of Socialism*,[4] in 1988, has been to demonstrate that socialism in all its forms is untenable, and that the good society must be one governed by liberal institutions upholding the market economy and the rule of law. Indeed as one recent author has commented, Hayek had two intellectual personas:

> [H]e was a patient, thorough, wide-ranging scholar, who emerged as one of the most important and original thinkers of the century, but also as one of the century's most renowned ideologues, a leading critic of all forms of socialism and a passionate advocate of classical liberalism.
>
> ... Hayek's reputation as an ideologue has for long been a barrier to a wider appreciation of his intellectual contribution to social science. This

[3] See for example, John Gray, 'Hayek as a Conservative', in his *Post-Liberalism* (Routledge, London, 1993), pp32-9. Hayek himself, whilst recognising the similarities to conservatism in certain elements of his thought, was concerned to deny that he might be a conservative, see especially the postscript, entitled 'Why I am not a Conservative' to *The Constitution of Liberty* (Routledge & Kegan Paul, London, 1960), pp397-414.

[4] F. A. Hayek, *The Road to Serfdom* (Routledge, London, 1944); and *The Fatal Conceit: The Errors of Socialism*.

is hardly surprising. The two are hard to disentangle, because Hayek for the most part saw no reason to keep them apart. His ideological views flow from the same methodological assumptions as his scientific work and his writings are all part of the same intellectual project.[5]

The unacknowledged dichotomy between Hayek the ideologue and Hayek the scholar is what is centrally problematic about his thought. Although Hayek's theory seeks to offer both normative and allegedly empirical scientific justifications[6] for making liberty the foremost value in society, neither is ultimately successful - or so I shall seek to show. Hayek attempts to do two things. First, he tries to show, through his epistemology and psychology, that a free society offers the best opportunity for progress, prosperity and the fulfilment of the diverse and proliferous wants of individuals. This is an empirical claim about the value of liberty and it offers a reason, other than suggesting that liberty is an end in itself, why liberty is valuable. Second, he attempts to offer a normative defence of liberty that does in fact claim that liberty is of value as an end in itself, rather than in terms of the effect that it might have on the material well-being of individuals. I shall argue that his attempt fails in two ways.

First, he does not succeed in demonstrating that his model of society as a rule-governed, purposeless, spontaneous order - the product of human action but not of human design - is in fact neutral in the sense of being free from value-laden notions of the good society. While the putative neutrality of Hayek's work rests on the idea that, as 'spontaneous order' describes how things *are*, the rules which emerge unintentionally to regulate them do not have a normative element and hence are neutral between the premeditated competing conceptions of the good of individuals, the very fact that he argues that intervention in certain types of order can create or improve the qualities of those orders in such a way that their efficiency - in meeting the diverse and proliferous wants of individuals - is improved suggests that, underlying the notion of 'spontaneous order', is some form of instrumental good. That instrumental good, however, assumes an object and that is material well-being, that is to say a substantial good. Second, Hayek offers no consistent moral defence of the maintenance of what he describes as a free society. His justification for his political programme of maintaining and

---

[5] Andrew Gamble, *Hayek: The Iron Cage of Liberty*, pp1-2.

[6] To claim that Hayek uses empirical justifications for his defence of liberty is not to claim that he is in the empiricist tradition; rather he makes a series of claims for the benefits of liberty which can be tested empirically. See in particular F. A. Hayek, *The Constitution of Liberty*, pp41, 48, and 259. Other writers have also seen Hayek in this light, for example, Gamble, cited above and Jeremy Shearmur, *Hayek and After: Hayekian Liberalism as a Research Programme* (Routledge, London, 1996).

promoting liberty through the free market is that it is such a system that allows the survival, in relative material prosperity, of a greater number of people than would otherwise be the case - again what we have is an assumed substantive conception of the good. The survival in relative material prosperity of a greater rather than a smaller number of people is neither self-evidently nor necessarily a good, difficult though that thought might be: consider, for example, the ascetics of various religious and philosophical traditions. Hayek uses three types of argument to defend freedom. The first, implied by the contention that a free society with a free market allows a greater number of people a better quality of material life, is consequentialist. The second, which is related to the first, offers what is in fact a conservative defence of the established order, based on a psychology and epistemology which tells him that as there is no archimedean point whence societies can stand back and objectively reform themselves by reason, they are more likely to retain their freedom, and hence their material prosperity, by adhering to established traditions and institutions. Both these arguments are teleological, a justification of the morality of the liberal order on the basis of the ultimate well-being of individuals. The third argument is a Kantian one, based on the idea that liberty is a worthwhile end in itself. Difficulties, however, arise from the combination of these arguments: for they are clearly inconsistent with each other. On the one hand, attempting to maintain and secure a system - based on what Michael Oakeshott described as the 'plausible ethics of productivity'[7] - is not neutral between competing conceptions of the good; and on the other, if liberalism fails to deliver the prosperity promised, then it cannot be empirically justified on that basis. Nor can Hayek then fall back on his Kantian defence of freedom, because its rationalist basis contradicts his (earlier) empirical psychology and epistemology. It might be supposed, however, that I have misconstrued the problem for the tension I have described is evident only if Hayek's two lines of argument are understood as either/or possibilities; but, as Hayek after all insists, the claim that liberalism is the most effective way of satisfying human wants is not a moral claim; and thus the notion that freedom is valuable in itself could be seen as an additional reason for adopting liberalism. To put it more formally,[8] there is no actual inconsistency between (a) the notion that liberalism is the most effective way of satisfying the aggregate of human wants, as a reason for espousing it; and (b) that freedom is valuable in itself, as an additional reason for espousing it. We only get into meta-ethical problems if we claim (a) is a moral claim - i.e. if (a) - that

[7] Michael Oakeshott, 'The Claims of Politics', *Scrutiny*, 8 (1939-1940), pp146-51.

[8] I am grateful to my PhD supervisor, Ms. Susan Khinzaw of the Open University, for making this point.

liberalism is the most effective way of satisfying the aggregate of human wants - is a *moral* reason for espousing it. And this is precisely what Hayek wants to avoid claiming as (a) is meant to be value neutral. But this objection assumes that (a) *can* be regarded as other than a moral claim, as Hayek indeed intends. It is only if we assume a liberal view - and indeed Hayek's version of it - that (a) could be seen as not a moral claim. On a liberal view the claim that 'liberalism is the most effective way of satisfying the aggregate of human wants' can be other than a moral claim because 'most effective' is understood as either an empirical or value-free claim, or at any rate as one which does not rest on any substantive 'good'. But that is precisely the point at issue. What is simply 'most effective' for Hayek might well be morally outrageous for, for instance, a stoic or a pre-medieval Christian. Moreover, the very possibility of regarding the claim as value neutral, is already to subscribe, at least to the viability of liberalism's alleged neutrality concerning the good as itself a good.

To reiterate, the problem Hayek faces is that he is attempting to run an empirical and an ethical argument simultaneously. The empirical claim is founded on empirical psychological and epistemological evidence about the nature of society which he claims demonstrates that the most effective order for satisfying human wants is a liberal order; and moreover, because these claims explain how the world actually is, they are value-free and neutral, consequently, if liberalism fails to deliver prosperity the justification fails. By contrast, Hayek's normative argument claims that liberty is of value in itself, whether or not it promotes human material good. The empirical argument, however, cannot do the work demanded of it because the evidence does not support it; while the normative argument - being normative - requires a justification of the relevant values which Hayek does not provide. Thus Hayek's attempt to provide a foundation for the vision of a society founded on individual liberty fails: but, I shall argue, such a vision might more plausibly defended on a conservative understanding of the empirical evidence.

### 3.1 'Spontaneous order' and the value of liberty

Hayek, then, sees his work as an attempt to restate and refine the ideas of classical liberalism. Although he is not a natural rights theorist, he would accept Locke's contention that the reason why individuals associate with others in society is the '*Preservation* of their lives liberties and estates'.[9] What Hayek attempts to do is to show that states which confine themselves

[9] John Locke, *Two Treatises of Government* (Mentor, London, 1963), II, Chapter 9, p395.

to such roles not only preserve liberty by limiting coercion to ensure that people obey the law, but that such states are not *coercive* at all. To overcome this apparent contradiction Hayek argues that, provided the rules established to protect liberty are general and can be applied universally, the state which administers them is both neutral between competing conceptions of the good and does not itself have a substantive purpose. Where does this leave the idea that the purpose of entering political society and placing oneself under government is the 'preservation of lives liberties and estates'? His answer is that no one, or no institution seeks security of person or property as an end in itself. Security of person or property is always a good that is needed in order to achieve other substantive goods.

Hayek suggests that only those forms of association governed by internally abstract universal rules can achieve the security of lives, liberties and estates.[10] The maintenance of these rules is not what a theorist like Michael Oakeshott - who bears certain similarities to Hayek in this respect - would describe as a 'substantive' independent purpose, but is rather a pre-condition which allows citizens to pursue their own ends. The addition of the adjective 'substantive' is important here. Substantive means subsisting separately and independently apart from the individual ends of the citizens of a state.[11] Thus on Hayek's preferred model, the state must not have a separate independent purpose from the individual purposes of the citizens who live under its jurisdiction if it is to maintain the liberty of its citizens. The state is a compulsory institution in that no one has a choice whether or not to be a member: if it has a specific purpose of its own, beyond allowing individuals to pursue their own purposes, then it imposes on its citizens its own particular goals and so destroys the liberty it was established to protect. The nature of this type of purposive state can be made more explicit by comparing it with an organisation. Organisations such as sports clubs, community associations or charities unite their members in the pursuit of a common goal: if they did not share that goal, they would not be members of the organisation. The rules of the organisation exist to facilitate members in the pursuit of this common end. By contrast, in Hayek's terms, the rules of a state exist to prevent individuals and organisations clashing in the pursuit of their own self-set goals.

---

[10] See F. A. Hayek, *The Constitution of Liberty*, pp149-52.

[11] Oakeshott uses the term 'substantive' to apply to the difference between 'civil association', that is association without substantive purposes, and 'enterprise association', that is association in terms of a common goal or objective. In *On Human Conduct* (Clarendon Press, Oxford, 1975), Oakeshott describes 'enterprise association' as a 'relationship in terms of the pursuit of some common purpose, some substantive condition of things to be jointly procured, or some common interest to be continuously satisfied'. - p114.

The arena in which individuals pursue these self-set goals is civil society. Civil society is a complex association of individuals joined together with one another in a series of relationships shaped by personal interest, economic inter-dependence, conventions and laws. Included within civil society are associations of individuals linked in pursuit of common goals through commerce, charitable institutions or community groups; or in enjoyment of common pastimes such as sport or art; or as communicants of various religions. Specifically excluded from civil society are political relations and the institutions of the state. But the state is, nevertheless, responsible for the maintenance of civil society through enforcing sets of general universal rules. These rules, however, are not coercive, inasmuch as they do not restrict individual purposes; they merely state universal conditions that must be taken into account when acting. One way of understanding how Hayek's ideal non-purposive rules would work is to compare them to the laws in existing states that regulate traffic. Such laws do not specify the destination of any journey that is undertaken; rather they specify the conditions which must be taken into account if the traveller is going to reach his or her destination safely and without risking the lives of other travellers. Similarly, Hayek's universal rules do not impose the purposes of the state upon us. As they are general, they provide the necessary conditions under which we may pursue our own purposes without arbitrary restriction by others or by the state. They work in the same way as the rules of the road, in that they will allow us to pursue our own goals without risk of harm or improper hindrance from others.

If states do not possess such a character, then, to a greater or lesser extent, they coerce their citizens. Although Hayek declares that liberty is the foremost value in society, a significant element in the case he makes for liberty surrounds the damage done by coercion. Indeed, Hayek begins his fullest account of individual liberty by saying: '[T]he state in which a man is not subject to coercion by the arbitrary will of another or others is often distinguished as 'individual' or 'personal' freedom, and whenever we want to remind the reader that it is in this sense that we are using the word 'freedom' we shall employ that expression.'[12]

At this point, Hayek cites F.H. Knight to the effect that 'coercion' is the term that really needs to be defined,[13] and in the definition cited above he has specified the coercion he has in mind, namely the 'coercion by the arbitrary will of another or others'. The rule of law, according to Hayek, is not arbitrary, but general and universal; and is therefore not a restriction on

---

[12] F. A. Hayek, *The Constitution of Liberty*, p11.
[13] ibid., note 3, p421.

individual liberty - for Hayek, the rule of law is not coercive. It has been argued by some that Hayek's insistence on universality as a basis for law will not protect individual spheres of liberty, and overlooks some forms of coercion.[14] However, Hayek's position is that the rule of law is not coercive, and that furthermore it is only the version of the rule of law that Hayek espouses which will allow society to flourish.

In order to make his case that his conception of the rule of law is non-coercive, Hayek makes a distinction between spontaneous order and organisation.[15] Hayek claims that laws are neutral and non-coercive because they are products of orders in society that he declares to be 'spontaneous': that is, the product of human action but not of human design. The conception of the 'spontaneous order' is at the heart of Hayek's social theory and is the foundation of his neutralist claims. For Hayek, 'the formation of spontaneous orders is the result of their elements following certain rules in their responses to their immediate environment'.[16] Furthermore, '[T]he individual responses to particular circumstances will result in an overall order only if the individuals obey such rules as will produce an order. Even a very limited similarity in their behaviour may be sufficient if the rules, which they all obey, are such as to produce an order'.[17] Hayek developed his idea of a 'spontaneous social order', '[T]o explain how an overall order of economic activity was achieved which utilised a large amount of knowledge which was not concentrated in any one mind but existed only as the separate knowledge of thousands or millions of different individuals'.[18] This point was to show how a market society could function without the co-ordination of a central authority: and his answer is that: '[A]n adequate insight into the relations between the abstract rules which the individual follows in his actions, and the abstract overall order which is formed as a result of his responding, within the limits imposed upon him by those abstract rules, to the concrete particular circumstances which he encounters.'[19]

From this passage it seems that the mechanism on which 'spontaneous order' rests has two components. 'Spontaneous order' first arises out of the routine observance of general rules of behaviour; and second, from the modifications which individuals make in response to local conditions. The orders established by such rule-governed behaviour can be distinguished

---

[14] See for example, Ronald Hamowy, 'Law and the Liberal Society: F.A. Hayek's *Constitution of Liberty*', *Journal of Libertarian Studies*, 2 (1978), pp287-97.

[15] F.A. Hayek, *Law, Legislation and Liberty Vol. I Rules and Order*, pp36 and 37.

[16] ibid., p43.

[17] ibid., p44.

[18] F.A. Hayek, *Studies in Philosophy, Politics and Economics* (Routledge & Kegan Paul, London, 1967), p92.

[19] ibid.

from the type of order formed by organisations.

The distinction between 'spontaneous order' and organisation is foundational for Hayek's social theory. According to Hayek, however, it is a distinction which goes against the widely held belief that society, and the social orders which comprise it, are all constructed by conscious human design. People have 'anthropomorphic habits of thought',[20] and this inclines them to think that all social orders are deliberately created by human beings in order to serve substantive human purposes, that they are all organisational in character. However, to regard all social formations in this way, as social corporations based upon hierarchical relations of a command and obedience, is a mistake. Of course, many social institutions are 'organisations' - e.g. companies, clubs, charities even families[21] - but they are integrated into an all-encompassing social order that is not itself hierarchically structured and must not be mistaken for an organisation. This 'overall order'[22] of society is the most extensive spontaneous order that Hayek identifies in social life, but it is not the only one. Other examples of spontaneous social orders are '[m]orals, religion and law, language and writing, money and the market',[23] and the thing that all of these orders have in common is an intersubjective process of mutual discovery through exchange.[24] The crucial difference between spontaneous order and organisation is that spontaneous orders, because they are the products of human action but not of human design, do not have purposes: therefore they cannot coerce their members - unlike organisations, which operate by command in order to achieve collective goals.

Five elements distinguish spontaneous orders from organisations. The first distinction is one of origin. The origin of spontaneous orders is not intentional, unlike that of organisations, as we have seen spontaneous order is the 'result of human action but not of human design'.[25] It is the product of self co-ordination among its members, each seeking their own objectives but not making any deliberate efforts to establish an order. By contrast, co-ordination in organisations is the product of central direction in order to achieve collective goals: hence, unless unanimity can be reached on the nature of these, individuals who dispute the validity of, or who oppose, collective goals must be coerced. The second distinction lies in the nature of the co-ordinating medium. The co-ordination between individuals that exists

[20]F.A. Hayek, *Law, Legislation and Liberty Vol. I Rules and Order*, p36.
[21] ibid., p46.
[22] ibid., p47.
[23] ibid., p43 and pp55-6.
[24] ibid.
[25] ibid., p20.

in spontaneous orders is a product of rules: individuals co-ordinate their activities by accepting rules that specify conditions to be taken into account when acting. The order that emerges is the result of both the regular observation of these *rules of conduct* by individuals; and of individuals adjusting to the specific circumstances in which they find themselves whilst following the *rules of conduct*. To clarify this point, it is important to understand that one reason why Hayek values spontaneous orders is that their regularity allows us to co-ordinate our actions with the actions of others without the necessity of coercion. We can do that only if we can predict the actions of others within certain given parameters. The *rules of conduct* provide these parameters, and as a result the responses of individuals to their environment will not be random but will be, to a certain extent, predictable. That is why, for Hayek, spontaneous orders are indeed *orders* and not a series of disconnected responses to isolated singular events. In an organisation, by contrast, co-ordination is achieved either by commands from those in charge, for example, a committee, a manager, or a commander; or by the will of a majority of organisation members; these commands coerce those who are not voluntarily part of the organisation. The third element of difference between spontaneous orders and organisations surrounds the nature of purposes that they allow individuals to pursue. A spontaneous order facilitates the pursuit of many individual purposes: 'not having been made it *cannot* legitimately be said to *have a particular purpose*, although our awareness of its existence may be extremely important for our successful pursuit of a great variety of different purposes'.[26] This is clearly distinct from the purposive nature of an organisation established to serve a specific objective defined in advance, and this distinction determines the nature of the co-ordinating devices on which spontaneous orders and organisations rely. The rules of conduct, which are the co-ordinating medium for spontaneous orders, are 'negative', merely framing a sphere of allowed individual activity, but leaving members free to choose their ends according to their own plans.[27] The commands that ensure co-ordination in an organisation, on the other hand, determine members' activities in order to further the organisation's established collective goal as effectively as possible, whether or not these conflict with the goals of individuals. The fourth difference is their level of complexity. Hayek believes that there are no inherent limits to the complexity which spontaneous orders can acquire. By contrast, organisations are 'confined to such moderate degrees of complexity as the maker can still survey'.[28] Finally,

---

[26] ibid., p38.
[27] ibid., pp36-7.
[28] ibid., p38.

only spontaneous orders raise genuine explanatory problems and thus require explanatory social theory: their intricacy and variety, according to Hayek, requires explanatory social theory so that the mechanisms they use to co-ordinate the multiplicity of activities of individuals may be understood. Social theory is further necessary here because, unlike in the case of organisations, these spontaneous orders: 'do not obtrude themselves on our senses but have to be traced by our intellect. We cannot see or otherwise intuitively perceive this order of meaningful actions, but are only able mentally to reconstruct it by tracing the relations that exist between the elements.'[29] It is the task of social theory to undertake such reconstruction: 'Social theory begins with - and has an object only because of - the discovery that there exist orderly structures which are the product of the action(s) of many men but are not the result of human design.'[30] The specific task of social theory is to discover the rules, the observance of which has led to the evolution of the spontaneous order. In Hayek's view organisations do not pose similar social theoretical problems because their complexity is limited to what can be understood by the mind, or group of minds, which has consciously designed the organisation. The co-ordination of activities taking place in an organisation is explained by reference to the intentions of those that establish and direct it.

If Hayek's model is accurate, spontaneous orders - unlike organisations - are non-coercive and neutral because they do not impose external purposes on individuals. Hence Hayek's claim to neutrality between the pursuit of individual purposes depends on the validity of his distinction between spontaneous order and organisation. Two questions arise. First, is the distinction between organisation and spontaneous order as clear-cut as Hayek supposes? Second, is the spontaneous order as bereft of purpose as he supposes? If not then the claim that the rules of conduct governing spontaneous orders are value-free is called into question. If this is indeed the case then the validity of Hayek's claim that liberty is the foremost value in society comes to rest on his normative justification of liberty as an end in itself.

Hayek himself is equivocal about whether orders are to be classified as *either* a spontaneous order *or* an organisation; or whether spontaneous order and organisation are characterisations of two ideal types of social co-ordination. Even in the course of a single chapter[31] Hayek demonstrates the ambiguity of his position. After presenting spontaneous order and

[29] ibid.
[30] ibid., p37.
[31] See ibid., Chapter 2.

organisation as a dichotomy,[32] and establishing that one of the fundamental differences between the two is that the co-ordination of spontaneous order is rule governed while that of organisation is command centred, he says:

> [T]o some extent every organisation must rely also on rules and not only on specific commands. The reason here is the same as that which makes it necessary for a spontaneous order to rely solely on rules: namely that by guiding the actions of individuals by rules rather than by specific commands it is possible to make use of knowledge which nobody possesses as a whole. Every organisation in which members are not mere tools of the organiser will determine by commands only the function to be performed by each member, the purposes to be achieved, and certain general aspects of the methods to be employed, and will leave the detail to be decided by the individuals on the basis of their respective knowledge and skills.[33]

Hayek appears to be arguing that an organisation, if it is to operate successfully using the knowledge and skills of its members, must possess at least some of the features of a spontaneous order, especially in respect of individuals being guided by general rules rather than by specific commands. The problem is that he obscures his own distinction between 'spontaneous' and 'made' orders. One example is that cited above, where he notes that organisations also depend on rules. More significant is that Hayek suggests that changing the rules may influence the general character of a spontaneous order: '... even where, as is true of a society of human beings, we may be in a position to alter at least some of the rules of conduct which the elements obey, we shall thereby be able to influence only the general character and not the detail of the resulting order'.[34] Further confusion is generated when Hayek discusses the possibility of inducing a spontaneous order by designing and introducing appropriate rules:

> ...it is possible that an order, which would still have to be described as spontaneous, rests on rules which are entirely the result of deliberate design. In the kind of society with which we are familiar, of course, only some of the rules which people in fact observe, namely some of the rules of law (but never all, even of these) will be the product of deliberate design, while most of the rules of morals and custom will be

[32] ibid., pp36-8.
[33] ibid., pp48-9.
[34] ibid., p41.

spontaneous growths.[35]

Hayek has blurred the boundaries between organisation and spontaneous order, which he had previously argued were unequivocal. If a spontaneous order is designed, even in part, or its general character is to be changed, even in part, then the designers of the order, or those who wish to change its character, must have some reason for doing so. He starts by arguing as follows: '[M]ost important, however, is the relation of a spontaneous order to the conception of purpose. Since such an order has not been created by an outside agency, the order as such also can have no purpose, although its existence may be very serviceable to the individuals which move within such an order'.[36] And intervention in the spontaneous order can be extremely damaging because: '[T]he spontaneous order arises from each element balancing all the various factors operating on it and by adjusting all its various actions to each other, a balance which will be destroyed if some of the actions are determined by another agency on the basis of different knowledge and in the service of different ends.'[37] In conclusion he claims that:

> What the general argument against 'interference' thus amounts to is that, *although we can endeavour to improve a spontaneous order by revising the general rules on which it rests*, and can supplement its results by the efforts of various organizations, *we cannot improve the results by specific commands that deprive its members of the possibility of using their knowledge for their purposes.*[38]

So the reason why Hayek believes that amending of the general rules of a spontaneous order is justified is that it allows people to utilise their own knowledge to their own advantage. That being the case, those who wish to preserve the spontaneous order in some way must be happy with the spontaneous order *as it is*: and those who wish to restore or amend a spontaneous order must believe a restored or amended order will be *better* in the sense that it will allow individuals to use their own knowledge in their own way. There is clearly, then, a normative dimension to spontaneous orders. If they can be changed or designed they must have the capacity to be evaluated. If they are to be evaluated, it must be against some conception of what is or is not good, in this case the individual utilisation of knowledge.

---

[35] ibid., p46.
[36] ibid., p39.
[37] ibid., p51.
[38] ibid., emphasis added.

And if this is so, then the conception of spontaneous order cannot be neutral: it must have a normative dimension.

The reason why Hayek wishes to induce or otherwise adapt spontaneous orders is to promote liberty and prevent coercion. He believes that association in terms of spontaneous order - and governed by the rule of law - is the only mode of human order that does not coerce its members by imposing external purposes upon them. Hayek's normative position, therefore, must be that liberty is good and coercion is bad: and he offers three types of justification for this position. The first is an instrumental defence of liberty: liberty is justified because it is the means to achieve other values, such as prosperity, or perhaps an overall increase in a happy population. This defence emerges from Hayek's philosophy of mind and theory of knowledge. The second is built on the same intellectual foundations: because we can never know our own mind, we must distrust the 'constructivist rationalism' which claims that reason can tell us how to build idealised versions of societies. Thus we must hold a prejudice in favour of the established institutions and traditions which have allowed liberty, and with it the ability of individuals to use their own tacit knowledge, to flourish. Again, this defence of liberty is instrumental: the societies which have in the course of their natural (spontaneous) development maintained market economies, and have an established rule of law, have usually enjoyed more material prosperity, and hence have been able to maintain greater populations in greater relative comfort than those which have not. Hayek's third type of justification is this: liberty has an intrinsic moral value of its own; intrinsically it is so precious that other values must be sacrificed so that it can be protected. This mixture presents three related problems for Hayek. First, his instrumental positions can neither be neutral, nor ultimately offer any secure normative justification for liberalism: for if they happen to fail in providing the desired ends, then it would be legitimate to replace the liberal order with an order that did deliver them. Second, Hayek's approach does not offer the defence of liberty as the foremost value in society that he needs because it rests on questionable empirical assumptions, and ones that confirm Hayek's subjectivism. Finally, Hayek is left with a combination of two types of theoretical argument, normative and empirical, which he attempts to run together but which cannot be run together. A consistent philosophical case for a particular view of society such as Hayek's can be based *either* on the consequences of what liberty can produce in measurable terms, such as prosperity, increase in population, or, most famously, happiness (an instrumental view): *or* it can be based on the moral value of liberty, which should be secured, irrespective of whether or not it promotes other valuable ends (a Kantian view). But it cannot be based on both together. In the remainder of the chapter I shall examine each in turn.

## 3.2 The empirical case for liberty

What is the basis of Hayek's empirical case? And why can't it be neutral? To explain the problems of Hayek's empirical case its foundation in his philosophy of mind and epistemology must first be examined. For his instrumental defence of liberty rests on his empirical psychology and epistemology, the conclusions of which lead him to assert that the only way for human society to flourish is to have liberty as the foremost value in society. Hayek's most complete version of his empirical psychology and its relationship to his epistemology appears in *The Sensory Order*,[39] in which he wants to discover 'the kind of process by which a given physical situation is transformed into a certain phenomenal picture'.[40] In other words, the question that Hayek is addressing is this: why is it that the way we perceive the world through our senses is different from the way we might describe the world in the language of science? Hayek's answer to this question is the beginning of his theory of how the mind operates.

For Hayek, the mind is a product of two evolutionary processes, one physical, the other cultural. According to Hayek the physical structure of the brain has evolved in certain ways that are reflected in the consistency of perception that most human beings share. At the same time, the environment and experiences of particular people will lead individual minds to evolve in different directions and guide perceptions in different ways. As people live, the various experiences they encounter all affect their mental evolution and development, so that at any given point the mind can be seen as the product of these historical and experiential events. Thus the mind is a cultural product that evolves from a particular physical structure.[41] Hayek would accept that there is a physical basis to the mental order, but he believes that the mind cannot be reduced to simple physical categories. The self-organising properties of the mind take it beyond our ability to understand in physical terms, despite its ultimately physical basis.

The neural order of the mind is, for Hayek, largely an 'apparatus of classification'.[42] To recognise something as a distinct sensory 'datum' it must be differentiated from other sensations. Hayek's theory suggests that the mind has evolved to perform this function - the mind is a 'process that

[39] F.A. Hayek, *The Sensory Order* (University of Chicago Press, Chicago, 1952).
[40] ibid.
[41] Hayek also makes this point in *The Fatal Conceit: The Errors of Socialism*, pp22-3.
[42] F.A. Hayek, *The Sensory Order*, p53.

creates the distinctions in question'.[43] The various combinations of neural firings that comprise a given mental event have evolved as the means by which we interpret the world. The mechanism of that evolution is the success of any given picture of the world in guiding individual actions in that world. Sets of classification that do not successfully guide actions (that is, ones that do not in some sense correspond to the physical world) will prevent the organism whose actions are being guided from thriving. Classification processes which survive are those which most accurately conform to external events.

Hayek employs the metaphors of 'map' and 'model' to describe the mental order more precisely.[44] The 'map' refers to the semi-permanent neural connections and linkages the brain has built up as the result of past experience. In some sense it is the classifying structure that drives mental functions. The 'model' refers to the 'pattern of impulses which is traced at any moment within the given network of semi-permanent channels'[45] derived from the specific environment in which the person is currently placed. The map generates the model. Based on previous sensory experience, the mind gives us a model of the present environment that serves as the backdrop for classifying incoming sensory information in the current context. The model is also forward-looking in that it enables actors to anticipate the likely consequences of both their own actions and of external events. Hayek envisions a feedback process between the two, as input from the various existing environments can eventually change the map, while the map is what creates any specific model. Hence, the mind is both the product of experience and what classifies that experience.

What is Hayek's purpose in presenting this account of the operation of the human mind? At the beginning of this chapter I pointed out that his goal was to restate and refine the arguments of the early thinkers of classical liberalism. Moreover, Hayek particularly points to Hume and Kant as his two most important intellectual progenitors.[46] From Hume comes Hayek's emphasis on spontaneous order and the empirical basis of society and morality. From Kant comes Hayek's emphasis on freedom and the importance of universal rules of justice. Indeed, Chandran Kukathas[47] interprets Hayek's project as one that attempts to bridge Hume and Kant in

---

[43] ibid., p48.
[44] ibid., pp112-18.
[45] ibid., p114.
[46] See, for example, 'The Confusion of Language in Political Thought', Chapter 6 of *New Studies in Philosophy, Politics, Economics and the History of Ideas* (Routledge & Kegan Paul, London, 1978).
[47] Chandran Kukathas, *Hayek and Modern Liberalism* (Clarendon Press, Oxford, 1990).

order to achieve an integrated theory of the liberal order:

> [H]ayek's critique of constructivist rationalism, and his account of the evolution of rules of conduct in the theory of the spontaneous order are strikingly Humean in character. His political philosophy is, to a considerable extent, founded in Humean assumptions about the nature of society and the place of justice within it. He sees morality as a social institution composed of rules of conduct which have evolved within the social order and derive their legitimacy, ultimately, from the fact they facilitate the co-ordination of human activities and enhance society's prospects of survival. He thus follows Hume in regarding justice as an institution which enables man to cope with his circumstances and denying that the rules of justice can be discovered by reason. At the same time, however, Hayek appears to reject the ideas of such a 'conservative' justification of the liberal order. In attempting to uncover the *principles* of a liberal social order he turns to a Kantian emphasis on the importance of freedom as the master of the Great Society. His conception of freedom as 'independence of the arbitrary will of another' is indeed strikingly Kantian, emphasising as it does that liberty means 'the absence of a particular obstacle-coercion by other men'.[48]

For Hayek, the mind is a classification system in the Kantian sense where the classes are part of the structure of the mind, not of the world itself. However, there is also a Humean dimension to Hayek's theory of mind, for he denies that these Kantian categories are a *permanent* part of the structure of the mind. Rather, the categories are the product of biology interacting with empirical experience,[49] that is, they evolve as the particular human actor grows and learns. Hayek's theory of mind, then, tries to provide an empirical explanation for the source and continuing evolution of these *a priori* categories. It is in this way that he is trying to straddle Hume and Kant. The mind, for Hayek, is what enables the to world appear organised and sensible to individuals, rather than as a chaotic blur of random images and movement. The orderliness of the world is a product of the mind, not a feature of the world itself. Human understanding of the world is orderly because the mind orders sensations - hence 'the sensory order'. The mind, therefore, does not translate sensations into a mental picture; it is the means by which we classify sensations in the first place. It is not, however, an unchanging, universal classificatory structure, but itself an empirical phenomenon.

---

[48] ibid., p45.

[49] F.A. Hayek, *The Sensory Order*, p119.

The most important implication of this 'Humeo-Kantian' theory for Hayek's social and political views is that individuals can never fully explain their own minds. If the mind is the way in which individuals classify the world around them, they can never step back and attempt to view the mind itself as a sensory input. As Hayek says, 'any apparatus of classification must possess a structure of a higher degree of complexity than is possessed by the objects which it classifies ... therefore, the capacity of any explaining agent must be limited to objects with a structure possessing a degree of complexity lower than its own'.[50] Therefore, he concludes, 'there also exists ...an absolute limit to what the human brain can ever accomplish by way of explanation'.[51] The corollary of the fact that no one can ever fully know his or her own mind is that not all human knowledge can be fully articulated. Hayek's psychology declares that the order of connections in the mind is

> ...modified by every new action exercised upon it by the external world, and since the stimuli acting on it do not operate by themselves but always in conjunction with the process called forth by the pre-existing excitatory state, it is obvious that the response to a given combination of stimuli on two different occasions is not likely to be exactly the same. Because it is the whole history of the organism which will determine its action, new factors will contribute to this determination on the latter occasion which were not present at the first. We shall find not only that the same set of stimuli will not always produce the same responses, but also that altogether new responses will occur. [52]

The crucial point here is that the knowledge that allows the mind to evolve is not built up by itself, but through selection amongst mechanisms producing different patterns. The mind's evolution is blind. It depends not on premeditated objectives or foresight, but on a process of evolution or discovery procedure that gropes through the space of what is possible and in some instances chances upon rules that fit the requirements of survival and flourishing:

> [I]t seems to me that the organism first develops new potentialities for actions and only afterwards does experience select and confirm those which are useful as adaptations to typical characteristics of its environment. There will thus be gradually developed by natural

[50] ibid., p185.
[51] ibid.
[52] ibid., p123.

selection a repertory of action types adapted to standard features of the environment. Organisms become capable of ever greater varieties of actions, and learn to select among them, as a result of some assisting the preservation of the individual or the species, while other possible actions come to be similarly inhibited or confined to some special constellations of external conditions.[53]

Thus it is impossible to state or communicate all of the rules which govern our actions, including our communications and explicit statements.

The limits of explicit human knowledge form the basis for Hayek's political and social thought. Social co-ordination processes and the institutions that comprise them ultimately consist in the communication and use of knowledge.[54] The problem of social co-ordination is the problem of how best to discover and utilise the diverse and fragmentary pieces of knowledge embedded in individual minds. In the same way that classical economics focuses on the role of markets in co-ordinating the division of labour so that the economy can grow, Hayek emphasises the division of knowledge inherent in complex social orders and argues that spontaneously evolved institutions, such as the market, are the only way to achieve the epistemological co-ordination necessary for economic growth, and hence prosperity. This point is fundamental to Hayek's epistemological and empirical psychological case for the liberal order. The necessity of the role of spontaneously evolved institutions lies in this, that only they can enable a society to make use of the knowledge possessed by individual economic actors, because a substantial portion of that knowledge is tacit and cannot be consciously known and communicated linguistically.

Hayek's case for the rule of law, and his demand that the remit even of thoroughly democratic governments be limited, follow directly from his epistemology and theory of mind. As I shall now show, however, the flaws in Hayek's empirical defence of liberty also emerge from these arguments. If Hayek's analysis is accurate, then his two instrumental defences of freedom flow from his explanatory social theory. The first is consequentialist. Freedom produces good results. In *Knowledge, Evolution and Science*[55] he claims that the measure of the success of a social system is the number of people it is able to sustain. His theory of human evolution is that of the

[53] See, for example F. A. Hayek, 'The Primacy of the Abstract', p42, Chapter 3 of *New Studies in Philosophy, Politics, Economics and the History of Ideas* and also, *The Fatal Conceit: The Errors of Socialism*, p15.

[54] F.A. Hayek, *Individualism and the Economic Order* (University of Chicago Press, Chicago, 1948), p91.

[55] F.A. Hayek, *Knowledge, Evolution and Science* (Routledge & Kegan Paul, London, 1983), p49.

'natural selection' of traditions which enhance the group's survival prospects. The exercise of liberty under the rule of law is valuable because it offers the best opportunity for every individual to utilise their own tacit knowledge. The utilisation of this widely dispersed knowledge facilitates the increased productivity that allows both human population and their level of material prosperity to increase. Such arguments have led John Gray to classify Hayek as an indirect utilitarian.[56] Roland Kley also understands Hayek as offering an instrumental justification for the liberal order:

> ... it is ultimately his view that the institutions together forming the basis of the liberal market society can be shown to be morally legitimate by demonstrating that they alone are capable of co-ordinating social and economic life in a way that prevents mass hunger, produces general prosperity, and ensures social peace.[57]

This point is crucial for Hayek's first instrumental argument for the defence of liberty. Any instrumental defence of liberty automatically leads to the question that, if the liberal order fails to deliver the goods of preventing mass hunger, promoting general prosperity and maintaining social peace, should the liberal order not then be discarded in favour of a society which does produce those goods? This is a dilemma for Hayek; and its implications for his theory will be examined later in the chapter. For the moment I shall put that aside and concentrate on Hayek's positive argument for liberty and the liberal order.

The liberal order is a dynamic order characterised by what Hayek describes as 'progress'. The 'progress' facilitated by the liberal order is a process of development and transformation of the human intellect. It is an adaptive, educative process in which wants and values constantly change. However, what are the consequences of this constant change? And, if Hayek is to have a coherent instrumentalist moral theory, then by what norms are such changes to be evaluated? The difficulty which Hayek faces is that 'progress' brings with it changes, not only in the form of individual accomplishments, but also in terms of individual goals: these are no less subject to the dynamic process of 'progress'. It is therefore doubtful whether the new circumstances created by 'progress' can be seen as 'better' than what has gone before. Individuals' goals are constantly changing; even if the liberal order is indeed the most effective way of facilitating the pursuit of individual goals, there is no way of evaluating whether or not individuals are better off for having achieved them. Hayek concedes this when he says:

---

[56] John Gray, *Hayek on Liberty*, Second Edition (Blackwell, Oxford, 1986), pp 59-61.
[57] Roland Kley, *Hayek's Social and Political Thought* (Clarendon Press, Oxford, 1994), p211.

> ... often it [progress] also makes us sadder men. Though progress consists in part in achieving things we have been striving for, this does not mean that we shall like its results or that we shall all be gainers. And since our wishes and aims are also subject to change in the course of the process, it is questionable whether the statement has a clear meaning that the new state of affairs that progress creates is a better one. Progress in the sense of the cumulative growth of knowledge and power over nature is a term that says little about whether the new state will give us more satisfaction than the old. The pleasure may be solely in achieving what we have been striving for, and the assured possession may give us little satisfaction. The question whether, if we had to stop at our present stage of development, we would in any significant sense be better off or happier than if we had stopped a hundred or a thousand years ago is probably unanswerable.[58]

Hayek is here denying the possibility of a normative ranking of 'states of affairs' - as he has to on the basis of his philosophy of mind. Hayek cannot rank states of affairs because of the claims he makes about the inarticulable nature of human knowledge and the impossibility of individuals knowing their own mind. Hayek's whole empirical psychology and epistemology denies the possibility that, by using reason, an individual or group of individuals can somehow stand outside an existing social order and evaluate competing social 'states of affairs'. For Hayek, as Kukathas notes:

> [R]eason cannot provide us with the criteria by which to compare states of affairs; it is merely a capacity which is produced or created (and modified) by progress. Thus reason can identify inconsistencies among rules within a situation (or tradition) of behaviour but cannot stand outside the evolutionary process to evaluate the different states of affairs that rational action might lead to.[59]

Hayek's criticism of 'constructivist rationalists' is based on the idea that it is impossible for anyone to have the complete knowledge required to 'evaluate the different states of affairs that rational action might lead to'. Their argument is based 'on the fiction that all relevant facts are known to some one mind, and that it is possible to construct from this knowledge of the particulars a desirable social order'.[60] Thus, according again to Kukathas:

---

[58] F.A. Hayek, *The Constitution of Liberty*, p41.
[59] Chandran Kukathas, *Hayek and Modern Liberalism*, p197.
[60] Hayek, *Law, Legislation and Liberty, Vol. I Rules and Order*, p14.

> Hayek's defence of the liberal order is based not on the claim that its rules will produce end-states we would choose if we knew what alternatives were available, but on the contention that the rules of the liberal order enable us to adapt to a changing environment which is always creating states of affairs which we can never wholly anticipate, let alone choose.[61]

Hayek, then, is definitely neither a rule nor an act utilitarian. Is it possible that his critique of 'constructivist rationalism' might still accommodate some other form of consequentialist moral theory? But how can Hayek be seen as a consequentialist of any sort if he denies the possibility of comparing and choosing between states of affairs? Indeed, '[I]f there can be no comparative evaluation of alternative states of affairs, it is difficult to show how a liberal order (which facilitates adaptation to a changing environment) can be regarded as superior or preferable to that condition in which a non-liberal order sustains an impoverished and diminishing population'.[62] Whatever form of consequentialism one adopts, it has to allow for one state of affairs to be identified as superior or preferable to another, and Hayek's theory explicitly excludes such a possibility.

By contrast, Hayek's insistence on the limits of reason allows an instrumental defence of liberty - but only in those societies which have an already established liberal tradition, because it is established liberal orders that have allowed liberty to flourish. This is what I term Hayek's conservative defence of freedom, a defence which emerges from his insistence that the power of reason is limited because of the impossibility of complete knowledge, and the inability of individuals to know their own mind. Having shown that Hayek's philosophy of mind is in tension with his consequentialist argument, I shall show how it supports a conservative normative defence of liberty within established orders.

### 3.3 The conservative case for liberty

Before going on to do that, however, it is important to establish what might allow a defence of the liberal order to be described as a conservative one. A good point to begin a discussion of putative conservatism in relation to Hayek is with Michael Oakeshott, the conservative whose ideas bear the closest resemblance to those of Hayek's liberalism. Oakeshott states:

---

[61] Chandran Kukathas, *Hayek and Modern Liberalism*, p197.

[62] ibid., p198.

> [T]o be conservative, then, is to prefer the familiar to the unknown, to prefer the tried to the untried, fact to mystery, the actual to the possible, the limited to the unbounded, the near to the distant, the sufficient to the superabundant, the convenient to the perfect, present laughter to utopian bliss. Familiar relationships and loyalties will be preferred to the allure of more profitable attachments; to acquire and to enlarge will be less important than to keep, to cultivate and to enjoy; the grief of loss will be more acute than the excitement of novelty or promise. It is to be equal to one's own fortune, to live at the level of one's own means, to be content with the want of greater perfection which belongs alike to oneself and one's circumstances.[63]

What Oakeshott is saying is that conservatives value those practices and institutions which subsist here and now. This is clearly different from Hayek's view that liberty is valuable because it allows 'progress', which in Hayek's terms is a restless dynamic process, a process that facilitates change and innovation.[64] Oakeshott, however, does offer one important proviso, namely that the inclination to conservatism will, 'if the present is arid, offering little or nothing to be used or enjoyed' be 'weak or absent'.[65] The inclination to conservatism 'asserts itself characteristically when there is much to be enjoyed, and it will be strongest when this is combined with an evident risk of loss'.[66] This has been a constant theme within conservatism since it emerged as a recognisable tradition in Western thought. It is a point made most famously by Burke when he said of attempts to overthrow established government that 'it is with infinite caution that any man ought to venture upon pulling down an edifice which has answered in any tolerable degree for ages the common purposes of society, or on building it up again, without having models and patterns of approved utility before his eyes'.[67] Contemporary conservatives take a similar line. Irving Kristol, for instance, notes that 'institutions which have existed over a long period of time have a reason and a purpose inherent in them, a collective wisdom incarnate in them, and the fact that we don't perfectly explain why they "work" is no

[63] Michael Oakeshott, 'On being Conservative', in *Rationalism in Politics and other Essays*, p169.
[64] Hayek, *The Constitution of Liberty*, p40.
[65] Michael Oakeshott, 'On being Conservative', in *Rationalism in Politics and other Essays*, p169.
[66] ibid.
[67] Edmund Burke, *Reflections on the Revolution in France* (Penguin, Harmondsworth, 1982), p152. Burke also offers a striking parallel with Hayek when he discusses the limits of human reason. See ibid., p183.

defect in them, but merely a limitation in us'.[68] This implies of course that conservatism is fundamentally a subjective[69] doctrine, that there is no need for the social or political order to be objectively justified. Indeed, it cannot be thus justified because 'objectivity' is itself internal to tradition. On the basis of Hayek's contention that it is impossible rationally to choose between states of affairs his doctrine too is subjective, matching the strong subjectivist strand within conservatism which, again, originates with Burke: '[A] state without the means of some change is without the means of its conservation.'[70] Equally, Burke makes clear that whether a value like liberty is good or bad depends on circumstance.[71] And that there are limits to human reason: '[W]e are afraid to put men to live and trade each on his own private stock of reason; because we suspect that this stock in each man is small, and that each man would do better to avail themselves of the general bank and capital of nations and of ages.'[72] These comparisons indicate a *prima facie* case for suspecting that Hayek's normative outlook is conservative. Now, how good is this *prima facie* case? Let us start by pursuing the comparison with Oakeshott's 'mainstream' conservatism.

His most important justification of conservatism is that people within an existing order have a disposition to maintain that order because they enjoy the benefits which accrue from it. But, beyond that basic contention, Oakeshott offers a series of arguments about why people should be attached to already extant institutions and orders. These arguments bear a striking resemblance to Hayek's anti-rationalism. Oakeshott, like Hayek, believes that there are two types of knowledge, knowledge of technique that can be articulated, like the knowledge in a cookery book, and practical knowledge embodied in skills, such as driving a car, which cannot. Furthermore, immanent within Oakeshott's epistemology is a critique of rationalism based on the impossibility of possessing complete knowledge.[73] Finally, Oakeshott,

---

[68] Irving Kristol, 'Utopianism, Ancient and Modern', in his *Two Cheers for Capitalism* (Basic Books, New York, 1978), p185.

[69] By 'subjective' I don't mean a necessarily individualistic subjectivism: rather I use it simply in contrast to an 'objective' view, namely one which is capable of disinterested justification.

[70] Edmund Burke, *Reflections on the Revolution in France*, p106. This point also raises interesting parallels between conservatism and post modernism which are beyond the remit of this book.

[71] ibid., p90.

[72] ibid., p183.

[73] Oakeshott, *Rationalism in Politics*, pp7-11 Note particularly the following:

> ... every human activity whatsoever, involves knowledge. And universally, this knowledge is of two sorts, both of which are always involved in any actual activity.... The first sort of knowledge I will call technical knowledge or knowledge of technique... In many activities this technical knowledge is formulated into rules which are, or maybe, deliberately learned, remembered, and, as we say, put into practice; ... its chief

like Hayek, also identifies two ideal forms of human association: civil association (which corresponds in some ways to Hayek's spontaneous order); and enterprise association (which parallels Hayek's notion of an organisation).

Oakeshott's conservative defence of the established order stems from the dichotomy he identifies between civil association and enterprise association. Civil association is a formal relationship, while enterprise association is a substantive relationship. Oakeshott explains the distinction in the following terms. All actions and choices have a substance and a form. The substance of an action is a performance in which an individual seeks to achieve a satisfaction: for example, the performance of playing the violin, selling a house or asking directions. The form of an action is not what is done (the performance) but the manner in which it is done: playing in or out of tune, selling legally or fraudulently, asking the way politely or impolitely. The form of an action is the action in respect of its acknowledgement of a procedure: musical pitch, law, or good manners.[74] Oakeshott calls the procedure acknowledged in an action a 'practice'.[75] A practice is a set of formal considerations to be taken into account when acting. These formal considerations may be maxims, principles, rules, manners, uses, observances, offices or customs. They do not identify or specify what choices an individual shall make; they are considerations to be taken into account when acting. They qualify but do not determine substantive choices and performances: the rules of music do not tell a violinist to play a particular tune, they invite him or her to play in tune; the law governing property transfer does not tell some one to whom they may sell their house, or at what price, but that they must not misrepresent what it is they are selling; good manners do not tell an individual what to say, simply the manner in which it should be said. When individuals act they use a practice or set of practices composed of various procedural considerations. However, they also do something in particular - to return to the example used earlier in relation to Hayek, the form of driving does not specify the substance of a destination. For Oakeshott, when individuals are associated in virtue of acknowledging a common practice their relationship is formal. Civil association, as Oakeshott defines it, is one such relationship; it is the formal

---

characteristic is that it is susceptible of precise formulation ... The second sort of knowledge I will call practical, because it exists only in use, is not reflective and (unlike technique) cannot be formulated in rules. This does not mean, however, it is an esoteric sort of knowledge. It means only that the method by which it may be shared and becomes common knowledge is not the method of formulated doctrine. - pp7-8.

[74] Michael Oakeshott, *On Human Conduct*, pp38-40, pp41-46.

[75] ibid., p54.

relationship of individuals who acknowledge a system of law.[76] This system includes a legislative procedure for making, repealing and amending law, a judicial procedure for resolving uncertainties and disputes about whether or not on any particular occasion a law has been adequately subscribed to, and a procedure for enforcing and administering law.[77]

Oakeshott further describes civil association as a moral practice.[78] It is non-instrumental in that it is not in any way concerned with the success or failure of substantive transactions and enterprises. It is not concerned with the satisfaction of wants, but solely with the terms under which the satisfaction of wants is sought. Civil association is association devoid of substantive purposes, therefore, and does not impinge on the freedom of individuals to pursue their own purposes. However, although there are similarities between civil association and spontaneous order, civil association differs from the latter in two important respects. On the one hand Oakeshott makes clear that civil association is an ideal type, that no state has ever confined itself exclusively to association in terms of a manner of living, or in terms of rules. All states combine, in different proportions, the character of the purposeless state, civil association and the purposive state, enterprise association.[79] The advantage of states where civil association is dominant is that they may be expected to afford the citizen

> … the right to pursue his chosen directions of activity as little hindered as may be by his fellows or by the exactions of government itself, and as little distracted by communal pressures. Freedom of movement, of initiative, of speech, of belief and religious observance, of association and disassociation, of bequest and inheritance; security of person and property; the right to choose one's own occupation and dispose of one's labour and goods; and overall the 'rule of law': the right to be ruled by a known law, applicable to all subjects alike.[80]

Furthermore, the rules of civil association are recognised in terms of their authority, rather than their desirability. The rules of civil association do not ask to be approved, they are not designed to persuade and they do not offer reasons why they should be obeyed. They are authoritative prescriptions and as such they neither require nor solicit approval.

---

[76] ibid., pp127-30.
[77] ibid., p132.
[78] ibid., p59.
[79] ibid., pp200-1.
[80] Michael Oakeshott, 'The Masses in Representative Democracy', in A. Hunold (ed) *Freedom and Serfdom: An Anthology of Western Thought*, pp156-7.

Individuals may argue about a rule and they may try to persuade their fellow citizens that the rule is good or bad, but the rules themselves do not argue or persuade. Citizens of the state as civil association (or *cives* as Oakeshott describes them) are related in virtue of recognising civil rules for what they are in themselves, namely authoritative proclamations of law. In other words they recognise the terms of their association, the rules, as authoritative.

The normative element of civil association derives from the approval of these terms, not simply of law, although law does play an important part. The approval of the practice of civil association is general and formal rather than the approval of specific purposes. Not every single rule or law needs to be approved by all individuals. But whether the desirability of a specific rule is accepted or not, members of civil associations accept its authority and they recognise that, until it has been changed or amended by the authoritative procedure for changing rules, it must be obeyed. Most significant, though, is that if the character of the way of life is enjoyed, rules that dramatically change that character must be avoided. Let me illustrate this point with a sporting analogy. Take the game of cricket. Some players and followers of the game may think that the current 'leg before wicket' law is inconsistent and needs to be amended. Nonetheless, until the body recognised as being authoritative alters it, players and spectators accept that a batsman trapped 'leg before wicket' is out. Such amendments are often debated and an adjustment in such a law would not dramatically change the nature of the game that players enjoy playing and spectators enjoy watching. What is not debated or discussed is change to the law which forbids the bowler throwing the ball at the opposing batsman instead of bowling it at him; for to do so would be to entirely change the nature of the game which players and spectators enjoy and appreciate.

Oakeshott's defence of the state as civil association stands on two pillars, then, both of which have an instrumental element. The first is the typically conservative approach, that we maintain this type of association because, imperfect as it is, we have it and we value it: '[W]hat is esteemed is the present; and it is esteemed not on account of its connections with a remote antiquity, nor because it is recognised to be more admirable than any possible alternative, but on account of its familiarity.'[81] In other words we seek to maintain what is for no better reason than it is there and it affords us sufficient enjoyment for us to want to keep it. The second defence is also instrumental, but it is more complex. Oakeshott's fullest account of this

[81] Michael Oakeshott, 'On being Conservative', in *Rationalism in Politics and other Essays*, p168.

defence is in 'The Masses in Representative Democracy'[82] where he traces the emergence of individuality in Europe, being concerned to explain that the emergence of individuality was an historical process, as 'artificial' and as 'natural' as the landscape:[83]

> [T]he character of the individual who emerged was determined by the manner of his generation. He became unmistakable when the habit appeared of engaging in activities identified as 'private'; indeed, the appearance of 'privacy' in human conduct is the obverse of the desuetude of the communal arrangements from which modern individuality sprang. This experience of individuality provoked a disposition to explore its own intimations, to place the highest value upon it, and to seek security in its enjoyment. To enjoy it came to be recognised as the main ingredient of 'happiness'. The experience was magnified into an ethical theory; it was reflected in manners of governing and being governed, in newly acquired rights and duties and in a whole pattern of living.[84]

The emergence of individuality is the pre-eminent event in modern European history. Thus individuality, and hence the freedom to express it, are the product of the European intellectual tradition. Individuality and freedom are worth defending for no other reason than that they are the product of this particular tradition.[85] The potential clash between individuality and freedom and order are reconciled in Oakeshott's thought (as in Hayek's but in a slightly different way) by the recognition that, if individuality is to be enjoyed, rules must exist to prevent individuals impinging on the protected domains of other individuals.

Similarly Oakeshott sees no moral defence for what he describes as 'modern representative democracy'. 'It [modern representative democracy] is not to be understood... as an approximation to some ideal manner of government.... It is simply what emerged in Western Europe where the aspirations of individuality upon medieval institutions of government were greatest.'[86] Furthermore, the boundaries of representative, or indeed any other form of government which defends individuality cannot be determined by reasoning from first principles; they can be established, always provisionally

---

[82] Oakeshott, 'The Masses in Representative Democracy', in A. Hunold (ed) *Freedom and Serfdom: An Anthology of Western Thought.*

[83] ibid., p157.

[84] ibid.

[85] See Michael Oakeshott, *Morality and Politics in Modern Europe*, chapter 6, especially pp84-5.

[86] ibid., pp155-6.

and never indisputably, only by reasonings that are circumstantial and which invoke precedents, judgements and practices that are present in current political life. Oakeshott fundamentally rejects liberal rationalism. Although he would be in agreement with Hayek's non-rationalism, he would not share. his account of its foundation: as he says in *Rationalism in Politics*, Hayek's theories are simply a species of doctrine, although a marginal improvement on the rest.[87] It is also clear that Oakeshott has Hayek in mind when he rejects 'the saddest of all misunderstandings of the state as "civil association"'.

> ... that in which it is properly presented as association in terms of non-instrumental conditions imposed upon conduct and specified in general rules from whose obligations no associate and no conduct is exempt, but defended as the mode of association more likely than any other to promote and go on promoting the satisfaction of our diverse and proliferant wants.[88]

Oakeshott's defence of 'civil association' and hence of freedom, is consequentialist, but of a different sort from Hayek's. Hayek recommends liberty as the only system which will maintain prosperity and an increased population, while Oakeshott recommends it because it is what we have and value. He also recognises that in the event of it ceasing to be valued or appreciated, change is inevitable, although it is probably undesirable, as there is no guarantee that change will be for the better, and there is always the possibility that things that are valued will be lost by change. Thus, for Oakeshott, or any conservative for that matter, while change is inevitable, it must be slowly mediated and in tune with existing traditions of behaviour, and it is always accompanied by a sense of loss.

Let me make clear that I am not claiming that this conservative position can be simply foisted on Hayek. Rather, it illustrates that what I have described as Hayek's conservative instrumental defence of liberty bears a striking resemblance to the work of a conservative philosopher like Michael Oakeshott. It is a resemblance that both Oakeshott and some of his interpreters also recognise.[89] However, although elements of Hayek's thought - such as the limitations he places on the power of reason and his epistemology - support a conservative conception of the good, other elements in his thought conflict with conservatism, in particular his notion of

---

[87] Oakeshott, *Rationalism in Politics*, pp21-2.

[88] Oakeshott, 'Talking Politics', *The National Review* 27 (5th December, 1975), pp1426-27.

[89] See previous footnote; and Paul Franco, *The Political Philosophy of Michael Oakeshott* (Yale University Press, New Haven, 1990), p231.

progress and - because for a conservative the liberal order cannot be shown to be intrinsically better than any other established form of political or social order - his attempted vindication of the 'Great Society' as capable of justification.

Hayek defends liberty because it secures 'progress', a term he uses in two senses. In one sense it denotes the advance in material well being that can be seen in societies enjoying economic growth: the value of progress lies in the higher living standards and reduced distributive inequality that it brings.[90] In a second sense, however, it refers not to directly materialist instrumental goals, but to the existence of the conditions of individual freedom; conditions which allow individuals opportunities to experiment and learn to use their knowledge for their own purposes. 'Progress' in this sense is characterised as a 'process of formation and modification of human intellect, a process of adaptation and learning in which not only the possibilities known to us but also our values and desires continually change':[91]

> [W]hat matters is the successful striving for what at each moment seems attainable. It is not the fruits of past success but the living in and for the future in which human intelligence proves itself. Progress is movement for movement's sake, for it is the process of learning, and in the effects of having learned something new, that man enjoys the gift of his intelligence.[92]

Hayek's view of progress here is peculiar and contradictory. His psychology and epistemology laud the value and necessity of tradition in ensuring liberty, and hence progress, but nothing is more likely to undermine traditions and render tacit knowledge valueless than the type of restless striving which characterises Hayek's view of progress. It is a question of progress *for its own sake* - and such a conception of progress is manifestly not conservative.

The second reason why Hayek's theory cannot simply be reconciled with conservatism lies with Hayek's own 'constructivist rationalism': and in the postscript to *The Constitution of Liberty* he explicitly explains why he is not a conservative.[93] Hence Oakeshott's peremptory dismissal of Hayek:

> [T]he main significance of Hayek's *Road to Serfdom* [is] not the

[90] Hayek, *The Constitution of Liberty*, pp45 and 48.
[91] ibid., p40.
[92] ibid., p41.
[93] ibid., pp397-415.

> cogency of his doctrine but the fact that it is a doctrine. A plan to resist all planning may be better than its opposite, but it belongs to the same style of politics. And only in a society deeply infected with rationalism will the conversion of traditional resources of resistance to the tyranny of Rationalism into a self-conscious ideology be considered a strengthening of those resources.[94]

Oakeshott, as a conservative, rejects not only a theory of progress such as Hayek's, but also the very idea that general principles can be used to direct political conduct. Hayek for his part regards conservatism as 'a useful practical maxim, but one which does not give us any guiding principles which can influence long-range developments'.[95] For Hayek, the decisive objection to any conservatism is that it is unable to offer an alternative to any direction in which society is moving;[96] so that the fate of conservatives is to be dragged along a path not of their own choosing. Hayek, as a liberal, wants to guide the direction along which society is moving; he wants not just to understand how society functions as a spontaneous order, but also how the processes of a spontaneous order might be utilised to facilitate human progress. Hayek's criticisms of rationalism and rationalists are not criticisms of rationalism *per se*, as in the case of Oakeshott, but are directed at those who do not see limits to the extent to which society can be directed by reason.

Hayek, that is to say, is against rationalism only in so far as it is unlimited. If it can promote liberty - and hence progress - then 'constructivist rationalism' is fine. Thus Hayek's 'conservative' defence does not offer a coherent explanation of the value of liberty: although we must hold a prejudice in favour of established institutions and traditions which have allowed liberty, in societies where these traditions are under threat, or do not exist, rules can and should be made, or remade, which will create or revitalise society as a spontaneous order. The problem with this defence, however, is that Hayek is attempting to impose an objective purpose, the defence of liberty, on what in fact is a subjectivist tradition of thought. At best his 'conservative' defence of liberty can be used only to justify existing successful liberal societies: where people are satisfied with their standard of material well-being and there is no clamour for change. It could not be used to promote liberty even in a society governed by a regime as repressive as, say, contemporary China, provided that that regime continued to retain the tacit support of the mass of the population and continued to offer the

[94] Oakeshott, *Rationalism in Politics*, pp21-2.
[95] Hayek, *The Constitution of Liberty*, p411.
[96] ibid., p398.

opportunity of material progress to most of its citizens. Although this cannot be what Hayek had in mind, it is nonetheless the best this type of defence of liberty can offer. While Hayek is not a conservative in the same way as Oakeshott or Burke, it is only conservatism which can fill the chasm between his epistemology, psychology and a valid defence of liberty.

### 3.4 Hayek's putative Kantianism

Two, then, of the three justifications which Hayek offers for the defence of liberty fail. This leaves Hayek's final defence of freedom, his Kantian approach. Two of the most distinguished commentators on Hayek, John Gray and Chandran Kukathas, claim that his philosophy, in fact, has firmly Kantian foundations.[97] Gray argues that: '[T]he entirety of Hayek's work - and, above all his work in epistemology, ethics and the theory of law - is informed by a distinctively Kantian approach. In its most fundamental aspect, Hayek's thought is Kantian in its denial of our capacity to know things as they are, or the world as it is.'[98] Furthermore,

> [I]n all of his [Hayek's] writings, ... the distinctively Kantian flavour is evident in his strategy of working with postulates in regulative ideas, epistemological and normative, which are as metaphysically neutral, and as uncommitted to specific conceptions of the good life, as he can reasonably make them. It is this minimalist or even formalist strategy of argument that most pervasively expresses Hayek's Kantian heritage.[99]

However, it is not apparent that Hayek is as unequivocally Kantian as Gray supposes despite its being an intellectual debt which Hayek explicitly acknowledges: 'I ... will not enlarge here on ... the obvious relation of all this to Kant's conception of the categories that govern out thinking - which I took rather for granted.'[100] And in *The Fatal Conceit* he writes:

> [A]lthough I attack the *presumption* of reason on the part of socialists, my argument is in no way directed against reason properly used. By 'reason properly used' I mean reason that recognises its own limitations and, itself taught by reason, faces the implications of the astonishing fact, revealed by economics and biology, that order generated without

[97] John Gray, *Hayek on Liberty*, and Chandran Kukathas, *Hayek and Modern Liberalism*.
[98] Gray, ibid., p4.
[99] ibid., p8, cf. Kukathas, *Hayek and Modern Liberalism*, chapter 5.
[100] F.A. Hayek, 'The Primacy of the Abstract' in *New Studies in Philosophy, Politics, Economics and the History of Ideas*, p45, footnote 14.

design can far outstrip plans men consciously contrive. How, after all, could I be attacking reason in a book arguing that socialism is factually and even logically untenable?[101]

The sympathy is clear with Kant's argument that: '[T]he greatest and perhaps sole use of all philosophy of pure reason is therefore negative; since it serves as a discipline for the limitation of pure reason.'[102] Hayek also offers a Kantian approach in *The Sensory Order*, where he disavows any concern for 'how things really are in the world', affirming that '... a question like "what is X?" has meaning only within a given order, and within ... this limit it must also refer to the relation of one particular event to other events belonging to the same order'. For Hayek, as for Kant, the limits of reason must be established internally, through reason itself. For both, the limitations of reason indicate the limits of possible knowledge. Hayek indicates that these are logical, not empirical, speaking of 'the permanent limitations of our factual knowledge'.[103] He is perhaps at his most Kantian in the *Constitution of Liberty* when he writes:

> The recognition that each person has his own scale of values which we ought to respect, even if we do not approve of it is part of the conception of the value of the individual personality ... believing in freedom means that we do not feel entitled to prevent him [an individual] from pursuing ends of which we disapprove so long as he does not infringe the equally protected sphere of others.
>
> A society which does not recognise that each individual has values of his own which he is entitled to follow can have no respect for the dignity of the individual and cannot really know freedom.[104]

But Hayek's Kantian approach neither offers the defence of liberty as the foremost value in society that he needs nor is as close to Kant as Gray thinks: for it rests only on empirical assumptions so that his position is in the end subjective. But since these are subject to contingency it is impossible for Hayek to argue to an objective - properly Kantian - viewpoint from which to

---

[101] Hayek, *The Fatal Conceit*, p8. Hayek also offers a Kantian approach in *The Sensory Order*, where he disavows any concern for 'how things really are in the world', affirming that '....a question like "what is X?" has meaning only within a given order, and within ... this limit it must also refer to the relation of one particular event to other events belonging to the same order'. - pp4-5.

[102] Immanuel Kant, *Critique of Pure Reason* (Macmillan, London, 1929), p795.

[103] Hayek, *Law, Legislation and Liberty Vol. I Rules and Order*, p11.

[104] Hayek, *The Constitution of Liberty*, p79.

develop a universal and immutable moral defence for liberty.

On the one hand what Hayek purports to show with his putative Kantianism is that liberty is valuable in itself; that is, that the material consequences which arise from the establishment of an order based on liberty are completely irrelevant to the issue of whether or not liberty is a good. On the other hand, - if Hayek had really adopted a Kantian position - he would have had to argue that there are universal and immutable moral truths on the basis of which to establish the liberty of the individual. But Hayek argues, rather, that there are certain specific sets of circumstances that are favourable to liberty and which should be maintained, not because they are expressions or instantiations of universal immutable rules, but because they have, *as a matter of fact*, established liberty in particular sets of circumstances, and because they have, *as a matter of fact*, been successful in establishing conditions which allow the survival in relative comfort of a greater number of people than would otherwise be the case. Hayek's subjective case for liberty, therefore, rests on empirical and matter of fact claims about the value of liberty in increasing the number of, and improving material conditions of, human populations. In brief Hayek is attempting to run a deontological and a teleological argument simultaneously. He is arguing that liberty is both valuable as an end in itself and for the consequences that result from it.

In order to explain fully the failings of Hayek's putative Kantianism let us remind ourselves of some central points within Kant. His belief in the unknowability of the rules that govern the human mind stems from the dualism between phenomenon and noumenon, phenomenon being the appearance of a thing, and noumenon being the thing in itself. What lies behind this distinction is Kant's conviction that the thing in itself is unknowable, whereas the phenomenon, or the thing as it appears, is knowable:

> ... the phenomenon is knowable because Kant believes it derives from the human mind. In other words, the thing appears as it does because of the unifying activity the ego undertakes on the manifold of experience, forming it into an object. The noumenon, is on the other hand, unknowable since it simply provides the permanent basis of experience.[105]

The distinction between the phenomenon and the noumenon underlies Kant's concept of man, who has:

---

[105] Howard Williams, *Kant's Political Philosophy* (Blackwell, Oxford, 1983), p52.

> two points of view from which he can regard himself and from which he can know laws governing the employment of his powers and consequently governing all his actions. He can consider himself first - so far as he belongs to the sensible world - to be under the laws of nature (heteronomy), and under laws which being independent of nature, are not empirical but have their ground in reason alone. [106]

For Kant, we have a dualistic nature. We belong to the world of sense or the phenomenal world, and to the noumenal world. The two worlds give rise to the related worlds of everyday life and the world of morality. In everyday life, individuals are part of the world of sense, with a noumenal substratum not open to knowledge. However, with respect to the moral life, individuals are independent of this unknowable substratum. According to Kant, because individuals are dealing with values and motives, which fall within thought alone, our knowledge is not limited. In their moral life, individuals can consider themselves as noumena when they are dealing with the moral self, for if individuals consider themselves as part of the intelligible world, they cannot understand the causality of their own wills except through the Idea of freedom; because to be independent of determination by causes in the sensible world is to be free. Free will, that is to say, is the product of understanding ourselves as intelligible beings.[107] The implication of such a position is that, for Kant himself, morality is not the product of tradition and evolution, but is produced *a priori* by reason.

Despite this problem however - for Hayek, as we have seen, is avowedly anti-rational - Gray maintains that Hayek is essentially Kantian. Kukathas, to some extent, recognises that there are difficulties in interpreting Hayek this way, noting the implications of the flaws in Hayek's Kantianism for his defence of liberty. Kukathas believes that there are three major claims in Hayek's account of justice which suggest that his is a fundamentally Kantian moral philosophy:

1. The most basic and important test of justice lies in the principle of universalisability.
2. Laws are just in so far as they are not arbitrary commands imposed by others (but laws we would give to ourselves).
3. Justice is concerned with the distribution not of benefits and burdens, but of freedom.[108]

---

[106] Immanuel Kant, *Groundwork of the Metaphysic of Morals*, trans. H.J. Paton (Harper and Row, New York, 1964), p120.
[107] Howard Williams, *Kant's Political Philosophy*, pp53-4.
[108] Chandran Kukathas, *Hayek and Modern Liberalism*, p168.

While Kukathas does not directly pursue the nature and extent of Hayek's Kantianism, arguing rather that Hayek's ambitious project to combine Humean and Kantian ethical claims in a coherent moral theory of liberalism ultimately fails, his claims nonetheless offer a ready means of exploring the difficulties to which I have alluded.

The first indication that Hayek's purportedly Kantian defence of liberty is unsustainable - because he vitiates that very Kantianism - arises from his prerequisite that laws, to be just, must fulfil a universalisation requirement. Hayek seems to understand this requirement in two related, but different ways. He says that '[T]he appropriate interpretation is suggested by the manner in which Immanuel Kant approached the problem, namely by asking whether we can "want" or "will" that such a rule be generally applied.'[109] However, he also says that 'as a test of the appropriateness of a rule, the possibility of its generalisation or universalisation amounts to a test of consistency or compatibility with the rest of an accepted system of rules'.[110] As Kukathas points out,[111] although Hayek doesn't recognise it, he [Hayek] is considering 'universalising' a rule in two different contexts, each producing its own distinctive results:

> [I]f universalization takes place in the context of a system of accepted rules and the problem is regarded as one of deciding whether or not the rule in question can also be accepted as consistent and compatible with existing rules, the test of universalization does not exclude rules of distribution if the accepted system is a system of distributive procedures. All that would be required of the new rule is that it not come into conflict with existing (distributive) arrangements. If, however, universalization does not take place in the context of a system of accepted rules but is a test applied to every rule, and so is not a test concerned to reconcile a new rule with an established system but a test whether the rules of conduct within any system can be universally willed, then universalization would (in Hayek's view) render rules of distribution unjust. Certain rules cannot apply equally to all since some would be required to obey laws (of taxation, for example....) that others were not. This argument is unsound since there is no reason why a conditional principle or rule ('if you are rich you must pay more tax') cannot be universalized. It is clearly this second understanding of universalization that Hayek has in mind when criticizing the idea of

[109] F.A. Hayek, *Law, Legislation and Liberty Vol. II The Mirage of Social Justice*, p28.
[110] ibid.
[111] Chandran Kukathas, *Hayek and Modern Liberalism*, p169.

social justice...[112]

However, there is also a simpler point to be made here. What both these two interpretations have in common, and what conflicts sharply with Hayek's claim that law and justice are the product of social evolution, is that any adjudication of the universalisability of a rule, by either method, requires the ability to stand back to some archimedean point to judge either whether or not it is consistent or compatible with the rest of the accepted system of rules, or whether or not we can 'want' or 'will' that such a rule be generally applied. But Hayek has ruled out such an approach with both his epistemology and his philosophy of mind. But perhaps Hayek might not understand universalising a rule in quite the same sense as Kant.

Kant intended the idea of universalisability to capture and express the substance of morality: the universalisation test would reveal whether or not a particular maxim or a principle of action was a rule of morality.[113]Kant defines universalisation thus: '[E]very action which by itself or by its maxim enables the freedom of each individual's will to co-exist with the freedom of everyone else in accordance with a universal law is *right*.' Kant goes on to argue that 'if my action or my situation in general can co-exist with the freedom of everyone else in accordance with a universal law, anyone who hinders me in either does me an injustice; for this hindrance or resistance cannot co-exist with freedom in accordance with universal laws'.[114] This, as Gray puts it, amounts to the position that 'if a rule or a maxim is to be acceptable as just, its application must be endorsed by rational agents across all relevantly similar cases'.[115] Hayek's view, given his evolutionary psychology, is rather different, however. Whereas the Kantian version of the test of universalisability adjures individuals to deliberate as rational beings and members of the world of reason, Hayek wants individuals to do so as members of existing liberal orders, or of potential liberal orders. The criterion that Hayek actually offers for the universalisability of a rule, i.e. whether it should be accepted as just, is in the functional contribution it makes to the generation of spontaneous economic order. Thus the Hayekian universalisation turns out to be an

> [I]mmanent ... criticism that moves within a given system of rules and judges particular rules in terms of their consistency or compatibility

[112] ibid., p169.
[113] Immanuel Kant, 'The Metaphysics of Morals', in Hans Reiss (ed) *Kant's Political Thought* (Cambridge University Press, Cambridge, 1977), p133.
[114] ibid.
[115] Gray, *Hayek on Liberty*, p7.

> with all other recognised rules in inducing the formation of a certain kind of order of actions.[116]

> The great body of rules which in this sense is tacitly accepted determines the aim which the rules being questioned must also support; and this aim ...is ...the maintenance or restoration of an order of actions which the rules tend to bring about more or less successfully.[117]

In these passages, Hayek is using the test of universalisability in the context of an already established system of rules. Although the system is not directly specified in his discussion of the Kantian test, the system he has in mind is that of the liberal order which has evolved over time. The practical thrust of Hayek's test is simply to keep on refining, or in the case of non-liberal orders, establishing, the institutional framework of a liberal order. As I explained earlier, Hayek's rules of just conduct are requirements for co-ordination and efficient co-operation and are moral or just to the extent to which their observance contributes to the generation and maintenance of a liberal order:

> ... justice is an attribute of human conduct which we have learnt to exact because a certain kind of conduct is required to secure the formation and maintenance of a beneficial order of actions. The attribute of justice may thus be predicated about the intended results of human action but not about circumstances which have not been deliberately brought about by men. Justice requires that in the 'treatment' of another person or persons, i.e. in the intentional actions affecting the well-being of other persons, certain uniform rules of conduct be observed. It clearly has no application to the manner in which the impersonal process of the market allocates command over goods and services to particular people: this can be neither just or unjust, because the results are not intended or foreseen, and depend on a multitude of circumstances not known in their totality to anybody. The conduct of the individuals in that process may well be just or unjust; but since their wholly just actions will have consequences which were neither intended nor foreseen, these effects do not thereby become just or unjust.[118]

Crucially, he goes on:

---

[116] F.A. Hayek, *Law, Legislation and Liberty Vol. II: The Mirage of Social Justice*, p24.
[117] ibid., p25.
[118] ibid., p70.

> [T]he fact is simply we consent to retain, and agree to enforce, uniform rules for a *procedure which has greatly improved the chances of all to have their wants satisfied*, ... With the acceptance of this procedure the recompense of different groups and individuals becomes exempt from deliberate control. *It is the only procedure yet discovered in which information widely dispersed among millions of men can be effectively utilized for the benefit of all - and used by assuring to all an individual liberty desirable for itself on ethical grounds*. It is a procedure which of course has never been 'designed' but which we have learnt gradually to improve after we had discovered how it increased the efficiency of men in the groups who had evolved it.[119]

What Hayek is saying here is that we adopt universalisable rules for the liberal and/or market order because it is a procedure that has 'greatly improved the chances of all to have their wants satisfied' - and this could hardly be more different from Kant's position. This dispersed knowledge, which constitutes the mechanism by which such want satisfaction is achieved, can be guaranteed only by ensuring that everyone is guaranteed individual liberty, and not for the consequential reason of satisfying wants. It is 'desirable for itself on ethical grounds'. Now that appears Kantian; but the appearance is deceptive, for Hayek does not at all mean by this what a Kantian would - or should. His 'ethical grounds' are not Kantian givens but rather the outcome of empirical claims about want-satisfaction. For the point is that if something is to serve as additional justification it cannot at the same time contradict the original justification. Hayek, then, has made two claims here: on the one hand he has claimed that the liberal order is the most efficient order for satisfying human wants; on the other he claims that liberty is valuable for its own sake - but this would itself have to rest on a successful empirical claim regarding the value of the liberal order in satisfying human wants.

### 3.5 Hayek's inconsistency

As I argued earlier, Hayek's empirical defences of liberty are inconsistent: his claim, then, that the liberal order is the only procedure yet discovered in which information widely dispersed among millions of men can be effectively utilised for the benefit of all, cannot be accepted as an empirical one. His only remaining defence of liberty is what looks like the Kantian idea that liberty is an end in itself, a point he makes forcefully in *The*

[119] ibid., pp70-71, emphasis added.

*Constitution of Liberty,* where he says that '[liberty] demands that it be accepted as a value in itself, as a principle that must be respected without our asking whether the consequences in the particular instance will be beneficial'. But in the next sentence there is an important qualification: '[W]e shall not achieve the results we want if we do not accept it as a creed or presumption so strong that no considerations of expediency can be allowed to limit it.'[120] Liberty, that is to say, should be 'accepted as a value in itself'; but the reason why we should accept it as such are not at all Kantian. That 'we shall not achieve the results we want' if we fail to do so is a transparently instrumental argument. Hayek is again putting together a deontological with a teleological argument. A truly deontological, or Kantian, argument would hold that liberty is valuable *whatever* the results and not just because it gives us 'the results we want'. At best Hayek seems to be adopting a species of indirect utilitarianism rather than Kantianism. Of course, given Hayek's contention that the test of universalisation amounts to a 'test of consistency or compatibility with the rest of an accepted system of rules', his argument might be acceptable in conservative terms. For the 'accepted system of rules' to which Hayek is referring is the 'liberal order', so that, in effect, he is enlisting Kant in defence of an existing system of rules. Hayek in the end interprets universalisation in a political rather than in a metaphysical or moral sense. And that is precisely what marks an argument for certain political values as a conservative - for example Oakeshottian - one. Such an interpretation, whatever else might be said about it is, inimical to liberalism's espoused meta-political neutrality.

In order to demonstrate more clearly the problem Hayek has, it is worth reminding ourselves of the distinction made by Rawls, amongst others, between deontological and teleological moral theories.[121] A deontological theory asserts that what is right does not depend on, but is independent of, what is good. So, for example, that we should keep our promises is not determined by the good consequences of doing so; right conduct requires us to keep promises, and this injunction is in no way dependent on any good consequences that come from keeping promises. Promise keeping is good because it is right; it is not right because it is good or because it produces good results. Teleological moral theories, on the other hand, maintain that what is right depends upon what is good. If promise keeping is right, it can only be so because it leads to good. The character of deontological moral theories thus contrasts sharply with the alleged deontological nature of Hayekian rules of just conduct. These rules depend on contingent empirical

---

[120] Hayek, *The Constitution of Liberty*, p68.

[121] John Rawls, *A Theory of Justice*, pp22-33.

circumstances. If they happen to be such that a principled intervention (i.e. a change of the rules) is believed to produce superior outcomes, that is a better result, in Hayekian terms, then it is entirely legitimate for rules to be changed. Now, this argument must be invalid unless Hayek's empirical case for liberty is proved beyond doubt - and it is apparent from previous discussions in the chapter that it is not. Hayek is therefore left with no satisfactory defence for the priority of liberty ahead of other values.

This presents a major problem for Hayek's project of defending the liberal order. His theory of human evolution as the 'natural selection' of practices which enhance the group's survival prospects leads him to argue that institutions like justice and property have value because, by making possible the utilisation of dispersed knowledge, they facilitate increased productivity, and so on.[122] This would not be a problem for Hayek if he really did present a coherent normative case for liberty as the foremost value in society; but he does not. The difficulty this constitutes becomes clear in his critique of socialism. Hayek's dispute is not with the socialist aims of reducing inequality and abolishing poverty, but with the socialist method of redistributive intervention.[123] Many of his arguments against socialism attempt to show that socialist aims and socialist methods are incompatible:[124] '[S]ome of the aims of the welfare state can be realised without detriment to individual liberty, though not necessarily by the methods which seem most obvious'.[125] What Hayek manifestly fails to demonstrate is that these contentions are empirically sound. In the same way his reliance on contestable empirical claims leaves him open to the allegation that, should his empirical claims for liberty be demonstrated to be dubitable, then his theory only has a very weak normative basis to fall back on.

Without a normative basis, and lacking any proof of the empirical validity of his claims, Hayek's liberalism rests simply on those preferences that individuals agree upon as useful for their subjective purposes. In a recent article Tibor Machan summed up the difficulty faced by liberalism without normative foundations:

> [A]ny judgement of morally or politically good or bad, as well as right and wrong, comes to no more than a preference, a positive or negative feeling of the agent, lacking any objective moral import. Is the favourite political principle of classical liberals itself a mere subjective value?

---

[122] F.A. Hayek, *Knowledge, Evolution and Science*, p49.
[123] Hayek, *The Constitution of Liberty*, p48.
[124] See, for example, Hayek, 'Individualism: True and False' in *Individualism and the Economic Order*, pp1-32.
[125] ibid., p259.

> The answer is 'yes' despite the fact that the right to individual liberty on first impression seems to be well supported by this radical individualism. But it is only a matter of convenience, something we have adopted but might just as easily not have; we might have with equal justifiability have adopted something else-say the right to equality or security.
>
> If this is all true, then people who prefer playing golf to defending freedom when the latter is in jeopardy do nothing wrong. Also, if someone ignores the plight of the hapless or the unjustly treated, there is nothing to be criticised about this choice. Feelings toward one's community or fellow human beings are in no way superior to feelings toward another visit to Las Vegas or playing tennis. Since there are no objective goods or objective values, neither the defence of liberty nor any other course of conduct is more important than any alternative.[126]

Machan encapsulates Hayek's dilemma. Unless it can be shown that liberty has a moral value beyond expediency, then it becomes a choice to be rejected or ignored, either when it becomes inconvenient that it should be supported, or if another alternative offers better opportunities for progress and material well-being.

If, on the other hand, Hayek's empirical defence of liberty were wholly convincing then the weakness of the normative dimension to his thought would perhaps not matter too much. But it is not. Indeed the evidence, where it exists, is elsewhere. Now, whilst it is beyond my scope to offer a comprehensive empirical evaluation of Hayek's theory, one point is particularly germane. In the contemporary world economy most progress, in terms of technological advancement, is not originating in those societies closest to the liberal free-market model that Hayek advocates. Rather it is - or has been - occurring in the so-called 'tiger economies' of the Pacific Rim: but these societies are hardly liberal: they permit little individual choice and autonomy, and practice large scale government intervention in the economy. But that does not mean that Hayek would want Britain and the USA to adopt the Singaporean model of society and government. His whole system is predicated on the assumption that the western liberal order is uniquely valuable insofar as it expresses in some sense the essence of human nature through liberty and individuality. Hayek's problem is that in all his elaborate arguments and his competing defences of liberty, he never actually *finally justifies* this point. In effect he gets no closer than Oakeshott in doing so.

[126] Tibor Machan, 'Individualism v. Classical Liberal Political Economy', *Res Publica*, Vol. I, no. 1 1995, pp3-23, p7.

Now for Oakeshott, as a conservative, this does, at least arguably, not matter. He can defend his position on the basis of just such a set of subjective values: it is ours, we have found much to value in it, and we are prepared to defend it against too radical and rapid innovation. But Hayek cannot have such a defence for two reasons: first he is advocating a universalist system; and second, one of the elements he values most about liberalism is its ability to promote change and progress.

Both Hayek's critique of socialism, and his attempt to establish an unchallengeable basis for a rule-governed liberal order are based on his epistemology and philosophy of mind. As John Gray has noted, Hayek's deepest insight has been to develop the political implications of the limits of human knowledge.[127] The confusion and contradiction in Hayek's thought begins when he attempts to build upon that foundation an edifice which, for all times and all places, proves that the liberal order is the sole, universal version of the good society to which all people must aspire. This is supererogation on a massive scale. Hayek's case would constitute a valid defence of the liberal order so long as he could establish three points. First, that there are convincing arguments that the liberal order works most effectively when individuals are allowed as much scope as possible to use their own tacit knowledge; second, because we cannot know our own minds or articulate all the knowledge we possess, that any doctrine which requires perfect knowledge and the rationalist reconstruction of social orders is (probably) doomed to failure; and third that sufficient people enjoy the conditions in a liberal order to want to maintain it.

Hayek's thought fulfils the first two criteria. But he does not consider that the liberal order can be defended simply on the basis that people enjoy making choices and seeking their own wants, and that the liberal order offers them such an opportunity. Ironically, it is precisely Hayek's restless conception of progress that undermines such a defence. To go back to Oakeshott's conservative defence of liberty: he notes that 'if the present is arid, offering little or nothing to be used or enjoyed',[128] then the inclination to preserve existing institutions and social orders will be absent or very weak. The 'restless striving' for progress which Hayek sees as an essential part of the liberal order is bound to damage the foundations of liberty which he has laid so carefully; for such 'restless striving' will undermine the sense of enjoyment people get from existing society, and will also invariably lead to constant criticism and re-evaluation of the traditions on which Hayek insists liberty rests. Hayek has, therefore, failed to provide a satisfactory normative

[127] John Gray, *Post-Liberalism*, p35.

[128] Michael Oakeshott, 'On being Conservative', in *Rationalism in Politics and other Essays*, p169.

foundation for the liberal order and has undermined a potentially convincing alternative.

To conclude then Hayek claims that his thought is neutral between competing conceptions of the good, and offers a universal justification for the liberal order. It can only be so if his epistemology and psychology can be proved to be empirically true. Hayek does not achieve this goal. However, his epistemology and psychology do offer a potent critique of rationalism in all its forms. It is this critique of rationalism which is incipiently conservative. Where Hayek's thought is unconvincing, is the point where he tries to bridge an unbridgeable gap between his anti-rationalist epistemology and psychology, and his rationalist attempt to provide universal justifications for the liberal order.

# 4 Challenges to Neutrality I: Liberalism with a Moral Foundation

What is common to the strands of liberalism earlier identified, in their partly overlapping and partly different foundations, is an avowed neutrality regarding the good. Even those liberals who are the subject of this chapter and the next, while they might variously have a notion of the good, still strive to retain in the foundations of their thought an element of neutrality on the basis of which they argue for the former. What differentiates these liberal thinkers in this regard, therefore, from, say, socialists or Marxists, is the extent to which their idea of the good is determined by their liberalism - rather than their idea of the good determining their politics. Their version of the good is derived from their liberalism, rather than their liberalism being derived from their idea of the good. This is what makes Hobhouse, for example, a socialist liberal rather than a liberal socialist. He believes that different forms of life, even if a liberal believes them to be in error, nonetheless have value:

> [L]et error have free play, and one of two things will happen. Either as it develops, as its implications and consequences become clear, some elements of truth will appear within it. They will separate themselves out; they will go to enrich the stock of human ideas; they will add something to the truth which he himself mistakenly took as final; they will serve to explain the root of the error; for error itself is generally a truth misconceived, and it is only when it is explained that it is finally and satisfactorily confuted. Or, in the alternative, no element of truth will appear. In that case the more fully the error is understood, the more patiently it is followed up in all the windings of its implications and consequences, the more thoroughly will it refute itself.[1]

Hobhouse's and Green's liberalisms lead them to a notion of the good. As I shall show through an examination of the Victorian discourse on character, the content of their notion of the good derives from the specific

---

[1] L.T. Hobhouse, *Liberalism* in J. Meadowcroft (ed) *Hobhouse; Liberalism and other Writings*.

context of Victorian Britain. Their liberalism is one which results in an understanding of the good that is local, and hence valid, if at all, only in the context from which it is derived (as contrasted with, say, a universalistic conception of the good which may, of course, be more widely valid).

## 4.1 The idea of 'character'

In fiction, economics, psychology, political theory, and above all in the popular moralism of a writer like Samuel Smiles, the idea of character dominated Victorian moral thinking.[2] The absence of neutrality from the thought of Green and Hobhouse stems from their adherence to the discourse on 'character' inherent in the social and intellectual context of Victorian Britain. Again, John Stuart Mill - whether willing or not - was the inspiration for the apparent abandonment of neutralism. A significant element in Mill's tacit conception of the good, for instance, is the idea of 'character': the idea that individuals should have 'strong impulses' but that they should be controlled by a 'strong will' that will produce the 'energetic characters' needed if society is to progress.[3] However, despite his firm desire to see individuals develop in such a way that they possessed a 'character', his position remains firmly voluntaristic in that he did not believe that good characters could be engineered. The difference between Mill and his late Victorian successors, however, is that much as he stresses the development of 'character', he is not prepared to sanction coercive state action (such as the prohibition of the sale of alcohol) to promote it; whereas Hobhouse and Green are prepared to countenance such action by the state. Green, for instance, was particularly energetic in his campaign to ban alcohol.[4] This more interventionist notion of 'character' is fundamental to social liberalism as it developed in late Victorian England. Its tensions are instructive: and in order to understand the social liberals' conception of the good it is necessary to explore these tensions, in response to which - at least in part - they developed their idealist - (in the case of Green) and socialist - (in the case of Hobhouse) influenced liberalisms.

'Character' in the Victorian sense had two dimensions, one descriptive,

[2] Samuel Smiles, *Self Help* (London, 1859); *Thrift* (London, 1876); *Duty* (London, 1880); and Matthew Arnold, *Culture and Anarchy*, in Stefan Collini (ed) Matthew Arnold, *Culture and Anarchy and other Writings*, see especially Chapter 3, Barbarians, Philistines, Populace.

[3] Mill, *On Liberty*, pp124-5.

[4] See Richard Bellamy, *Liberalism and Modern Society*, pp40-1.

and one evaluative.[5] In the descriptive sense, 'character' referred to the 'sum of the mental and moral qualities that distinguish an individual or race viewed as a homogeneous whole'; whereas in the evaluative sense it referred to 'moral qualities strongly developed and strikingly displayed';[6] and although 'moral qualities' could refer equally well to vice as to virtue, for the Victorians it was confined to the possession of those moral qualities which met with ethical approval. 'Character', then, was used to refer to the possession of certain highly valued moral qualities. The working class friendly societies of Victorian Britain which adopted the idea of 'character' wholeheartedly became a powerful social force in the nineteenth century. Not all friendly societies retained a character building dimension but those that did, such as the Grand United Order of Oddfellows (the leading friendly society in the North West of England) and the Ancient Order of Foresters (a leading national friendly society), had, by 1910, almost 3 million members.[7] The discourse on character that permeated working class friendly societies, was simply a reflection of the preoccupation with character in Victorian intellectual life.[8] The Oddfellows encouraged new members to make the moment of joining not only a time of self-criticism but also an occasion for remoulding the character: '[I]t is desired that you should make the event of your Initiation a time for strict self-examination; and if you should find anything in your past life to amend, I solemnly charge you to set about that duty without delay, let no immoral practice, idle action, or low and vulgar pursuit, be retained by you.'[9]

The moral qualities prized by Victorians were, first, the exhibition of strenuous effort, perseverance and courage in the face of adversity; and second, underpinning these qualities, the demonstration of self-restraint at all

---

[5] For a more detailed discussion of the Victorian idea of character see Stefan Collini, *Public Moralists: Political Thought and Intellectual Life in Britain 1850-1930* (Clarendon Press, Oxford, 1991), Chapter 3.

[6] ibid., p96.

[7] David Green, *Reinventing Civil Society* (IEA Health and Welfare Unit, London 1993), p42.

[8] See Stefan Collini, *Public Moralists: Political Thought and Intellectual Life in Britain 1850-1930*, Chapter 3. Collini justifies the preoccupation of Victorian intellectuals with the notion of character in the following way:

> [V]ictorian intellectuals were self-consciously members of a society in the van of progress: the first arrivals in the future cannot be sure what to expect, and no particular technical expertise can be guaranteed in advance to be relevant. Where circumstances are known or can reliably be predicted ... then particular substantive virtues tend to figure more prominently among the moralist's desiderata. Seen thus, character may be said to represent a set of 'second-order' virtues, or even an acquired form of what a later age would call a 'personality-type', which would provide the best chance of first order virtues being upheld in unknown circumstances. - p114.

[9] Grand United Order of Oddfellows, *Ritual of the Grand United Independent Order of Oddfellows* (1865), p41.

times, combined with an abiding sense of duty. Self-restraint was contrasted with behaviour that was random, impulsive and feckless. Within the Victorian discourse on character the notion of duty was fundamental: individuals had an abiding duty to their family, to others and to themselves. The friendly societies, again, offer a representative view that duty went beyond simple self-reliance and attending to the well-being of a man's family. The initiation ceremony of a new member of the Grand United Order of Oddfellows made this clear: '[W]hoever enters this Order for the mean and selfish object of paying his contributions and receiving its pecuniary benefits, without, so far as in him lies, aiding the arduous labours of conducting the business of his Lodge, is to be regarded as an unworthy intruder; but we trust that you will run a nobler and truer course; proving by your conduct that you are worthy of the Order.'[10] The character-building nature of friendly societies is apparent also in the initiation ceremony to the Ancient Order of Foresters:

> [W]e are united together not only for the wise purpose of making provision against those misfortunes which befall all men, and of assisting those who require our aid, but for the moderate enjoyment of friendly intercourse and the temperate exchange of social feeling.... We encourage no excess in our meetings, and enforcing no creed in religion or code in politics, we permit neither wrangling nor dissension to mar our harmony or interrupt our proceedings.[11]

Moreover, such behaviour was not to be confined just to the lodge: 'In your domestic relationships we look to find you, if a husband, affectionate and trustful; if a father, regardful of the moral and material well-being of your children and dependants; as a son, dutiful and exemplary, and as a friend, steadfast and true.'[12]

What is apparent from the writings on character of what might be described as the *haute* intelligentsia, John Stuart Mill, Matthew Arnold and John Morley;[13] the work of popular sages like Samuel Smiles; and from the rules of various working class friendly societies, is that character was not simply the pursuit of individual self-interest. Even the author of *Self-Help*, the most well known testament to Victorian self-reliance, Samuel Smiles praises the value of philanthropy in a later work entitled *Duty*:

---

[10] Grand United Order of Oddfellows, *Initiation Ceremony* (1864), pp42-3.
[11] Ancient Order of Foresters, *Ceremony of Initiation* (1879), pp22-3.
[12] ibid.
[13] See particularly Arnold, *Culture and Anarchy*, Chapter 2, 'Doing as One Likes'; and Mill, *Utilitarianism*, pp20-1.

> [S]ympathy, when allowed to take a wider range, assumes the larger form of public philanthropy. It influences man in the endeavour to elevate his fellow-creatures from a state of poverty and distress, to diffuse the results of civilisation far and wide among mankind, and to unite in the bonds of peace and brotherhood every man's duty, whose lot has been favoured in comparison with others, who enjoys the advantages of wealth, or knowledge, or social influence, of which others are deprived, to devote at least a certain portion of his time and money to the promotion of the general well-being.[14]

Victorian discourse on character held within it a strong commitment to the welfare of others. Above all, having a 'character' meant that an individual chose to be a certain type of person, and that qualities such as self-restraint, duty to others and of courage in the face of adversity were qualities individuals displayed in conformity to this ideal.

It was widely believed, furthermore, that the possession of a good character would allow individuals to transcend their circumstances. A distinguished economist of the period wrote: 'I have always held that poverty and pain, disease and death are evils of greatly less importance than they appear, except in so far as they lead to weakness of life and character.'[15] The question that all Victorian thinkers on the question of character address, but to which they seldom find satisfactory answers, was how to promote good character amongst the masses. It was disputes over how to build up strong and righteous characters that dominated much thinking about the role of the state in the late nineteenth century. Thus, according to the *Encyclopaedia of Social Reform*: '[The reason] why individualist economists fear socialism is that they believe it will deteriorate character, and the reason why socialist economists seek socialism is their belief that under individualism character is deteriorating.'[16]

The tensions in the Victorian discourse on character are exemplified in the work of John Stuart Mill. *On Liberty*, while inspired by Mill's concern that the tyranny of public opinion would lead to the pinched and hidebound type of character which Mill believed was then prevalent, especially amongst Non-conformist middle classes,[17] is ambivalent about how such a character might be discouraged. For Mill is quite negative about the idea of self-restraint. Indeed, *On Liberty* is itself a plea against the idea of restraint even

---

[14] Samuel Smiles, *Duty*, p261.

[15] Alfred Marshall, correspondence with Helen Bosanquet, published in the preface to, Helen Bosanquet, *The Strength of the People: A Study in Social Economics* (London, 1902), pviii.

[16] W.P.D. Bliss (ed) *The Encyclopaedia of Social Reform* (London, 1898), p895.

[17] John Stuart Mill, *On Liberty*, pp146-9.

for the sake of promoting 'better' character formation:

> [P]rotection... against the tyranny of the of the magistrate is not enough; there needs also to be protection against the tyranny of prevailing opinion and feeling, against the tendency of society to impose, by means other than civil penalties, its own ideas and practices as rules of conduct on those who dissent from them; to fetter the development and, if possible prevent the formation of any individuality not in harmony with its ways, and compel all characters to fashion themselves upon the model of its own.[18]

Later in *On Liberty* Mill is directly critical of Calvinism as a 'strong tendency' behind a 'narrow theory of life' which states that: '[W]hatever is not duty is a sin.'[19] The major difficulty that Mill faces he shares in common with most other Victorian theorists of character: how to contrive that citizens would pursue aims which were of value only if pursued voluntarily? The second difficulty is that Mill believes that the self-abnegation promoted by the ideal of character would lead to precisely the type of social conformism he condemns in *On Liberty*. How then should government promote this higher type of character? Mill attempts to solve this problem voluntaristically, arguing that individuals, once exposed to the higher pleasures through their good character, will not sink back into the pursuit of the lower. However, while Mill accords individuals a high degree of autonomy in the creation of their own moral characters - indeed he insists on freedom of choice, however it might be exercised in relation to 'character' - he also opens the door to the idea of the possibility of an autonomy-maximising paternalism. Mill himself is able to avoid having explicitly to bring such a notion into his argument because of the interdependence within the Victorian liberal idea of character of liberty and self-development. Such a combination of ideas implies that only an individual of established virtue could be wholly free.[20]

Mill's view of human self-development is most clearly set out in his work on socialism. In his earliest writings on socialism, in the first edition of the *Principles of Political Economy*,[21] Mill is comparatively unsympathetic to the idea. However, in both his *Autobiography*[22] and the posthumously

[18] ibid., p63.
[19] ibid., p126.
[20] John Stuart Mill, *A System of Logic*, p547.
[21] John Stuart Mill, *Principles of Political Economy*, First Edition (London, 1848), Book II, Chapter 1, Book III, Chapter 7.
[22] John Stuart Mill, *Autobiography* (Penguin, Harmondsworth, 1989), pp149 and 175-6.

published *Chapters on Socialism*[23] he seems to be more in sympathy: indeed, Mill admits in the *Autobiography* that his views on socialism had changed:

> [I]n those days I had seen little further than the old school of political economists into the possibilities of fundamental improvement in social arrangements. Private property as now understood, and inheritance, appeared to me as to them, the *dernier mot* of legislation: and I looked no further than to mitigating the inequalities consequent on these institutions, by getting rid of primogeniture and entails. The notion that it was possible to go further than this in removing the injustice - for injustice it is whether admitting of a complete remedy or not - involved in the fact that some are born to riches, and the vast majority to poverty, I then reckoned chimerical; and only hoped that by universal education, leading to voluntary restraint on population the portion of the poor might be made more tolerable. In short I was a democrat, but not the least of a Socialist.[24]

The problem with democracy is the problem that Mill identified in his review of Tocqueville's *Democracy in America*,[25] and the ultimate remedy could be some form of socialism. Referring to himself and his wife Harriet Taylor, Mill writes:

> [W]e were now much less democrats than I had been, because so long as education continues to be so wretchedly imperfect, we dreaded the ignorance and especially the selfishness and brutality of the mass: but our ideal of ultimate improvement went far beyond Democracy, and would class us decidedly under the general designation of Socialists.[26]

If socialism is to be achieved there needs to be a social transformation. However, in order to achieve that transformation the characters of individuals also need to be changed

> ...to render any such social transformation either possible or desirable, an equivalent change of character must take place both in the uncultivated herd who now compose the labouring masses, and in the immense majority of their employers. Both these classes must learn by practice to labour and combine for generous, or at all events for public

[23] John Stuart Mill, *On Socialism* (Prometheus Books, Buffalo, 1987).
[24] John Stuart Mill, *Autobiography*, p175.
[25] John Stuart Mill, 'M. de Tocqueville on Democracy in America', in Geraint L. Williams (ed) *John Stuart Mill on Politics and Society*, pp214-5.
[26] John Stuart Mill, *Autobiography*, p175.

and social purposes, and not, as hitherto, solely for narrowly interested ones. But the capacity to do this has always existed in mankind, and is not, nor is ever likely to be, extinct. Education, habit, and the cultivation of sentiments will make a common man dig or weave for his country, as readily as fight for his country. True enough, it is only by slow degrees, and a system of culture prolonged through successive generations, that men in general can be brought up to this point.[27]

The 'deep rooted selfishness' that forms 'the general character of the existing state of society'[28] could be changed only by experiments in collective action and co-operative living. Education into a more collaborative mode of life could come only from practical attempts to co-operate:

> ...we welcomed with the greatest pleasure and interest all socialistic experiments by select individuals (such as the Cooperative societies), which, whether they succeeded or failed, could not but operate as a most useful education of those who took part in them, by cultivating their capacity of acting upon motives pointing directly to the general good, or making them aware of the defects which render them and others incapable of doing so.[29]

This is the method that Mill believed would ultimately lead to human self-realisation. While he 'repudiated with the greatest energy the tyranny of society over the individual which most Socialistic systems are supposed to involve',[30] he believes that through education, experiment, development and rational discussion a society based on socialist principles would evolve:

> ...we yet looked forward to a time when society will no longer be divided into the idle and the industrious; when the rule that they who do not work shall not eat, will be applied not to paupers only, but impartially to all; when the division of the produce of labour, instead of depending, as in so great a degree it now does on the accident of birth, will be made by concert, on an acknowledged principle of justice;[31]

Mill believed that he could dispense with the need to use government as an autonomy-promoting paternalist agency to achieve these goals because he

---

[27] ibid., p176.
[28] ibid.
[29] ibid., p177.
[30] ibid., p175.
[31] ibid.

optimistically believed that 'once mankind had become capable of being improved by free and rational discussion',[32] individuals would ultimately reject the selfish pursuit of self interest[33] and pursue their interests as collaborative progressive beings. After Mill's death however, when his virtuous community still showed no signs of being established, 'new' liberals like Green and Hobhouse attempt to promote action by government to create the type of conditions to allow Mill's virtuous community to flourish. They rely explicitly on what Mill rejects in order to realise what Mill had left problematic. However, to do that they both had to present much more explicit conceptions of the good than does Mill. Even more importantly, they had to justify to a public, reared on the character-building virtues of self-help, the legitimacy of state action to promote their vision of the good. The good that they espouse was in fact based on the notion of character.

## 4.2 Green on 'character'

Classical liberalism customarily argues that a liberal society is a good society because it allows individuals to pursue *their own* good and does not impose any external notion of the good upon them. Where Green and Hobhouse differ from Mill and from that tradition is in their insistence on an *explicit* conception of the good, one that is not at all a matter of individuals' own (notions of) good. Rather they do exactly what Mill had eschewed - namely they work with, and on the basis of, a substantive notion of the good in the light of which the growth of individual character could come to be seen as a 'good', as could collective action to create conditions which would allow individuals to develop fine characters. Such a task represents a very considerable departure for classical - i.e. British - liberalism, of course. More immediately, however, they face two major problems: first of all that their notion of the good is limited to the context of Victorian Britain; and second the localised nature of their good undermines liberalism's claim to neutrality.

Green offers an idealist justification of this notion of the good. He argues that as power could not create right, any normative theory must be able to distinguish *what is*, from *what ought to be*. His normative theory, then, begins with a criticism of classical liberal theories of political obligation which, whether they be natural rights or utilitarian theories, cannot account for a distinction between *what is* and *what ought to be*. Their error, as Green diagnosed it in the *Prolegomena*, is the classical liberal belief

32 Mill, *On Liberty*, p69.

33 John Stuart Mill, *Autobiography*, p176.

in a natural science of ethics.[34] But such theories cannot account for the use of 'ought' in cases where a moral obligation exists to resist the powers that be, or to take an action that leads to unpleasant consequences. For Green, the source of the good is reason, which declares that the end of an unconditional good is self-realisation:

> [T]he idea of the absolutely desirable ... arises out of, or rather is identical with, man's consciousness of himself as an end to himself. It is the forecast, proper to a subject conscious at once of himself as an absolute end, and of a life of becoming, of constant transition from possibility to realisation, and from this again to a new possibility-a forecast of a well-being that shall consist in the complete fulfilment of himself.[35]

This unquestionably constitutes a substantive conception of the good. Moreover, it is Kantian in that it does not allow for 'hypothetical' moral imperatives. [36] *On Liberty* lacks just such a substantive notion of the good because what constitutes a good society for Mill depends on contingent circumstances; whereas for Green the good is what it is regardless of circumstances. Green knows what his vision of the good society is, and what is outside that vision, such as strong drink, is ruled out. In Green's view it is not up to individuals to pursue their own good in their own way. Rather it is up to the individual to pursue self-realisation in accordance with reason, since that is what the good consists in. To fulfil that end, Green, like Kant,[37] is prepared to coerce individuals in the event of their undertaking actions which obstruct their consciousness of themselves as ends in themselves, because such actions are contrary to the nature of the good.

According to Green, individuals can develop a good character, and hence realise themselves, only within society: '[O]nly through society is anyone enabled to give that effect to the idea of himself as the object of his actions, to the idea of a possible better state of himself, without which the

---

[34] T.H. Green, *Prolegomena to Ethics*, Introduction, pp1-13.

[35] ibid., para. 199.

[36] Hypothetical imperatives are those which have to be fulfilled if something else is to be the case. We must do something if we are to attain certain ends. Kant's categorical imperative has no such 'if' attached to it; its demands are non-hypothetical. The maxims or principles that should govern our moral action are of the categorical kind. It is not just that we ought to keep our promises if a desired result is to be obtained; we ought to keep them without qualification. See, Immanuel Kant, 'The Metaphysics of Morals', in Hans Reiss (ed) *Kant's Political Thought*, p137.

[37] T.H. Green, *Prolegomena to Ethics*, Fourth Edition, para. 325-6; and Immanuel Kant, 'The Metaphysics of Morals', in Hans Reiss (ed) *Kant's Political Thought*, p134.

idea would remain like that of space to a man who had not the senses of sight or touch.'[38] Personal identity is not a product of biological or psychological states of affairs: rather, it is the product of living in a community which itself consists of shared ways of experiencing and explaining the world, through which an individual's personal objectives and preferences are developed. However much individuals attempt to isolate themselves from society, they will still retain culturally and socially conditioned norms when undertaking any actions other than those relating to the most basic biological necessities.[39] Thus, individuals can realise themselves only within society. Green's good - the rational unfolding of self-realisation - was to be instantiated by the 'common pursuit of self-realisation by the members of a given society'.[40]

Self-realisation can take place only within society. Social relations are essential to the idea of self-realisation in two ways. First, individuals have interests by virtue of being human; and second, because of these interests they have interests in other persons:

> [N]ow the self of which a man thus forecasts is not an abstract or empty self. It is a self already affected in the most primitive forms of human life by manifold interests, among which are interests in other persons. These are not merely interests dependent on other persons for the means to their gratification, but interests in the good of those other persons, interests which cannot be satisfied without the consciousness that those other persons are satisfied. The man cannot contemplate himself as in a better state, or on the way to the best, without contemplating others, not merely as a means to that better state, but as sharing it with him.[41]

This is a social interest and it implies the consciousness of the self and others as persons, and therefore the consciousness of a permanent well-being in which the well-being of others is included. The social interest human beings have in the well-being of each other, furthermore, has implications for Green's view of freedom. Freedom should not be simply the freedom to pursue the satiation of desire, but freedom to pursue the gradual realisation of the better self:

> ...when we ... speak of freedom, we... do not mean merely freedom from restraint or compulsion. We do not mean merely to do as we like

[38] T.H. Green, *Prolegomena to Ethics*, para. 190.
[39] ibid., para. 184.
[40] Richard Bellamy, *Liberalism and Modern Society*, p37.
[41] T.H. Green, *Prolegomena to Ethics*, para. 199.

irrespectively of what it is we like. We do not mean a freedom that can be enjoyed by one man or one set of men at the cost of a loss of freedom to others. When we speak of freedom as something to be so highly prized, we mean a positive power or capacity of doing or enjoying something worth doing or enjoying, and that too is something that we do or enjoy in common with others.[42]

In particular, freedom has to be limited so that individuals can attain a fine character.[43] Building on Mill's view that individuality and self-development require certain conditions, Green outlines what the conditions for the pursuit of 'self-realisation' might be. Some factors, such as the capacity for rational thought, are clearly internal to the individuals in question. Others, such as the availability of worthwhile choices, are dependent upon social conditions. What is particularly important, for Green as for Mill, is the range of available options from which individuals can choose, for the development of character depends on the choices made. Here Green faces the same problem as Mill: the choices one makes are dependent on the choices that are available. According to classical negative libertarian theory the availability of choices does not matter; what matters is the absence of compulsion or coercion. But such a position is unacceptable for Mill and Green because individuals cannot develop a character either by accepting circumstance and custom, or by simply facing a constant struggle for survival against poverty and disease, but only through deciding a course of action from a range of worthwhile opportunities. However, neither Green nor Mill believe that the state can impose a good character on an individual: '[N]o one can convey a good character to another. Everyone must make his character for himself. All that one man may do is to remove obstacles, and supply conditions favourable to the formation of a good character.'[44] Green, like Mill believes that the possession of character will lead to individuals behaving as rational moral agents. Thus the role of the state is to secure sufficient personal freedom for its members to act as such. In practical terms Green converts 'the removal of obstacles' to individuals behaving as 'rational moral agents' into a positive but limited agenda for government. Part of this agenda includes improving the moral and social well being of the masses through improvements in education and other social reforms.

Where Green most famously departs from Millian voluntarism, and

---

[42] T.H. Green, *The Works of T.H. Green*, R.L. Nettleship (ed) 3 Vols. (London, 1885-8) Vol. III, pp370-1.

[43] See T.H. Green, *Lectures on the Principles of Political Obligation* in *Works*, Vol. II, para. 21.

[44] T.H. Green, *Prolegomena to Ethics*, para. 332.

where he offers an example of his willingness to use coercion in pursuit of his substantive conception of the good, is on the temperance question. He is happy to recommend a large measure of interference with the freedom of any individual to do whatever they like in the matter of buying or selling alcohol. Green justifies this intervention

> ... on the simple ground of a recognised right on the part of society to prevent men from doing as they like, if, in the exercise of their peculiar tastes in doing as they like, they create a social nuisance. There is no right to freedom in the purchase and sale of a particular commodity, if the general result of allowing such freedom is to detract from freedom in the higher sense, from the general power of men to make the best of themselves.[45]

Thus the province of Green's limited government agenda concerns whatever 'is really necessary to the maintenance of the material conditions essential to the existence and perfection of human personality'.[46] For instance, freedom is valuable only in that it allows people to make the best of themselves in order to develop a fine character, along the lines suggested above. Despite his support for temperance, Green believes that restraint should be limited and he recognises that in some social circumstances restraint can be positively damaging to the self-realisation of individuals; restraints in the shape of regressive laws and institutions can inhibit the possibility of personal realisation to such a degree that substantial or even revolutionary change might be required to remedy or improve the prevailing state of affairs.[47] State action and restraint are legitimate only if they create an environment where it is easier for individuals to pursue the gradual realisation of a better self.

Green develops this theme about the function of government, and especially legislation, through the elaboration of his theory of rights. He rejects what he described as the 'older individualism' and the classical notion of natural rights that went with it because (wrongly in Green's view) it supposes that political society was established to secure these rights.[48] This notion of natural rights determines the standard for defining proper relations among people, as well as the conditions under which individuals ought to submit to the state. Green describes the results of this individualist tradition with evident distaste:

---

[45] T.H. Green, *Works*, Vol. III, p383.
[46] ibid., p341.
[47] T.H. Green, *Lectures on the Principles of Political Obligation* in *Works*, Vol. II, p339-46.
[48] ibid., para. 6-8.

> [T]he popular effect of the notion that the individual brings with him into society certain rights which he does not derive from society ... is seen in the inveterate irreverence of the individual toward the state, in the assumption that he has rights against the society irrespective of his fulfilment of any duties to society, that all 'powers that be' are restraints upon his natural freedom which he may rightly defy as far as he safely can.[49]

By contrast, rights, for Green, are the mutually recognised conditions of realising a moral end in society:

> [T]he claim or right of an individual to have certain powers secured to him by society, and the counter-claim of society to exercise certain powers over the individual, alike rest on the fact that these powers are necessary to the fulfilment of man's vocation as a moral being, to an effectual self-devotion to the work of developing the perfect character in himself and others.[50]

This is the heart of Green's substantive conception of the good. In pursuit of it he is prepared to advocate state intervention in entrenched liberal rights to property and freedom of contract.[51] Furthermore, he is also prepared to countenance the idea of social harm that Mill explicitly rejected in *On Liberty*.[52]

Green's position is complex. Through his Idealism he is moving in the direction of a theory of community, but a strong residual individualism - derived from both his theology and his liberalism - leads him to deny that morality can be attributed to anything other than the character of individuals. This denial immediately creates a presumption against moral enforcement by law. Of course law can compel individuals to perform certain actions, but these actions are external; they do not ensure that people undertake actions because they are moral, since they might do so because they are coerced, on account, that is, of a hypothetical, and not a categorical, imperative. Law

---

[49] ibid., para. 50.
[50] ibid., para. 21.
[51] ibid., pp531-5.
[52] John Stuart Mill, *On Liberty*, indeed Mill says of social harm:

> [S]o monstrous a principle is far more dangerous than any single interference with liberty; there is no violation of liberty which it would not justify; it acknowledges no right to any freedom whatever, except perhaps to that of holding opinions in secret, without ever disclosing them; for the moment an opinion which I consider noxious passes anyone's lips, it invades all the 'social rights' attributed to me.... The doctrine ascribes to all mankind a vested interest in each other's moral, intellectual, and even physical perfection, to be defined by each claimant according to his own standard. - pp157-8.

cannot make individuals moral because morality depends upon freely willed actions, on performing an act for the right reasons. Therefore there must be a presumption against the use of law when voluntary action is possible. The role of law is to maintain the conditions under which will and reason may be exercised, and which, according to Green, do not include the wide and free availability of alcohol. Only those acts should be enjoined by law that are 'so necessary to the existence of society in which the moral end stated can be realised that it is better for them to be done or omitted from that unworthy motive which consists in fear or hope of legal consequences than not to be done at all'.[53] Yet Green's attitude towards the proper function of law and institutions is not purely negative. As noted above, his criticism of classical liberal individualism is based on his contention that its theory of obligation, founded on self-interest, would provide reasons for resisting positive reforms favourable to the moral life. In *The Lectures on the Principles of Political Obligation* he attempts to find a way of reconciling individuality with community. Using the normative foundations laid out in the *Prolegomena to Ethics*, Green argues that society is based not on contract or utility, but upon the spontaneous recognition by persons of other persons as ends in themselves, and the further recognition that the interests of those others is involved in their own interest. Such recognition of the common good is in his view the essence of both morality and political obligation. What is important is not just that that is the case, however; it is no less important to stress that recognition acquires its normative status on the basis of Green's substantive conception of the good, the self-realisation demanded by reason.

Green's idea of the good is therefore intimately related to the idea of character. The unfolding of self-realisation leads to the development of fine character. Individuals are allowed freedom so that they can achieve this good, and for no other reason. This is a conception of the good that is manifestly not neutral, being derived from Green's idealist notions of community and self-realisation. As such, it presents a vision of some form of collective pursuit of the good which must present conceptual problems for liberalism, a doctrine that customarily sees the good as facilitating the pursuit of individual goods.

### 4.3 Hobhouse's 'harmonic principle'

Green's notion of the collective pursuit of the good rests upon his Idealism, which he developed so that he could provide normative foundations for state action to deal with what he believed was the decline in the physical and

[53] T.H. Green, *Lectures on the Principles of Political Obligation* in *Works*, Vol. II, pp340-2.

moral conditions of the British lower orders. The normative foundations of another nineteenth century advocate of the liberal good, L.T. Hobhouse, are somewhat different, although he sought solutions to the same social problems as Green. Hobhouse is perhaps the most famous liberal advocate of the collective pursuit of the good of the individual and he also attempts to offer coherent normative foundations for a liberal good, influenced by the need to provide justification for state action to deal with the social problems of late Victorian industrial society. In that sense a direct parallel can be drawn between the nineteenth century liberalism of Hobhouse and the liberalism of contemporary thinkers like Reiman and Galston, who will be examined in the next chapter, and who also attempt to find a normative base for proactive state action to deal with social problems. Hobhouse rejects the Idealism of Green for a synoptic empirical approach to the social problems of his day. His lifelong concern was to reveal laws and principles of social evolution, in particular the growth in the historical process of a social mentality, in effect a rational collective mind in terms of which individuals progressively recognise their mutual involvement in the common good.[54] The theoretical basis for the argument that Hobhouse offers is an idea of evolutionary growth tied to an ethic of individual fulfilment that entails a substantial degree of control over the social environment. For Hobhouse, any valid theory has to rest on a scientific basis, and in Hobhouse's day that meant the theory of evolution: 'I was convinced that a philosophy that was to possess more than a speculative interest must rest on a synthesis of experience as interpreted by science, and that to such a synthesis the general conception of evolution offered a key.'[55]

While the process of evolution had been spontaneous in the natural world and in the early stages of human development, Hobhouse believes that there comes a point in human development where the mind becomes able to master material shortage and physical handicap and so intervene in that process. Science had begun to regulate our environment, and ethics and religion had begun to form 'ideas of the unity of the race, and of the subordination of law, morals and social constitutions generally to the needs of human development which are the conditions of the control that is required'.[56] For Hobhouse, evolution is the process of the development of consciousness and self-consciousness and the resultant domination of mind over the conditions of life to ensure that harmony, co-ordination and

[54] See, for example, L.T. Hobhouse, 'The Ethical Basis of Collectivism', *International Journal of Ethics*, VIII (1897-8), pp137-56, pp150-1 and pp154-5.
[55] L.T. Hobhouse, *Development and Purpose: An Essay towards a Philosophy of Evolution* (London, 1913), pxviii.
[56] ibid., ppxxii-xxiii.

adjustment increasingly pervade human existence.[57] Specifically, social progress is understood in terms of the development of the mind that enables the individual to grasp the importance of the social framework within which he or she exists and also the need for rational, conscious regulation of the social order.[58]

The objective Hobhouse seeks to achieve by regulation of the social order is the 'common good' of all the individuals in society. What is more, individual rights could not conflict with the common good because the rights and duties of individuals are understood in terms of the common good. Yet Hobhouse is far from clear by what he means by the 'common good':

> 'the common good to which each man's rights are subordinate is a common good in which each man has a share. This share consists in realizing his capacities of feeling, of loving, of mental and physical energy, and in realizing these he plays his part in the social life... he finds his own good in the common good.'[59]

Two inter-related points need to be clarified here. First of all it is important to realise that what Hobhouse means by the common good is, in actual fact, a substantive notion of the good rather than an aggregate of individual preferences. If the 'common good' were, *per impossible*, indeed no more than an aggregate of individual preferences, which is the usual classical liberal approach to ideas of the common good, individuals' preferences would establish what the common good actually was: it would be no common good at all. In Hobhouse's terms, the common good is different, in that individuals find their own good, not by pursuing their own individual preferences, but by discovering the common good of the community. This is related to the second point, Hobhouse's view of the individual in society. For the individual, the good consists in the realisation of his or her potential in a balanced expansion of personality (to use Hobhouse's term, Green's would be character). For society, it lay in the simultaneous and mutually reinforcing fulfilment of each of its members. This was the thrust of Hobhouse's 'harmonic principle', which

> ... implies that ... fulfilment or full development of personality is practically possible not for one man only but for all members of a

[57] ibid., ppxxviii-xxix.

[58] L.T. Hobhouse, 'The Individual and the State', in J. Meadowcroft (ed) *Hobhouse; Liberalism and other Writings*, p152.

[59] L.T. Hobhouse, *Liberalism*, in Meadowcroft (ed) *Hobhouse; Liberalism and other Writings*, p61.

> community. There must be a line of development open along which each can move in harmony with others. Harmony in the full sense would involve not merely absence of conflict but actual support. There must be for each, then, possibilities of development such as not merely to permit but actively to further the development of others.[60]

So, for Hobhouse, on the one hand the various dimensions of an individual life should be harmonised in a well-rounded personality; on the other, the trajectories to self-realisation adopted by the different members of the community should harmonise in a general flourishing. It is not sufficient for Hobhouse that collisions among individuals should be avoided, as in the case of classical liberalism: 'true harmony' implies positive support so that each person could have 'possibilities of development' in order to 'actively further the development of others'.[61] Hobhouse indicates the substantive character of this harmonic principle, and hence of his conception of the common good, first by harking back to Green: 'the common good to which each man's rights are subordinate is a good in which each man has a share. This share consists in realizing his capacities of feeling, of loving, of mental and physical energy, and in realizing these he plays his part in the social life, or in Green's phrase, he finds his own good in the common good.'[62] Hobhouse clarifies matters further when he speaks of the relationship between liberty and the 'good':

> ... the fundamental importance of liberty rests on the nature of the 'good' itself, and that whether we are thinking of the good of society or the good of the individual. The good is something attained by the basal factors of personality, a development proceeding by the widening of ideas, the strengthening and extension of rational control. As it is the development of these factors in each human being that makes his life worth having, so it is their harmonious interaction, the response of each to each, that makes society a living whole. Liberty so interpreted cannot ... dispense with restraint; restraint, however, is not an end but a means to an end, and one of the principal elements in that end is the enlargement of liberty.[63]

Liberty, that is to say, understood as a value only because of the end, i.e. the good that it serves.

---

[60] ibid., pp61-2.
[61] ibid., p62.
[62] ibid., p61.
[63] ibid., pp63-4.

Hobhouse, like Green, or indeed Mill for that matter, believed that the fulfilment or full development of personality is practically impossible unless that individual lives within a community,[64] and he develops the metaphor of society as an organism to justify his contention:

> ... the human body is organic because its life depends on the functions performed by many organs, while each of these organs depends in turn on the life of the body, perishing and decomposing if removed therefrom. Now, the organic view of society is equally simple. It means that, while the life of society is nothing but the life of individuals as they act one upon another, the life of the individual in turn would be something utterly different if he could be separated from society. A great deal of him would not exist at all. Even if he himself could maintain physical existence by the luck and skill of a Robinson Crusoe, the mental and moral being would, if it existed at all be something quite different from anything that we know. By language, by training, by simply living with others, each of us absorbs into his system the social atmosphere that surrounds us.[65]

The relationship between the individual and the community determines the rights and duties of the individual. This relationship is fundamental for liberal theory and, according to Hobhouse, rights and duties alike are understood substantively in terms of the common good.[66] Rights are claims we make upon others; but Hobhouse argues, claims on their own are nothing. Whether or not a claim is to be respected as a right depends on whether or not it is acceptable to an 'impartial observer':[67]

> [B]ut an impartial observer will not consider me alone. He will equally weigh the opposed claims of others. He will take us in relation to one another, that is to say, as individuals involved in a social relationship. Further, if his decision is in any sense a rational one, it must rest upon a principle of some kind; and again as a rational man, any principle which he asserts he must found on some good result which it serves or embodies, and as an impartial man he must take the good of everyone affected into account. That is to say, he must found his judgement on the common good. An individual right, then, cannot conflict with the

---

[64] ibid., pp61-2.
[65] ibid., p60.
[66] ibid., p61.
[67] ibid.

common good, nor could any right exist apart from the common good.[68]

In Rawlsian terms what Hobhouse is saying is that the good determines the right; and such a position must lead Hobhouse to suppose that there is an objective criterion of the social good, which he described as an 'ethical harmony' to which individuals might aspire.

Two questions arise for Hobhouse's theory from this contention. On the one hand, what is the foundation of his idea of the common good? And on the other, what means does he advocate to achieve the common good? The answers to these questions are connected. From the quotation immediately above we can see that Hobhouse interprets liberty as the freedom to promote the common good; and liberty so interpreted becomes inseparable from restraint. However, 'restraint is not an end but a means to an end, and one of the principal elements in that end is the enlargement of liberty'.[69] This is the point where Hobhouse appears to desert Mill and his insistence that character and the higher pleasures are of value only if pursued voluntarily, and to join forces with Rousseau in insisting that men must be 'forced to be free'.

The parallel with Rousseau is even more striking when Hobhouse's means to achieve the common good are considered. Hobhouse in fact advocates a collectivist democratic paternalism to achieve the common good. The role of government is to 'forward the collective purpose of at least the majority of the individuals constituting the community'.[70] So, provided self-government is genuinely realised, the action of the state represents the combined will of all citizens and thus cannot be coercive. Achievements by a state that represents the will of the majority have as much moral value as if individuals themselves or voluntary associations such as friendly societies had performed them. Hobhouse justifies state action of this type by claiming that:

> when the reform of law depends on the deliberate resolve of the people themselves, when it is won at the cost of a hard fought political struggle, by the appeal to reason, by a contest involving widespread earnestness, some self-sacrifice, much serious attention to some social problem and the means of solving it, then the law is no magician's wand helping people out of trouble with no effort of their own. It is the reward of effort. It is the expression of a general resolve. It embodies a

[68] ibid.

[69] ibid., p64.

[70] L.T. Hobhouse, 'The Individual and the State', in J. Meadowcroft (ed) *Hobhouse; Liberalism and other Writings*, p156.

collective sense of responsibility. It is in a word, something that a mass of people have achieved by their combined efforts for their common ends, just as a well organized trade-union or a friendly society is an achievement won by combined effort for common ends.[71]

Even Hobhouse admits that this is an idealised picture of democracy,[72] and even if it were not, it is a picture that rests on a normative assumption which is not ethically neutral. Hobhouse's normative position is that serious, reasoned, democratic discussion would result in decisions that were somehow ethically 'right'. Hobhouse does not specify whether the decisions would be 'right' because they are democratic, or that a democratic process would produce 'right' decisions and he does not offer an ethical justification for either case. In effect, Hobhouse simply offers an unsubstantiated claim that participatory democracy will inevitably produce decisions which are ethical. He has no other normative foundation.

Hobhouse's and Green's arguments can be coherent only if they offer a valid argument for their normative foundations, that is to say for their notions of the good. However, it is impossible to see how these bases can be ethically neutral as liberalism requires and/or assumes. This is especially true inasmuch as both Green and Hobhouse attempt to provide normative bases for their liberalism in order to achieve a specific social purpose. Their liberalisms therefore directly contravene the idea that a liberal state and society should be neutral between competing conceptions of the good in order to avoid coercing individual citizens.

## 4.4 Green, Hobhouse and the moral foundation of liberalism

Let us look in more detail at how this comes to be so. The normative foundation of Green's conception of the good is idealist and Christian. He argues, in Kantian manner, that the view of the world essential to science, as a related series of objects and events, is not a product, but a pre-supposition, of knowledge. However, he goes beyond Kant to regard these relations not simply as features of our classifying and combining intelligence, but as explicable only on the assumption of the existence of a divine consciousness present in both mind and nature and guaranteeing their ultimate unity. He maintains, furthermore, that eternal consciousness reproduced itself in people's lives. Humankind's striving after self-realisation forms the operative force behind the transformation and development of human societies, the

[71] ibid., pp156-7.
[72] ibid., p157.

product of a progressive unfolding of the divine principle within the consciousness of individuals.[73] However, Green wishes to avoid the idea that history is the result of a teleological spirituality rationally ordering human affairs in a benign manner. Only individual effort could bring about the gradual moralisation of social relations. Moreover, the divine unity upon which it is premised remains beyond time and space, and hence is only imperfectly realised within existing institutions, which could regress from it no less than advancing towards its fulfilment. The divine unity that forms the normative foundation of Green's prescriptive philosophy clearly cannot form a satisfactory normative foundation for today's secular liberalism. In effect it rejects much of the tradition of liberalism as it developed during and after the Enlightenment: indeed Green is highly critical of the 'popular philosophy' of utilitarianism and classical economics which he believes undermined the moral dimension of liberalism:

> [T]he elimination of ethics, then, as a system of precepts, involves no intrinsic difficulties other than those involved in the admission of a natural science that can account for the moralisation of man. The discovery, however, that our assertions of moral obligation are merely the expression of an ineffectual wish to be better off than we are, or are due to the survival of habits originally enforced by physical fear, but of which the origin is forgotten, is of a kind to give us pause. It logically carries with it the conclusion, however the conclusion may be disguised, that, in inciting ourselves or others to do things because they ought to be done, we are at best making use of a serviceable illusion. And when this consequence is found to follow logically from the conception of man as in his moral attributes a subject of natural science, it may lead to a reconsideration of a doctrine [that of believing moral attributes to be a subject of natural science] which would otherwise have been taken for granted as the most important outcome of modern enlightenment.[74]

In a sense Green is returning to the original religious foundations of liberalism that can be found in Locke, who states: 'God hath certainly appointed Government to restrain the partiality and violence of Men.'[75] Green argues that the cause of men's obedience to the state or sovereign is their free recognition that customs, laws and institutions embody, however roughly, a notion of right that they all share. The legal sovereign does not

[73] T. H.Green, *Prolegomena to Ethics*, para. 83-85.
[74] ibid., para. 8.
[75] John Locke, *Two Treatises of Government*, Second Treatise, para. 13.

exercise an unlimited power of compulsion. It is effective only to the extent that the government is contributing to the common good. When Green is arguing in this way it is clear that he is analysing actual states, for he refers to the Roman Empire, British rule in India and the Russian Empire.[76] In all of these examples the sovereign authority was obeyed because it maintained a customary law recognised by the people as being in their common interest. Where there is conflict between law and what Green sees as the common good, for example the question of land-holding, then there would be some form of almost spontaneous self-regulation of societies.[77] What Green means by this becomes clear from his discussion of the collapse of the Greek *polis*: '[T]here is no clearer ordinance of that supreme reason, often dark to us, which governs the course of man's affairs, than that no body of men should in the long run be able to strengthen itself at the cost of others' weakness. The civilisation and freedom of the ancient world were short-lived because they were partial and exceptional.'[78] So when an institution such as land ownership was oppressive, as Green believed it to be, then laws would spontaneously evolve to reform the institution.

This is unconvincing, especially when one examines more closely the basis of Green's notion of rights as consisting in the pursuit of a fine character. Green attempts to shift the basis for rights from the theory of consent used by natural rights theorists to his own version of the common good. To this, as noted above, he introduces the idealist notion of social and conscious recognition as an essential ingredient of rights. What Green is arguing, when he uses the idea of recognition, is that a moral community will be one in which an individual will limit his or her claims to freedom in the light of recognised general social interests. The community itself will support these claims because the general well-being can be realised only by recognising certain individual rights to pursue the good. In Green's case, this of course means freedom to pursue a fine character. A right, furthermore, is a claimed power which should be granted if it promotes a good common to all those within a given political society. More: this power must be *recognised* as so doing by the members of the society, or be implied by existing practices and relationships themselves recognised as legitimate, both tacitly and explicitly. Green's account of slaves in a society which otherwise grants full rights to all its members demonstrates the weakness of his case. Slaves, by their use of rationality, and their affection for friends and family, demonstrate their right to be recognised as equal human beings by the larger community of which they are members. The community, if Green's concept

---

[76] T.H. Green, *Lectures on the Principles of Political Obligation* in *Works*, Vol. II, pp370-78.
[77] ibid.
[78] T.H. Green, *Works*, Vol. III, p372.

of recognition is valid, is thus obliged to recognise slaves as having the same rights as everyone else. If this is so, then 'recognition' has been transformed from the criterion of right into a process by which the validity of claims of right are measured. This is to assert that some rights exist which are not legally, but only tacitly, recognised. What, then, constitutes tacit social recognition? The presence of relationships that imply certain rights, for example the human relationships of the slave, imply that they should be treated equally with other humans. If slaves are not treated in this way, then those individuals who deny slaves the rights that they themselves enjoy deny the basis of their own claimed rights. But this introduces a question of logic into what Green had previously been presenting as a matter of fact. What if slave-owners fail to recognise their slaves' claim to rights? In the presence of conflicting views about which rights ought to be recognised, who will decide what are the rights immanent in the existing social system?

This position must be unsatisfactory, for a claimed power may contribute to some common good of all members of society, but not be recognised as doing so. Equally, such a power may be implied by existing social relationships, but resisting existing laws that deny that claim may demonstrably produce results inimical to the good of society as a whole. Green's account of recognition is also unclear. Suppose that after serious consideration an individual decides that a law does not promote a good common to all individuals within a given society, individuals must then decide how to register their protests. Green believes that in a country like Britain, with a popularly elected government and settled methods of enacting and repealing laws, the answer of common sense was enough. The individual should use all legal methods to have the law repealed but should not violate it. The good would suffer more from resistance to legal authority than from the individual's conformity to a bad law.[79] This model would work quite well in ordinary instances: but problems do not arise in 'ordinary instances', as Green's discussion of slavery referred to above demonstrates. Genuine difficulties arise in abnormal circumstances and Green's theory offers no means to resolve them.

Green has elided a formal and a substantive argument. What he considers as rights resemble those granted to British subjects in his own time. But he believes that the concept of recognition, in its idealist form, could both account for, and justify those rights: because all individuals want to be granted certain claims, they acknowledge similar claims on the part of others. But what grounds are there for believing that the claims actually

---

[79] T.H. Green, *Lectures on the Principles of Political Obligation* in *Works*, Vol. II, paras. 103-12.

recognised by individuals will resemble those rights actually granted by the governments Green deemed legitimate? The form of Green's argument is typical of attempts to give liberalism a moral foundation. He begins his theory with a radical agenda. Ultimately he makes clear that his theory of rights is based on socially acknowledged claims.[80] A theory of rights based on social acknowledgement can say nothing about the content of rights. If the members of a society recognised cannibalism as a practice, not only justified but mandatory in certain circumstances, no one, using Green's criterion, would have a right to object to being eaten under such specified conditions. Given the nature of Green's theory nothing could be more certain than that he would have rejected practices substantially at variance with the values of his own society. Yet on the basis of recognition alone, he could not have excluded as rights things that he manifestly would have wished to exclude, such as the right to buy and sell strong drink. Ironically, the essence of this liberal dilemma is captured most accurately by Green's own praise of Burke's critique of rationalism:

> [H]e almost alone among the men of his time caught the intellectual essence of the system which provoked him. He saw that it rested on a metaphysical mistake, on an attempt to abstract the individual from his universal essence, i.e. from the relations embodied in habitudes and institutions which make him what he is; and that thus to unclothe man, if it were possible, would be to animalise him.[81]

Green is admitting here that liberal individuals are a product of particular political and social traditions, and that, therefore, the flourishing of individuals is dependent on the flourishing of the social and political traditions that allowed the establishment and maintenance of individuality. The problem with Green's attempts to provide liberalism with a moral foundation is that they attempt to impose a universalistic normative framework on a particular liberal tradition.

By attempting to use recognition to justify the common good, Green has in fact offered an idealist justification of the existing social order. Green thus prefigures Hobhouse and contemporary liberals such as Galston, Reiman and Machan. They all fall foul of the same difficulty as Green: that is, they attempt to offer a moral foundation for liberalism, but end up offering a justification of existing social arrangements.

Hobhouse's conception of the good rests on six assumptions, all of which can be shown to be dependent on the intellectual context of late

---

[80] ibid., pp400-5, see especially para. 147.
[81] T.H. Green, *Works*, Vol. III, pp116-7.

Victorian and Edwardian Britain, and hence to vitiate his universalistic claims. The first assumption is that personal development, enabling individuals to become capable of self-direction, is a good.[82] Second, and following from the first, is that liberty is not simply letting people alone, but the duty to treat individuals as rational beings.[83] Third, if individuals behave rationally there will be an ethical harmony amongst individuals in a society.[84] Fourth, this harmony, as shown in the course of the discussion of Hobhouse's substantive conception of the good, will be represented by the will of the majority in a representative democracy.[85] Fifth, the rights, liberties - and hence justifiable restraint - of individuals are determined by what is required to maintain ethical harmony within society.[86] And sixth, as the restraint of individuals is legitimate in pursuit of the common good, the state - as the agency representing the majority - is justified in coercing individuals who oppose the pursuit of a 'common good', that is to say of Hobhouse's ethical harmony.[87] There is a single normative foundation on which these assumptions rest: the idea that the universal good to which all human beings ought to aspire is that of Hobhouse's rational individual, living in harmony within a community. What Hobhouse means by this is best summed up by Meadowcroft in his introduction to Hobhouse's *Liberalism*:

> [F]or the individual, the good consisted in the realization of his or her potential in a balanced expansion of personality. For society, it lay in the simultaneous and mutually reinforcing fulfilment of each of its members. This was the essential bearing of Hobhouse's 'harmonic principle': on the one hand, the various dimensions of an individual life should be harmonized in a well-rounded personality; on the other, the trajectories to self realization adopted by different members of the community should harmonize in a general flourishing.[88]

Hobhouse's notion of the 'harmonic principle' is teleological: he believes that society is evolving harmoniously in precisely the direction he believes to be valuable: toward the fulfilment of individuals within a liberal community. The problem then becomes this: how to deal with groups that reject his notion of liberal harmony. His attempted solution, as I shall demonstrate,

---

[82] L.T. Hobhouse, *Liberalism*, p60. and 'The Individual and the State', p162, both in J. Meadowcroft (ed) *Hobhouse; Liberalism and other Writings.*
[83] L.T. Hobhouse, *Liberalism*, p73.
[84] ibid., pp61-2.
[85] ibid., pp64-5.
[86] L.T. Hobhouse, 'The Individual and the State', pp161-2.
[87] ibid.
[88] J. Meadowcroft, Introduction, pxviii, *Hobhouse; Liberalism and other Writings.*

illustrates serious contradictions within his thought, particularly in relation to the rights of minorities and his definition of rights as those claims that an impartial (liberal) observer would grant; and this in turn has implications for any residual claims to neutrality.

Hobhouse begins his justification of his conception of the good by saying that the collective pursuit of self-realisation and the social control it must entail does not conflict with the evolutionary principle, but is part of a 'line of advance which educed the higher from the lower animal forms, which evolved the human out of the animal species and civilised from barbaric society'.[89] The necessary condition of evolution is not, Hobhouse believes, the struggle for survival, or even the competition leading to the 'survival of the fittest', but rather 'the rise and growth of a principle of organic harmony or cooperation which from the first rise of parental care begins to mitigate and finally to restrict the field of struggle'.[90] Hobhouse is on weak ground here and he obliquely acknowledges the fact:

> [M]erely to point to the existence of this tendency was not, we admitted, sufficient to justify it, but we urged that its existence and success suffice to prove the feasibility of the conscious effort, to carry through the harmonic principle in social life, and this is in fact the guiding principle of a rational social philosophy. To apply such a principle, we admitted is a matter of infinite practical difficulty, but it nowhere founders on any theoretic objections, for no essential element of social value has to be purchased at the expense of the fundamental and irrevocable loss of any other element of irrevocable value.[91]

Hobhouse admits the difficulty by pointing out that the tendency observed toward social harmony does not ethically justify its pursuit by a state or community, but he still urges that its 'existence and success suffice to prove the feasibility of the conscious effort to carry through the harmonic principle in social life, and that this is in fact the guiding principle of a rational social philosophy'.[92]However, despite contending that the 'existence and success' of the harmonic principle proved its feasibility, Hobhouse recognises that such a principle is practically difficult to apply. Despite these practical difficulties, he believes that there could be no theoretical objections to the notion of social harmony, because in his view no essential element of social value had to be purchased at the expense of any other valuable social

---

[89]L.T. Hobhouse, 'The Individual and the State', p165.

[90] ibid.

[91] ibid.

[92] ibid.

element. The whole point of the principle of social harmony is that Hobhouse believes social values do not conflict. The criticism that Hobhouse attempts to answer directly is that directed at liberal welfare reform by the Social Darwinists. The basis of Hobhouse's rejection of Social Darwinist argument demonstrates how utterly convinced he is of the validity and universality of his conception of the good:

> [T]he keenest critics of the feasibility of social progress... rest their case on the tendency of the higher social ethics to preserve inferior types and so lead to racial deterioration. But on this point... if it is true, which is not yet proved, that selection remains essential to social progress, the solution of the difficulty is to be found in the replacement of natural by social selection.[93]

With serene confidence Hobhouse concludes that

> the conception of social progress as a deliberate movement towards the reorganization of society in accordance with ethical ideas is not vitiated by any contradiction. It is free from any internal disharmony. Its possibility rests on the facts of evolution, of the higher tendencies of which it is the outcome. It embodies a rational philosophy, it gives scope and meaning to the best impulses of human nature, and a new hope to the suffering of mankind.[94]

Three key problems emerge, to none of which he has any answer. The first is the question of liberty and control. Hobhouse sees liberty as the organisation of constraints, and believes that liberty is the positive expression of the will of the majority. A progressive majority is entitled to impose their will on a minority. This is the antithesis of both Mill's voluntarism and his concern, expressed in his review of Tocqueville's *Democracy in America*,[95] that democracy would lead to the tyranny of the majority and the oppression of unpopular minority beliefs. This leads to the second problem. The only defence against such tyranny toward minorities is - in his view - that their rights, or claims against the majority, would be upheld if they would be deemed justified by an 'impartial observer':

> A may make a claim on B, and B may refuse the claim. The claim only becomes recognized as a right if some impartial third person, (C)

[93] ibid.
[94] ibid.
[95] John Stuart Mill, 'M. de Tocqueville on Democracy in America', in Geraint L. Williams (ed) *John Stuart Mill on Politics and Society*, pp214-5.

upholds A in making it, and on what ground can C as an impartial being base his judgement? As impartial he is looking at A and B just as two persons equally members of the community with himself. If there exists a rule recognized by the community which covers the case no question arises. But we are looking at cases in which no rule exists, and C has to frame his decision on first principles. To what in such a case can he look except the common good? If he maintains as a right a general principle of action incompatible with the good of the community, he must hold by that what is right is one thing and what is good is another, and that not merely by accidental circumstances of a peculiar case but as a matter of principle. Unless then we are to suppose such deep-seated ethical conflict in the ethical order we must regard the common good as the foundation of all personal rights.[96]

But the observer would not be impartial. In *Liberalism* Hobhouse is concerned that his argument of the impartial observer founding his judgement on what constitutes rights, on the common good, would be seen as making the individual too subservient to society. He denies that this would be so. However, his denial demonstrates the lack of impartiality in his idea of the impartial observer:

> [S]ociety consists wholly of persons. It has no distinct personality separate from and superior to those of its members. It has indeed a certain collective life and character. The British nation is a unity with a life of its own. But the unity is constituted by certain ties that bind together all British subjects, which ties are in the last resort feelings and ideas, sentiments of patriotism, of kinship, a common pride, and a thousand more subtle sentiments that bind together men who speak a common language, have behind them a common history, and understand one another as they can understand no one else. The British nation is not a mysterious entity over and above the forty odd millions of living souls who dwell together under a common law. Its life is their life, its well-being or ill-fortune their well-being or ill-fortune. Thus, the common good to which each man's rights are subordinate is a good in which each man has a share.[97]

The impartial observer was therefore adjudicating claims for rights within an existing tradition of political behaviour, the political tradition of

[96] L.T. Hobhouse, 'The Individual and the State' in J. Meadowcroft (ed) *Hobhouse; Liberalism and other Writings*, p160. Hobhouse makes the same point in *Liberalism*, see p61.
[97] Hobhouse, *Liberalism*, p61.

Britain in the late nineteenth and early twentieth centuries. He or she would be impartial in adjudicating claims only within that paradigm. When considering which claims should be regarded as rights, the impartial observer could operate only within the tradition that Hobhouse delineated; the British tradition of the period. Where there was conflict between competing claims the observer could not be impartial between, for instance, the claim of an individual to a right of free speech and the claim members of a non-native British religious confession to a right to have their religion and historic religious figures respected. Under such circumstances the observer could not be impartial.[98]

The third difficulty is the extent to which all members of a society can in fact adhere to a substantive conception of the good. Within the context of a homogeneous community, such as that of late Victorian and Edwardian England, it was perhaps possible to suppose that all members of a society might adhere to a particular substantive conception of the good, but even here there would be significant minorities who, although part of the homogeneous culture, rejected the imposition of homogeneity. The problem is, of course, far more acute within multicultural contemporary societies, and there are no obvious signs of the harmony that Hobhouse predicted coming to pass. What is more, on Hobhouse's teleological view of society, it is hard to see how he could fail to be prepared to coerce members of groups whom he deemed a regressive influence on a progressive society because he argued that the majority have a right to self-expression and action:

> [I]f liberty is among other things the right of self-expression, this is a right which masses of men may claim as well as minorities, and they will seek to use the means that lie at hand for effectuating their claim. Now it may be that legal machinery is the only efficient means for the purpose, and if the members of a majority are debarred from the use of such machinery, their will is to that extent frustrated and their right so far denied.[99]

However, Hobhouse's liberalism made him insist that it was legitimate for the rights of minorities to put a restraint on the self-expression of

---

[98] Hobhouse's problem here bears some similarity to the current debate within contemporary liberalism over how liberal theory can deal with the problems created by multicultural societies. For example, Will Kymlicka, *Multicultural Citizenship*; Joseph Raz, 'Multiculturalism: A Liberal Perspective', *Dissent*, Winter, 1994, pp67-79; Chandran Kukathas, 'Are there any Cultural Rights?' in Kymlicka (ed) *The Rights of Minority Cultures?*; John Gray, 'The Politics of Cultural Diversity', in *Post-Liberalism*.

[99] Hobhouse, 'The Individual and the State', p157.

majorities because of the risk of majorities coercing minorities.[100] Hence some means had to be discovered to establish when such restraint of the majority was justified:

> [T]he objections to the use of coercion in some directions may be, and for my part I should agree that they are so great that it is better that the majority should fail to get its way. But do not let us shut our eyes to the fact that to insist this in any case, whether for good and sufficient or for bad and insufficient reasons, is alike to put a restraint on self-expression, and to that extent upon liberty. The liberty of the minority in such a case is (as always) a restraint upon the majority.[101]

The method Hobhouse chooses to use to establish when such restraint was justified was that of the 'impartial observer' and the criterion the impartial observer had to use was Hobhouse's idea of the common good. For Hobhouse, the liberty of minorities depended on their rights as individuals. Rights were those claims granted by an impartial observer who can use only the criterion of the common good as the foundation for all personal rights.[102] But this criterion was itself the product of Hobhouse's own intellectual context. Hence he could offer no independent normative criterion on which to base his conception of the good other than the wishes of a 'progressive majority'. Hobhouse's conception of the good, like Green's, has no independent normative foundation other than that which was specific to a particular social and historical context.

---

[100] ibid.
[101] ibid.
[102] ibid., pp159-60.

# 5 Challenges to Neutrality II: Ethical Liberalism and Contemporary Debates

Victorian social liberalism, as I intimated in the previous chapter, possessed an explicit conception of the good that was derived from Idealism. It is not, however, the only species of liberalism to maintain an explicit conception of the good; contemporary liberals such as Tibor Machan, William Galston and Jeffrey Reiman[1] also argue in favour of such a liberalism - unorthodox as their position is in relation to the classical liberal tradition. Equally unorthodox is Richard Rorty: unlike Machan, Galston and Reiman, he believes that liberalism is ungroundable, but this does not stop him advocating a liberal good, however, it is a good founded not upon the putative neutrality of Enlightenment rationalism but upon the contingent circumstances within liberal states. This draws Rorty close, despite his left-wing credentials, to the 'liberal' conservatism of a writer like Michael Oakeshott. Finally I shall consider how communitarian discourse illustrates a conservative reversion within liberalism and hence attempt to explain why Rorty's attempt to conscript Oakeshott to the liberal cause is ultimately unsuccessful.

## 5.1 Galston, Reiman and Machan: contemporary advocates of a liberal 'good'

Certain contemporary advocates of a liberal good offer arguments that run parallel to those of Hobhouse and Green. Each address, in their different ways, a distinctive problem in contemporary liberal society that they believe undermines liberalism. For instance, the key dilemma Galston addresses is that of diversity within contemporary liberal societies. He holds that

[1] William Galston, *Liberal Purposes* (Cambridge University Press, Cambridge, 1991); Tibor Machan, *Capitalism and Individualism* (St. Martin's Press, New York, 1990) and 'Individualism Versus Classical Liberal Political Economy', *Res Publica*, Vol. 1, Number 1, 1995, pp3-23; Jeffrey Reiman, *Critical Moral Liberalism: Theory and Practice*.

liberalism, rightly understood, is about the protection of diversity.[2] Galston's method of tackling this particular issue is relevant for two reasons. First, the existence of illiberal minorities within liberal states has led to widespread debate within liberalism about how far liberal societies can, or indeed should, accommodate themselves to illiberal practices. And second, Galston's work is particularly germane in dealing with the question of liberal neutrality because, unlike others such as Kymlicka,[3] he sees the existence of diversity as an essential part of the liberal good that he seeks to promote: he attempts, therefore, to retain some degree of neutrality between liberal and non-liberal lifestyles in his formulation of the good, while Kymlicka simply argues that groups should not be allowed to impose illiberal internal restrictions with either the sanction or connivance of a liberal state.[4] Reiman's vision of the liberal good, in contrast, is concerned with autonomy rather than diversity.[5] In this sense Reiman bears similarities to communitarian critics of liberalism such as Charles Taylor and Michael Sandel,[6] who also believe that the flourishing of an individual depends on social circumstances. However, Reiman goes beyond the communitarians in arguing that his vision of the liberal good is universal because true community can thrive only in the space liberalism protects. Tibor Machan, finally, is unique amongst contemporary liberals in that he explicitly questions whether liberal neutrality is sustainable. What Machan is attempting to do is establish a foundation for liberalism that rests on explicit and decisively non-neutral claims.

While their starting points are all rather different Galston, Machan and Reiman, like Green and Hobhouse, share an explicit commitment to a universal liberal good in such a way as to undermine even the vestiges of neutralism their liberalism might retain. However, before going any further it

---

[2] William Galston, 'Value Pluralism and Political Liberalism', *Report from the Institute for Philosophy and Public Policy*, Volume 16, No. 2, Spring 1996, http://www.puaf.umd.edu/ippp/galston.htm 30/11/97, p3 of 8.

[3] Will Kymlicka, *Multicultural Citizenship*.

[4] ibid., pp35-6.

[5] Jeffrey Reiman, *Critical Moral Liberalism: Theory and Practice*:

> ...the individual who surrenders his sovereignty by becoming an addict under awful circumstances makes a choice to do so and thus is *causally* responsible for the addiction. He is not, however, morally responsible for it, where this refers to the sort of responsibility for an action that makes one rightly the object of moral blame or praise for it. Moral responsibility for the addicts choice passes to whomever it is who is responsible for creating or maintaining conditions evil and awful enough to make surrender of sovereignty rational. - p90.

[6] Charles Taylor, 'Atomism', in Shlomo Avineri and Avner de-Shalit (eds) *Communitarianism and Individualism* (Oxford University Press, Oxford, 1992) and Michael Sandel, *Liberalism and the Limits of Justice* (Cambridge University Press, Cambridge, 1982).

is important briefly to differentiate Galston, Reiman and Machan from two other noted critics of the neutralist and communitarian strands in contemporary liberalism with whose critiques they might be confused, Richard Rorty and Alasdair MacIntyre. Rorty rejects the search both for neutral foundations of liberalism, recognising that liberalism is contingent upon circumstances and not on ahistorical philosophical for the foundations of liberal practices and principles: instead he regards 'the justification of liberal society as simply a matter of historical comparison with other attempts at social organization - those of the past and those envisaged by utopians'.[7] As a consequence Rorty admits that there is 'no neutral, noncircular way to defend' liberal ways from Marxists or Nazis but, he argues, such a neutral argument is no longer necessary for the preservation of liberalism within those societies which possess liberal traditions.[8] Rorty has accepted that the liberal tradition is a good, but argues it is no longer necessary to use Enlightenment rationalism to defend it. MacIntyre, by contrast, rejects the whole Enlightenment project and liberalism with it. Towards the end of *After Virtue* he states:

> [M]y own conclusion is very clear. It is on the one hand we still, in spite of the efforts of three centuries of moral philosophy and one of sociology, lack any coherent rationally defensible statement of a liberal individualist point of view; and that, on the other hand, the Aristotelian tradition can be restated in a way that restores intelligibility and rationality to our moral and social attitudes and commitments.[9]

By contrast with Rorty and MacIntyre, Galston, Reiman and Machan adopt the same form of argument as Green and Hobhouse, but argue far more explicitly that liberalism must rely on a substantive notion of the good - and (in their different ways) that such a notion has *universal* validity. It is in that sense a notion that remains neutral - neutral between cultures, societies and so on - a possibility Rorty and MacIntyre reject. Galston, Machan and Reiman might be said to attempt to retain a historico-geographical neutrality while recognising (to an extent that varies between them) that liberalism both relies upon and advocates certain conceptions of human life - that is to say, certain substantive notions of the good.

Galston begins from the assumption that there are two master ideas in liberal thought. He describes them as the 'Enlightenment' and 'Reformation'

---

[7] Richard Rorty, *Contingency, Irony and Solidarity*, p53.
[8] ibid., p44 and p197.
[9] Alasdair MacIntyre, *After Virtue*, Second Edition, p259.

projects.[10] The Enlightenment project gives pride of place to autonomy, the experience of liberation through reason from centrally imposed authority. Within this project, the examined life is understood to be superior to reliance on tradition or faith, and preference is given to self-direction over any external determination of the will. The alternative, 'Reformation', project gives pride of place to diversity. The central tenet of this master idea of liberalism is that of accepting and managing diversity through mutual toleration within a framework of civic unity.

Problems arise, he argues, when liberals embrace the 'Enlightenment' project at the expense of that of the 'Reformation':

> [I]n my judgement social theorists - especially liberals - go astray when they give pride of place to an ideal of personal autonomy, understood as the capacity for critical reflection and for choice guided by such reflection. The inevitable consequence is that the state takes sides in the ongoing tension between reason and faith, reflection and tradition, needlessly marginalizing and antagonizing groups that cannot conscientiously embrace the Enlightenment project.[11]

Nonetheless, Galston recognises that there must be limits to how far diversity can go: and this gives rise to a particular difficulty. On the one hand he believes that where the imposition of liberal norms threaten the survival of civil associations such as churches, then a liberal politics guided by the principle of diversity should give priority to the claims of civil associations. On the other, he insists that not all religiously motivated practices are deserving of accommodation: for example, '[N]o civil association can be permitted to engage in human sacrifice: there can be no free exercise for Aztecs.'[12] The Aztecs, as they ceased to exist 500 years ago, are easily dismissed. Galston's problems in justifying diversity as the master idea of liberal thought stem from the existence of illiberal groups in liberal societies today. What he must do is to vindicate the differential treatment of non-liberal groups within liberal polities whilst maintaining a commitment both to the diversity, which he sees as the basis of the liberal good, and - somehow - to liberal neutrality between competing conceptions of the good. An example of the difficulties that Galston faces comes from his contention that (what he describes as) a civil association cannot endanger the basic

---

[10] William Galston, 'Value Pluralism and Political Liberalism', *Report from the Institute for Philosophy and Public Policy,* Volume 16, No. 2, Spring 1996, http://www.puaf.umd.edu/ippp/galston.htm 30/11/97.

[11] ibid., http://www.puaf.umd.edu/ippp/galston.htm 30/11/97, p3 of 8.

[12] ibid., http://www.puaf.umd.edu/ippp/galston.htm 30/11/97, p6 of 8.

interests of children by withholding medical treatment in life-threatening situations.[13] What, then of the rejection of blood transfusions by Jehovah's Witnesses and the refusal of ultra-Orthodox Jews in Israel to countenance organ transplants? In these cases, because the basic interests of children cannot be threatened by denying them life saving treatment, Galston would intervene against the desire of individuals and groups to pursue their own conception of the good. Yet this is surely to impose a secular liberal value system on groups with different (perhaps more spiritual) values and these individuals and groups would regard liberal intervention as both immoral and a contravention of their right to diversity.

In order to explain why Galston believes that there should be limits to how far liberals should tolerate diversity it is necessary to see exactly why he sees diversity as a good. Diversity is a premise in an argument for a protected zone of liberty. Galston argues that

> [S]ince there is no one uniquely rational ordering of incommensurable values, no one could ever provide a generally valid reason, binding on all individuals, for a particular ranking or combination. And, under what might be *called the principle of rational autonomy*, a generally valid reason of this sort, while not a sufficient condition for restricting the liberty of individuals to lead a range of diverse lives, is certainly a necessary condition.
>
> Note that this case for a zone of liberty is a claim about limits on coercive interference in individual or group ways of life. It is not an argument that each way of life must itself embody a preference for liberty.[14]

For Galston, it is the principle of diversity rather than autonomy that is at the heart of liberalism. Diversity is valuable within liberal polities because it allows the widest possible range of autonomy, including the autonomy to participate in faith-based and traditional ways of life. It also does not overly discriminate against minorities who reject the liberal value of autonomy and are committed to tradition and faith. Galston does not regard, as a higher order good in itself, the critical reflection that is so often seen as a crucial part of liberalism. However, if minorities are permitted to impose their

---

[13] ibid., Galston's use of the term civil association should not be confused with that of Oakeshott. Oakeshott uses the term to describe an ideal model of association in terms of moral non-instrumental rules (Michael Oakeshott, *On Human Conduct*), pp124-7 whereas for Galston civil associations are independent groups within existing societies.

[14] ibid., http://www.puaf.umd.edu/ippp/galston.htm 30/11/97, p2 of 8.

visions of the good on those around them, they contradict the very reasons for which they are permitted to do what they want to do. That is: they are only permitted to enact minority tastes because they live in a liberal polity. So, by being illiberal they contravene grounds for diversity. In effect, illiberal minority groups within a liberal polity take advantage of liberalism. Galston responds by distinguishing between private and public:

> … a liberal community may legitimately establish institutions to promote public health and require all citizens including Christian Scientists and individuals bent on suicide to maintain them through taxation. It does not follow, however, that a liberal community may compel these dissenters to make use of its public health facilities: coercion for public purposes is distinguishable from coercion directed at individual ways of life.[15]

Galston's argument here parallels Mill's distinction between self-regarding and other-regarding actions. However, Galston gives a very detailed account of the conditions under which tolerance is extended to illiberal groups:

> [T]heir [civil association's] norms may significantly abridge individual freedom and autonomy without legitimating external state interference. But these associations may not coerce individuals to remain as members against their will. Thus there is a form of liberty whose promotion is a higher-order political goal: the individual's right of exit from groups and associations that make up civil society. This liberty will involve not only insulation from certain kinds of state interference, but also a range of affirmative state protections.[16]

'Affirmative state protections' are required in order to provide conditions for a meaningful right of exit from 'civil associations'. These include, according to Galston,

> *knowledge* conditions, offering chances for awareness of alternatives to the life one is in fact living; *psychological* conditions, including freedom from the kinds of brain washing practised by cults; *fitness* conditions, or the ability of individuals to participate effectively in some ways of life other than the one they wish to leave; and *social diversity*,

[15] William Galston, *Liberal Purposes*, p10 (emphasis added).

[16] William Galston, 'Value Pluralism and Political Liberalism', *Report from the Institute for Philosophy and Public Policy*, Volume 16, No. 2, Spring, 1996, http://www.puaf.umd.edu/ippp/galston.htm 30/11/97, p7 of 8.

affording an array of meaningful options.[17]

His conditions offer a series of encouragements for individuals to embark on a liberal way of life and desert any faith-based or 'traditionalist' civil associations within a liberal state. Galston, like Mill, takes for granted that minorities will accept the private/public distinction and accept the imposition of conditions which will enable individuals to secede from their faith-based or traditionalist groups. The problem is, however, that many minority groups would not accept the public/private distinction - for instance some fundamentalist Christian or Islamic groups; nor would they accept that the rights of the individual should be prior to the rights of the religious confession or the family. This leaves Galston with precisely the same problem as besets classical liberals: the only groups whose diversity will be accommodated are those that can coexist with the liberal imperative without contravening its fundamental tenets. Galston himself sees this as a weakness:

> [I]t may be suggested that while autonomy poses clear challenges to faith, the moral philosophy of value pluralism is not straightforwardly hospitable to faith either. This is true. Some faiths purport to establish clear hierarchies of values, with universally binding higher-order purposes. Some faiths argue for sociopolitical domination against the idea of free civil space. Clearly value pluralism cuts against these claims.
>
> Still there are zones of overlap between value pluralism and religious belief. In practice, even well articulated faiths are characterized by internal value pluralism. And once the multiplicity of faiths is an irreversible fact, other considerations - many themselves faith-based - come into play to restrict state coercion on behalf of any single faith. *This is a kind of restraint on certain religious practices, and it may well stack the deck in favor of faiths that emphasize inward conscience rather than external observance.*[18]

Now, despite this recognised weakness, Galston maintains that the liberal state 'comes closer than any other form of association, past or present to accommodating human differences. It is "repressive" not in comparison with available alternatives but only in relation to unattainable fantasies of perfect liberation'.[19] This claim is tenable where someone is either an

[17] ibid., http://www.puaf.umd.edu/ippp/galston.htm 30/11/97, p7 of 8.
[18] ibid., http://www.puaf.umd.edu/ippp/galston.htm 30/11/97, p3 of 8 (emphasis added).
[19] William Galston, *Liberal Purposes*, p4.

adherent of a faith that emphasises individual conscience, or adheres to a political creed that values diversity and choice within society. However, it is not tenable if someone's conception of the good is the maintenance of a community. If Galston takes his conditions for exit from a 'civil association' to their logical conclusions they would seriously undermine the efforts of many faith-based communities to perpetuate themselves - for example, the way certain Islamic schools in the UK not only segregate the sexes but educate young women into specific social roles, including the acceptance of arranged marriages within a patriarchal community. In addition, the psychological and knowledge conditions that Galston advocates could be used to argue in favour of secular education in the place of religious schools in order to ensure that children are aware of forms of life other than that practised by their own traditionalist or religious group. If such encouragements were carried to their logical conclusion they could in fact thus interfere with the freedom that religious groups have traditionally had in liberal states to educate children in their own religion. Galston would obviously reject such infringements on diversity but nonetheless he must, like other liberals, demonstrate preference for groups and practices that abide by the liberal tradition. Illiberal groups are tolerated only to the extent that they do not transgress the rules and values of the liberal tradition. All liberals can do is fall back upon the argument that the laws of Britain (or any of other liberal democracy), and the mechanisms for amending them, are legitimate because such procedures have both the authority of history, and the tacit consent of the respective populations. As Green would say, obligation comes from the recognition that laws are just.

Reiman begins his account by stating that he wishes to defend the moral liberalism of Locke, Kant, Mill and Rawls.[20] He is concerned that much contemporary liberalism becomes a 'pared-down "political" liberalism that is scarcely more than a recipe for peaceful coexistence among people who can never be expected to agree about the moral good'.[21] Reiman describes his own version of liberalism as critical moral liberalism:

> [I]t is moral because it is neither neutral about the moral good, nor merely a set of rules for peaceful coexistence. Critical moral liberalism contends that living one's own life according to one's own rational

[20] In some ways this seems an odd grouping but in the Preface to *Critical Moral Liberalism* Reiman states:

> [T]he liberalism I have in mind is the moral liberalism that was defended by John Locke in the seventeenth century, by Immanuel Kant in the eighteenth century, by John Stuart Mill in the nineteenth and John Rawls in the twentieth - the liberalism that champions the moral right of individuals to live as they choose so long as they respect that right in others. - pix.

[21] ibid., px.

judgements is a condition of living a good life; that promotion of the ability to so live is a moral ideal that all societies should foster and the right of individuals to so live (as far as this is compatible with all individuals being able to do so) is a right that all human beings have a duty to respect. It is critical because it recognizes in the wake of Marxian and, more recently feminist analyses - that our knowledge of what threatens freedom and what is needed to protect it change in history, and therefore that any particular interpretation of what liberalism requires may, in effect, function ideologically to legitimate a situation characterized by unjust coercion. Critical moral liberalism takes this danger very seriously and therefore remains open to the idea that as-yet-unrecognized forms of coercion may be discovered and that new rights may be needed to defend freedom against them.[22]

Reiman holds that the moral principle at the heart of this doctrine is the 'ideal of individual sovereignty',[23] which contends that all human beings are entitled to the maximum ability to live their lives according to their own judgements, subject to the conditions necessary to realise this for everyone.[24] In this model of liberalism freedom is not the ultimate value: it has an instrumental value in that freedom is necessary if people are to live their lives according to their own judgements. Living self-governed lives is, according to Reiman, the chief value of critical moral liberalism. Crucially, Reiman says, 'it claims to identify a *universal* good and a *universal* moral right'.[25]

The foundation for this claim - bearing considerable similarity to Hayek's - is the universal rationality of all human beings, a rationality itself evidenced by their use of language. [26] Thus the universal condition to be

---

[22] ibid.

[23] ibid., p1.

[24] ibid.

[25] ibid. (emphasis added) See also,

> ... if community is to have moral worth, it must be more than people living near one another. People must share interests and concerns and feel toward one another some measure of affection. None of this is compatible with force.... Forced community is like forced laughter. It is to true community what forced religious observance is to true faith. Real community must be a free expression of shared commitment. But, to be free, it must arise in the space that liberalism protects. - p48.

[26] Reiman notes:

> [R]ationality is a universal capacity of human beings because, among other things, it is presupposed by the use of language. Language sounds to us like the direct transmission of sense or information, as if comprehending were merely a matter of direct perception, like seeing. But simple reflection shows that language must be more complicated. What reaches our ears is not sense but sound. Thus the comprehension of language must involve rational processing of sound to infer what their producer meant by them. We hear a series

applied in the treatment of human beings is to allow them to use their rationality to live according to how they judge best. For the most part this goal is achieved by leaving people alone and not blocking them in the pursuit of their goals provided they do not block others. The need to live self-governed lives, then, is a fundamental part of Reiman's conception of the good.[27] Drawing on Heidegger and Husserl, Reiman bases the need to live self-governed lives on existentialist ideas of human mortality. As people we have one chance to live. Mortality, and our consciousness of it, limits individual existence and so transforms living into living a life. Unusually, for a liberal, Reiman believes that existentialism offers valuable insights into the human condition that can be appropriated by his 'critical moral liberalism'.[28] According to secular tradition, life is the sum total of an individual's existence, 'bounded on the far side endless darkness and silence'.[29] Mortality, therefore, makes life into a special kind of challenge. As individuals are 'aware of the fact that they have one finite chance to be in all eternity'[30] they are confronted by the need to live a life whose worth satisfies them that they have used their chance well. Reiman contends that '[H]owever different we are, we all confront our lives as our once-in-eternity chance to live a life whose nature we care about',[31] and that this must establish a distinctive human good:

> [T]hat we live our lives in response to the challenge of mortality means that it is, above all, important in each person's life, not just that she lives some particular way or another, but that she *intentionally* lives a life that somehow *satisfies her* that it is worthwhile in the face of the inevitable nonbeing on the other side. No life can answer the challenge

---

of sounds and we rationally judge what someone who utters those sounds must be trying to get across. We do it so well and so quickly that we don't notice it except, of course, when communication breaks down and our capacity for deliberate review kicks in. We then check our beliefs about what the other is trying to say against other things she has said, or against our shared beliefs about the world, or, of course, by asking her what she meant. - p4.

[27] ibid., pp16-18.

[28] ibid.

> [W]hat I take from Heidegger, then, is the idea that the challenge of mortality, brought home to us in an ultimate way in the first person puts a distinctive shape on the human good. That we live our lives in response to the challenge of mortality means that it is, above all, important in each person's life, not that she lives some particular way or another, but that she *intentionally* lives a life that somehow *satisfies her* that it is worthwhile in the face of the inevitable nonbeing on the other side. No life can answer the challenge of mortality unless it is judged to do so by the one whose life it is. - p17.

[29] ibid., p16.

[30] ibid.

[31] ibid., p17.

of mortality unless it is judged to do so by the one whose life it is.[32]

Reiman's account implies that a necessary condition of any human life's being good is that the person whose life it is intentionally lives it in a way that he or she can recognise as good. But then it is a condition of living a good life that an individual's life be the outcome of their own rational judgements about how best to live. Thus rational self-governance is the condition of living a good life. In this sense Reiman is clearly part of that liberal tradition, originating with Kant, that sees rationality as opposed to wants as the basis of a liberal good, even Mill includes the notion of rational development as a good for individuals in his thought, although, of course, he desires to see such individual goods pursued voluntarily.

The major difficulty with Reiman's conception of the good surrounds his use of anti-rational existentialist arguments. He admits this difficulty and says:

> [R]eaders who are familiar with the writings of Heidegger will know that his philosophy is marked by a deep antirationalism, and that in response to mortality's challenge, he counsels 'resolve' an act of sheer will by which one undertakes to live one's own life 'authentically' rather than give in to the temptation of letting the world script one's life for one.[33]

Reiman's response is baldly to state that such anti-rationalism has no place in critical moral liberalism, and that such an act of sheer non-rational will has more in common with an unexpected accident than an individual's resolve to live their own life. In contrast; 'a true resolve to live one's own life would have to be marked by the sort of evaluation of one's nature and possibilities that can only be rational'.[34] What Reiman is saying is that to live a valuable life we must be constantly evaluating and re-evaluating what we do in order to establish whether or not we are fulfilling some sort of rationally decided intentional life plan. Therefore, Reiman's notion of the good society is one that allows individuals the best opportunity to formulate, evaluate and achieve intentional life plans in order to ensure our one shot at mortality is worthwhile.

Reiman has attempted to provide a universalist justification of autonomy on the basis of what he sees as the two crucial elements of what it is to be human: rationality and mortality. One problem with this argument,

---

[32] ibid., p17.
[33] ibid., p17.
[34] ibid.

however, is of course that it is not neutral: for Reiman's thought rests firmly on certain value laden assumptions about the nature of the individual and society. Although rationality and mortality are indeed defining elements of the human experience it is an assumption of liberalism that we can live worthwhile lives only if they are governed by ourselves rather than by others - being an acolyte of a religious faith, or in solidarity with others, or indeed in solidarity with what has gone before. Once that assumption is granted, of course Reiman - in keeping with the liberal tradition - remains neutral about how such self-governance might be realised, that is up to each individual, as we have seen. But, in the absence of an argument to show that his rationality condition has necessarily to be fulfilled through individuals' autonomy, the latter remains an assumption, and one which is clearly value laden. The value he places on living self-governed lives, and hence on autonomy, are products, and expressions of the very social circumstances he wishes his 'critical, moral liberalism' to criticise. It expresses not some universal 'human nature' but the liberal tradition's view of and/or insistence upon autonomy. It is thus not neutral, but an expression of liberalism's core values.

Reiman offers the most radical attempt to provide liberalism with a moral foundation. Reiman's radicalism is partly based on his belief that Marx made two important discoveries that profoundly affect our moral situation. He states:

> [F]irst, Marx has discovered the potentially unjust and coercive nature of social practices, such as, but not limited to, forms of property ownership. This discovery applies as well to the social maintenance of gender roles. ...
>
> Marx's second discovery is of the tendency of the coerciveness of social practices not to be recognized as such. Since social practices are all around us, they fade into the background like the smell of the air or the feel of your chair. This means that their coercion works effectively and doesn't feel unjustly coercive.[35]

This is the basis for the radical critique of liberalism as an ideology. Reiman notes that:

> [T]he general form of criticism of liberalism as an ideology is that *(a)* liberalism effectively defends freedom by establishing rights against recognized forms of unjust coercion; *(b)* there exist putatively unjust social practices (for example, property arrangements, sexism, racism,

[35] ibid., pp19-20.

> poverty) that limit people's choices coercively, but which are not recognized as doing so; and *(c)*, because of *(a)* and *(b)*, liberalism ignores (leaves unrecognized and thus unchallenged) these forms of coercion which then simply work through the existing system of liberal rights.[36]

He denies that this is an objection to liberalism as such. Rather, it appeals to liberalism's own core value, freedom. Hence, for Reiman, the critique of liberalism as an ideology is always a critique of an existing version of liberalism as not doing enough to protect individual freedom in the light of unrecognised and unjust coercion. There is on the face of it one obvious problem concerning coercion with this argument and one which Reiman in fact recognises:

> ... that a social practice coerces people is not enough to condemn that social practice morally. Established social practices are necessary for the smooth functioning of any society; and the way they narrow choices may be necessary for social life to be predictable and relatively conflict free.... The issue is whether the coercion works justly, that is, to everyone's benefit alike, or unjustly, that is, to force a disadvantage on some one for the benefit of others.[37]

To determine the justice of any coercion exercised, a test must be discovered to test the justice of established social practices. The device that Reiman proposes is a variation of Rawls's idea of the veil of ignorance asking

> ... whether it would be reasonable for (imaginary rational) people (interested in maximizing their ability to govern their lives by their own judgements, and supplied with the best available knowledge, but ignorant of how they in particular will fare under any particular social arrangement) to agree unanimously to live under that social arrangement *given the possible alternatives*.[38]

Two points are germane here. First, Reiman rests his case on the assumption that we can separate ourselves from our cultural and religious attachments; he has accepted Rawls's idea of the unencumbered self. Second, he has accepted that there is no absolutely ideal liberal model, but only the

---

[36] ibid., p20.
[37] ibid., p22.
[38] ibid., p23, emphasis added.

best of a series of possible alternatives. The first point is important because he has accepted the nature of human beings as essentially utility maximisers. The second point is important because, despite his attempt to rid liberalism of unintentional coercion, Reiman is accepting that whether unrecognised social practices are coercive or not depends not on objective criteria of justice, but on whether or not they are better than possible alternatives. Reiman's thought, despite its radical intent, therefore, is both value-laden and implicitly dependent upon contingent circumstances for its conception of the good.

It is the preservation of these core liberal values which concerns the final contemporary liberal to be examined, Tibor Machan. The justification that Machan offers of liberalism, then, is that it is the mode of human association which, given human nature, allows human beings the best opportunity to realise their true selves - one essential characteristic of which is their individuality. That individuality, however, is neither a developmental notion along Millian lines, nor a purely formal notion which admits of whatever content individuals might choose. Rather it explicitly expresses Machan's substantial conception of human nature. He thus offers both a critique of neutralist liberalism and a claim that liberalism *per se* is the most suitable mode of human political and social organisation because it most closely fits with human nature (as he finds it to be).[39] For the problem with neutralist liberalism is that it leaves liberalism defenceless from other intellectual challenges.

Machan begins his critique by encapsulating the liberal dilemma as follows:

> [A]ny judgement of morally or politically good or bad, as well as right and wrong, come to no more than a preference, a positive or negative feeling of the agent, lacking any objective moral import. Is the favourite political principle of classical liberals [liberty] itself a mere subjective value? The answer is 'yes', despite the fact that the right to individual liberty on first impression seems to be well supported by...radical individualism. But it is only a matter of convenience, something we have adopted but might just as easily not have; we might with equal

---

[39] Tibor Machan, 'Individualism Versus Classical Liberal Political Economy', *Res Publica*, Vol. 1 Number 1, 1995, pp9-10. Compare with *Capitalism and Individualism*:

> ...the main trouble with defending capitalism is the definition of the concept of 'human being' on which the defense usually relies. From this definition, put forward primarily by economists, it is not possible to generate a conception of the human good, except perhaps that most barren idea of subjective utility. In particular most economists hold the view that human behaviour always amounts to pursuing self-interest, trying to maximize wealth, seeking to satisfy desires. - px.

justifiability have adopted something else - say the right to equality or security.

If this is all true, then people who prefer playing golf to defending liberty when the latter is in jeopardy do nothing wrong. Also, if someone ignores the plight of the hapless or the unjustly treated, there is nothing to be criticized about this choice.[40]

In order to free liberalism from the subjectivism that such 'value-neutral' radical individualism entails, Machan argues it is necessary to return to the idea of what he describes as classical individualism, an individualism founded on the essential characteristics of human nature, of which the chief is individuality; and this must exclude certain (competing) conceptions of the good, prioritising others (those of that 'classical individualism') over what is in his view the sort of 'right' that these entail. The good he argues must take priority over the right.[41] The foundation for Machan's naturalistic individualism, then, is that human beings are primarily individuals.[42] 'Human nature', however, is a notoriously ambiguous concept and one that could point just as easily toward radical individualism, authoritarianism or collectivist egalitarianism. Recognising this problem Machan attempts to show that his conception of human nature nevertheless remains plausibly neutral (in the sense of not being ideological) yet without being neutral in the sense of allowing it just any content:

[W]hen we talk about the nature of something we should have in mind what is reasonably justifiable given what we know to be so beyond a reasonable doubt. The classification that we are entitled to make on the basis of evidence we have gathered - limited to the context and present state of our knowledge (provided that we are consistent and reasonably

[40] Tibor Machan, 'Individualism Versus Classical Liberal Political Economy', *Res Publica*, Vol. 1, Number 1, 1995, p7.

[41] ibid., p10.

[42] See ibid.

[there is] a capacity for self-differentiation ...albeit common to all *normal* human beings as well as features we all share ... that give rise to certain universal standards. It is by their own particular initiative, circumscribed by their family backgrounds, traditions habits customs, environment, opportunities, climate etc., that people must confront the living of their lives. So they must implement their individuality every moment of their lives, a point with serious implications for the best sort of polity for human living. Interestingly, this also points up the social nature of human life - being thinking animals implies that their flourishing is interwoven with their fellows. They will learn from them, find enjoyment and love from them, trade, play and carry on all the most exciting aspects of their humanity with them. - p12.

historically complete) - will yield a conception of what the nature of something is. And that is firm enough to guide us in our political, and even our personal lives; as firm a guide as we can expect the world to be from our knowledge of history and from common sense.[43]

A study of human nature reveals, according to Machan, that human beings have a stable nature as thinking animals who depend upon their essential quality as a thinking animal to live and to do well at the task of living. Where they go wrong is when they fail to act in accordance with their distinctive human nature through negligence, carelessness, evasion, imprudence, vanity and dishonesty.

However, there is a serious difficulty in Machan's approach, interesting as it is. For Machan's theory to be convincing he needs to show at the very least that the general principles of what he regards as a 'viable conception of human nature', although they may not hold for all eternity will be 'general enough to apply over time, to succeeding generations';[44] otherwise Machan can have no answer to critiques of substantive theories of human nature from Marxists, for example, which state that human nature is no more than the product of social environment. But by making the limited claim that he does, that the principles of human nature only need to be 'general enough to apply over time, to succeeding generations', Machan is admitting that these principles are the products of contingent circumstances rather than immutable foundations of human behaviour. But this makes it difficult to see how his conception of human nature can do the work demanded of it. Machan recognises that, as well as acting individually, human beings act in accordance with tradition, custom, habit and family background: he thus recognises that the principles of human nature he identifies are not immutable but dependent upon contingent circumstances. Machan's conception of human nature, therefore, remains tied to specific circumstances, cultures or societies. As such, it remains inescapably normative, rather than being the empirical basis he takes it to be. For it remains a contingent matter whether or not 'human nature' realises itself in any particular way; and inasmuch as any particular instantiation of it remains contingent on its context and circumstances, it cannot represent - universally - human nature 'as it is'. It is a recommendation and not merely a description of *how things are* (even though it may of course describe *how things happen to be* in certain cases). It thus turns out that Machan, therefore, has rejected neutrality only to adopt a highly debatable normativity.

Machan's conception of the good resembles Galston's in that its

[43] ibid., p11.
[44] ibid., p12.

foundation is only *purportedly* empirical. While Galston's conception is founded on the idea that observation of institutions and rules can allow the development of a series of pragmatic compromises that will underpin the institutions of the liberal state, Machan believes that the observation of human nature can perform the same task. Essentially they both attempt to offer conceptions of the good based on empirical observation: but these 'observations' are not 'pure'. They are made from a liberal vantage-point, assuming all the time the nature and importance of (liberal) 'individuality'. Such a position is like Hayek's in that it can only be valid - let alone non-normative - if the empirical assumptions on which the theory rests can be proven to be true. However, in the case of Galston and Machan, and for that matter in the case of Hayek, these assumptions are at best highly contestable. Moreover, the contestability of their assumptions shows that the attempt of contemporary liberal theorists like Galston, Reiman and Machan to provide liberalism with moral foundations does not succeed simply because their liberalism does not demonstrate the neutrality toward the good that a liberal approach demands.

## 5.2 The anomalous liberalism of Richard Rorty

This leaves the anomalous liberalism of Richard Rorty. Rorty is customarily associated with the Left in American politics but, as we shall see, he adopts metaphors and approaches in his philosophy which are more usually associated with the Right:[45] rejecting the liberal search for foundations, and accepting that liberalism is inevitably a matter of 'how we do things here' - a

---

[45] For example, consider Rorty's discussion of the self in *Objectivity, Relativism and Truth* (Cambridge University Press, Cambridge, 1991). He declares that the self is 'a network of beliefs, desires, and emotions with nothing behind the attributes. For purposes of moral and political deliberation and conversation, a person is just that network'. Rorty then cites Michael Sandel approvingly for realising that we cannot regard ourselves as Kantian subjects, capable of constituting meaning on our own without '...great cost to those to those loyalties and convictions whose moral force consists partly in the fact that living by them is inseparable from understanding ourselves as the particular people we are - as members of this family or community or nation or people, as bearers of this history, as sons and daughters of that revolution, as citizens of this republic'. Sandel, *Liberalism and the Limits of Justice*, p179. Rorty then makes clear his agreement with Sandel:

> I would argue that the moral force of such loyalties and convictions consists *wholly* in this fact, and that nothing else has *any* moral force. There is no 'ground' for such loyalties and convictions save for the fact that the beliefs and desires and emotions which buttress them overlap those of lots of other members of the group which we identify for purposes of moral or political deliberations, and the further fact that these are *distinctive* features of that group, features which it uses to construct itself-image through contrasts with other groups. - pp199-200.

conventionally conservative position - his left-liberal commitment stands in contradiction to his epistemic position.[46] Nonetheless he denies that this makes liberalism difficult to defend:

> [T]o say that convictions are only 'relatively valid' might seem to mean that they can only be justified to people who hold certain other beliefs - not to anyone and everyone. But if this were what was meant, the term would have no contrastive force, for there would be no interesting statements which were *absolutely* valid. Absolute validity would be confined to everyday platitudes, elementary mathematical truths, and the like: the sort of beliefs nobody wants to argue about because they are neither controversial nor central to everyone's sense of who she is or what she lives for. All beliefs which *are* central to a person's self-image are so because their presence or absence serves as a criterion for dividing good people from bad people, the sort of person one wants to be from the sort one does not want to be. A conviction which can be justified to *anyone* is of little interest.[47]

Moreover, the search for such foundations, he argues, is no more than a descent into metaphysics or theology:

> This book [*Contingency, Irony and Solidarity*] tries to show how things look if we drop the demand for a theory which unifies the public and private, and are content to treat demands of self-creation and of human solidarity as equally valid, yet forever incommensurable. It sketches a figure whom I call the 'liberal ironist.' Liberal ironists are people who include among ... ungroundable desires their own hope that suffering will be diminished, that the humiliation of human beings by other human beings may cease. For liberal ironists, there is no answer to the question 'Why not be cruel?' - no noncircular theoretical back up for the belief that cruelty is horrible. Nor is there an answer to the question 'How do you decide when to struggle against injustice and when to devote yourself to private projects of self-creation?' Anybody who thinks that there are well-grounded theoretical answers to this sort of question - algorithms for resolving moral dilemmas of this sort - is still, in his heart, a theologian or a metaphysician. He believes in an order

---

[46] Rorty's latest book, *Achieving Our Country: Leftist Thought in Twentieth-Century America* (Harvard University Press, Cambridge, Massachusetts, 1998) is an attempt to encourage the development of a democratic consensus around the ideas of a socially just and classless society, but on his grounds such encouragement can be no more than that; just encouragement.

[47] Rorty, *Contingency, Irony and Solidarity*, p47.

beyond time and change which both determines the point of human existence and establishes a hierarchy of responsibilities.[48]

Rorty's position is incipiently conservative; indeed in *Contingency, Irony and Solidarity* he associates himself with Michael Oakeshott (together with John Dewey and what might be described as the later Rawls) as thinkers who wanted to retain Enlightenment liberalism while dropping Enlightenment rationalism.[49] The nature and limits of Rorty's putative conservatism are best illustrated, in fact, by comparing him directly with Oakeshott:

> ...'moral principles' (the categorical imperative, the utilitarian principle, etc.) only have a point insofar as they incorporate tacit reference to a whole range of institutions practices, and vocabularies of moral and political deliberation. They are reminders of, abbreviations for, such practices. At best, they are pedagogical aids to the acquisition of such practices.[50]

This is remarkably similar to Oakeshott who insists that:

> [P]olitical enterprises, the ends to be pursued, the arrangements to be established (all the normal ingredients of a political ideology), cannot be premeditated in advance of a manner of attending to the arrangements of a society; *what* we do, and moreover what we want to do is the creature of *how* we are accustomed to conduct our affairs. Indeed, it often reflects no more than a discovered ability to do something which is translated into an authority to do it.[51]

Now Oakeshott is sometimes seen as a very 'liberal' conservative, but the idea the primacy of practice over theory and the contingency of circumstance have been fundamental to conservative theory since Burke. In the *Reflections on the Revolution in France*, for instance, he makes a statement with which both Rorty and Oakeshott would immediately concur:

> [T]he science of constructing a commonwealth, or renovating it, or reforming it, is, like every other experimental science, not to be taught *a priori*. Nor is it a short experience that can instruct us in the practical science; because the real effects of moral causes are not always

---

[48] ibid., pxv.
[49] ibid., p57.
[50] ibid., pp58-9.
[51] Michael Oakeshott, *Rationalism in Politics*, p120.

immediate; but that in which the first instance is prejudicial may be excellent in its remoter operations; and its excellence may arise even from the ill effects it produces in the beginning.[52]

Oakeshott, Rorty and Burke all hold a prejudice in favour of established arrangements, and agree on the importance of contingent judgements in political and moral considerations.

Rorty first drew on Oakeshott's ideas in *Philosophy and the Mirror of Nature*[53] where he uses Oakeshott's metaphor of conversation to explain how he believes philosophical issues whether moral or political should be discussed:

> [I]f we see knowing as not having an essence, to be described by scientists or philosophers, but rather as a right, by current, standards to believe, then we are well on the way to seeing *conversation* as the ultimate context within which knowledge is to be understood. Our focus shifts from the relation between human beings and the objects of their inquiry to the relation between alternative standards of justification, and from there to the actual changes in those standards which make up intellectual history.[54]

Rorty develops more fully his interpretation of Oakeshott's thought with respect to moral theory in *Contingency, Irony and Solidarity*.[55] In that work, Rorty praises Oakeshott for helping to undermine 'the idea of a transhistorical "absolutely valid" set of concepts which would serve as 'philosophical foundations' of liberalism'.[56] He cites Oakeshott approvingly when the latter likens morality to a language that has to be learned rather than a set of general principles; rather it is moral principles or precepts which are derived from the language. Indeed Rorty's overall conception of morality parallels that of Oakeshott very closely:

> [W]e can keep the notion of 'morality' just insofar as we can cease to think of morality as the voice of the divine part of ourselves and instead think of it as the voice of ourselves as members of a community, speakers of a common language. We can keep the morality-prudence distinction if we think of it not as the difference between an appeal to

---

[52] Burke, *Reflections on the Revolution in France*, p152.

[53] See Rorty, *Philosophy and the Mirror of Nature* (Princeton University Press, Princeton, 1980), pp389-94.

[54] ibid., pp389-90.

[55] Rorty, *Contingency, Irony and Solidarity*, pp57-6.

[56] ibid., p57.

> the unconditioned and an appeal to the conditioned but as the difference between an appeal to the interests of our community and the appeal to our own, possibly conflicting, private interests. The importance of this shift is that it makes it impossible to ask the question 'Is ours a moral society?' It makes it impossible to think that there is something which stands to my community as my community stands to me, some larger community called 'humanity' which has an intrinsic nature.[57]

Rorty actually invokes Oakeshott's notion of *societas*[58] - that is his view of the state as association in terms of a non-instrumental practice - as the ideal model of the liberal state.

Moreover, the notion of the constitutive nature of communities in establishing morality is not confined simply to a contemporary conservative such as Oakeshott: exactly the same theme is apparent in Burke when he points out the importance of affection for the locality and family as the 'first principle (the germ as it were) of public affection'.[59] This is a fundamental element in conservatism, which Burke clearly expresses in a famous section of the *Reflections*:

> [W]e begin our public affections in our families. No cold relation is a zealous citizen. We pass on to our neighbourhoods, and our habitual provincial connections. These are inns and resting-places. Such divisions of our country as have been formed by habit, and not by a sudden jerk of authority, were so many little images of the great country in which the heart found something which it could fill. The love to the whole is not extinguished by this subordinate partiality.[60]

Even more significant, in this context is Rorty's justification of this liberal society. '[I]t is a society whose hero is the strong poet and the revolutionary because it recognizes that it is what it is, has the morality it has, speaks the language it does, not because it approximates to the will of God or the nature of man but because certain poets and revolutionaries of the past spoke as they did.'[61] This is surely a conservative invocation of adhering to a tradition simply because it is ours. It is the ultimate result of Rorty's abandonment of the quest for rational coherent foundations for liberalism.

---

[57] ibid., p59.

[58] ibid., for Rorty, Oakeshott's *societas* is appropriate to a liberal society 'conceived as a band of eccentrics collaborating for purposes of mutual protection rather than as a band of fellow spirits united by a common goal'. - p59.

[59] Edmund Burke, *Reflections on the Revolution in France*, p135.

[60] ibid., p315.

[61] Rorty, *Contingency, Irony and Solidarity*, p61.

The problem for Rorty in adopting an incipiently conservative approach to contingency and community is that he does not adopt the conservative social authoritarianism that is required for its maintenance. Consider what he says about cruelty: what distinguishes liberals, he argues, is that they believe that 'cruelty is the worst thing we can do'.[62] But such a position, whatever the intention, will - because it remains ungrounded - allow almost anything to be justified. Take the example of one of Rorty's 'moral narcissists',[63] someone concerned with dressing to the height of fashion, drinking the finest wine, and eating the most exquisitely prepared food, but whose wealth was acquired from a legal, but disreputable, company specialising in lending money at exorbitant rates of interest to the very poor. An all powerful prankster decides to play a cruel joke on this particular person, to make him suffer by depriving him of his narcissistic lifestyle and make him, for a period of time, work in a factory, live on the same council estate as his company's clients and only have satellite television as entertainment. What is more, the prankster makes certain that he does not know whether or not he will return to his previous lifestyle. For a narcissist this would be horrendously cruel, but his lifestyle would still be better than those from whom he originally earned his money. I doubt many people would be able to summon much sympathy for the person in question, especially when many people, the homeless, the unemployed and people starving in the Third World, might regard such a lifestyle as the answer to their prayers. Even if 'cruelty is the worst thing we can do', then, the difficulty is to agree on exactly what cruelty consists in. And that, even if it does not perhaps depend on criteria universal across human cultures, it does depend on normative notions of human nature: consider the Inquisition, torturing people to death not, so they thought out of cruelty, but for the sake of people's eternal souls. They weren't being cruel, were they?

### 5.3 'Political liberalism', the 'liberal/communitarian' debate and conservatism: Bellamy, Rorty and Oakeshott

The continuance of the pressures giving rise to ethical liberalism can be discerned in the contemporary debate between the remaining adherents of liberal neutrality: the debate between deontological and communitarian liberals. This can be seen as the re-emergence of ethical liberalism in a muted or disguised form, for it is a last-ditch and ultimately unsuccessful response to the tensions within liberalism. These tensions have been

[62] ibid., pxv.

[63] Richard Rorty, *Objectivity, Relativism and Truth*, pp203-10.

exacerbated by what could be called the very success of the aspirations to neutrality of contemporary liberal society, namely its actual inclusion of illiberal groups within it, which challenge liberal preconceptions and values. The deontological/communitarian debate is an aspect of the attempt both to respond to these challenges and to determine how such groups should be treated. But the attempt is a failure in the end for liberalism can solve its problems only by resorting to conservatism *à la* Rorty.

Consider for example two groups who explicitly reject liberal ideals: religious fundamentalists and nationalists. Both nationalists and religious fundamentalists contest the liberal notion of the self because, for them, the self has meaning only as part of the national community or as an acolyte of a religious faith. For nationalism and religion, moral virtue consists in subordination of the self to the nation or religion. It follows that in religious or nationalist ethics, the individual, can if necessary, be sacrificed for the well being of the wider religious confession or national community. The self, then, for this community cannot be the autonomous, inviolate self of liberal tradition. By contrast and by definition deontological liberalism is an ethical theory because it insists on the priority of the rights of the individual over the good of the wider society.

The communitarian critique of deontological liberalism begins with a challenge to these notions of neutrality and of the self. Sandel and Taylor[64] argue that deontological liberalism rests on an atomistic conception of the self as prior to, and independent of, society. They maintain that deontological liberals fail to grasp the constitutive role of the community in our self-understanding and ultimately in the construction of the persons that we are. Now if this argument is valid, as I have suggested, then it must undermine liberalism's defences against the challenges it faces from outside its own tradition. According to Taylor,[65] the pursuit of neutrality between competing conceptions of the good must be abandoned for the joint pursuit of a 'common good'; conceived as a substantive conception of the good which defines a community's way of life. The public pursuit of shared ends that define the community's way of life is not, therefore, constrained by the requirement of neutrality between competing conceptions of the good. Yet for Taylor, the common good concerned is the maintenance of a community that allows the establishment of the ideal, liberal, rational, autonomous,

[64] See, for example, Charles Taylor, 'Atomism', in S. Avineri and A. de-Shalit (eds) *Communitarianism and Individualism*; Michael Sandel, *Liberalism and the Limits of Justice*; and 'The Procedural Republic and the Unencumbered Self', *Political Theory*, 12 (February, 1984), pp81-96.

[65] See, W. Kymlicka, *Liberalism, Community and Culture* (Oxford University Press, Oxford, 1989), p76.

choosing self. The obligation the individual owes to the community rests on the role it plays in nourishing this type of self. But a difficulty arises with communities that do the reverse, that is those communities whose existence depends on individuals subordinating their rationality and/or choices for the common good of nation or religion. Such communities actually undermine the individuality which a communitarian like Taylor would wish to see flourish. In such cases liberal communitarians face an unresolvable contradiction.

Liberalism, then, has so far proved inadequate to the practical challenges it currently faces. Partly, at least, this failure is due to the theoretical chaos currently haunting liberalism. In their different ways deontological liberalism and communitarianism have proved unable to mount an adequate defence against external challenges. Deontological liberalism, by its attempt to build a neutral, universal theory from the allegedly objective rights of competing individuals, opens liberalism to challenges that its theory is not neutral between individuals who *recognise themselves as individuals,* and those who can only identify themselves as members of a wider national community or a religious faith. Communitarianism is successful in that it points out the failure of deontological liberalism to recognise the role of community in constituting the rational, choosing, liberal self, but it fails in its attempt to offer a communitarian alternative foundation for liberal values. Liberalism, therefore, appears caught between two stools: an ethical doctrine that cannot take account of the community's role in creating the idealised liberal self; and a communitarian doctrine which cannot provide a moral foundation for liberal values, other than that they are *our* values.[66]

Seen in this light, the debate between communitarianism and deontological liberalism appears to have no satisfactory conclusion. Deontological liberalism cannot be neutral between those who adhere to theories of the unencumbered self, and those who say that only community can constitute the self. As Alasdair MacIntyre has observed, 'communitarians demonstrate the vulnerability of deontological liberalism by showing that the deontological ideal of the rational wanting self is not "natural" but is an underlying conception of the good created by specific communities in certain historical epochs'.[67] However, the communitarian defence of these communities rests on the historical record of these communities in producing

---

[66] See for example Richard Rorty, *Contingency, Irony and Solidarity,* especially the Introduction and chapter 3; and the critique of Rorty offered by Norman Geras, *Solidarity in the Conversation of Human Kind* (Verso, London, 1995), pp83-5.

[67] Alasdair MacIntyre, 'The spectre of communitarianism', *Radical Philosophy*, 70, 1995, p35.

the rational liberal individuals idealised by deontological liberals. But why do communitarians regard the production of this type of person as a good? They appear to be able to present no normative foundation other than this: we like the type of society we live in and the type of individuals we have become. This is a position which maintains that liberal values have proved worthwhile because they have created something we enjoy and see as worthwhile; and that societies which produce them should be maintained and protected for that reason alone. But this is a fundamentally conservative, rather than a liberal, position. Is this incipiently, even on occasion explicitly, conservative defence, the best defence that liberalism can offer?

Perhaps so: but one potential option remains, and that is the most sophisticated recent defence of liberalism, that of Richard Bellamy.[68] Bellamy accepts some of the communitarian critique of deontological liberalism. He believes that the presence of competing cultures and interests within modern societies renders an ethical conception of liberalism unacceptably offensive to too many people. This is true even of the allegedly neutral theories of deontological, liberalism because they can be shown to rely on the cultural assumptions of the societies where liberalism originated, principally in Britain, Western Europe and North America. However, the major problem that Bellamy identifies for contemporary liberalism is that these cultural assumptions can no longer be taken for granted even in the societies where they originated. In order to cope with this situation Bellamy argues that 'liberalism must transform itself from an ethical to a political theory, in which the central place is occupied, not by liberal values but by institutions or procedures capable of giving expression to a plurality of different points of view and arranging agreements between them'.[69] Bellamy challenges the pre-conception of deontological liberals that liberalism's foundations are ethical and that liberalism's political theory develops from its ethical theory. He believes that this is impossible because there can be no ethical agreement between individualist liberalism and belief systems which found their ethics on the common good or a vision of a good life. Bellamy suggests that the way forward, then, is neither the ethical theory put forward by the deontological liberals, nor the particularism of the communitarians, but a political liberalism based on Weberian realism that will accommodate ethical differences.[70]

How realistic is such a political liberalism? There are certainly incommensurable differences within existing liberal societies. The most obvious example of this type of conflict is the dispute between those

[68] Richard Bellamy, *Liberalism and Modern Society*.
[69] ibid., p7.
[70] ibid., p8.

Catholic and Protestant religious fundamentalists who believe that abortion is murder and that they have a moral duty to prevent it; and those who believe women have a right to control their own body. Superficially at least, it appears that no institution or procedure could square this particular circle. Bellamy's solution to the problem might be something like this: of course a liberal constitution, or institution, cannot solve this question: for it is an ethical question and liberalism must operate in the context of moral pluralism. A liberal constitution can provide only a political framework, which allows us to live with incommensurable ethical differences. In the case of abortion liberal institutions must impose tolerance of conflicting ethical positions on society. Abortion must not be imposed on those who oppose it; people who wish to have abortions must not be physically attacked. To those anti-abortionists who would find this position unacceptable Bellamy might say: you have accepted the benefits of liberal society, and one of the conditions for receiving those benefits is tolerance for others. You must therefore subject yourself to its rules; you must either accept this position or abandon the liberal polity. This position is strong insofar as it offers a criterion for dealing with ethical differences, but weak inasmuch as it is purely pragmatic and does not present a convincing argument to anti-abortionists why they should stop bombing abortion clinics. They would say, quite logically: yes, let us abandon a liberal polity, since a liberal polity that permits the mass-murder of unborn children is not worth protecting. Liberal theory, then, whether communitarian, deontological or political, seems to remain impotent in the face of contemporary problems. As MacIntyre observed: 'The spectre haunting contemporary liberal theorists is not communitarianism, but their own irrelevance'.[71]

Today's 'liberal/communitarian debate' signals a conservative reversion within liberalism rather than heralding a serious challenge to it, as certain somewhat aberrant liberals who reject liberalism's rejection of any substantive theory of the good seem partially to be acknowledging.[72] The liberal/communitarian divide, then, mirrors something far deeper and older than contemporary debates, namely liberalism's repeated resort to conservative values. Nowhere is this tension clearer, as we have seen, than in the work of Richard Rorty. To reiterate, Rorty's position is that the only defence of liberalism is pragmatic. Rorty believes that it is impossible to found liberal institutions on a metaphysical theory of the subject; rather, liberalism should be grounded in our shared intuitions about justice and our historic self-understanding. Rorty's fundamental point is that the practice of

[71] Alasdair MacIntyre, 'The spectre of communitarianism', *Radical Philosophy*, 70, 1995, p35.
[72] e.g. Tibor Machan, 'Individualism versus Classical Liberal Political Economy', *Res Publica*, 1,1, 1995, pp3-23; William Galston, *Liberal Purposes*, see chapter 8.

liberalism is prior to its theory and that the task of political philosophy is not to justify political institutions, but to *articulate* our shared intuitions and beliefs about politics. Rorty claims that he is engaged in reinterpreting liberalism on a more Hegelian and historical basis, abandoning the unencumbered self of deontological liberalism for a historically situated conception. He describes this favoured variety as 'post-modernist bourgeois liberalism'.[73]

The practice that Rorty favours is unquestionably the liberal practice of the promotion of liberty, respect for the individual, and recognition of the dignity of all human beings. But for Rorty, unlike for deontological liberals, such a claim depends on the individual's situation as part of a community, not on some metaphysical notion of the self. For Rorty human dignity becomes:

> ... the comparative dignity of a group with which a person identifies herself. Nations or churches or monuments are, on this view, shining historical examples not because they reflect rays emanating from a higher source, but because of contrast-effects, comparisons with other communities. Persons have dignity not as interior human essence, but because they share in such contrast effects.[74]

Rorty anticipates that there will be objections to such a position and says that:

> [T]he ... objection is that on my view a child found wandering in the woods, the remnant of a slaughtered nation whose temples have been razed and whose books have been burned, has no share in human dignity. This is indeed a consequence, but it does not follow that she may be treated like an animal. For it is part of the tradition of *our* community that the human stranger from whom all dignity has been stripped is to be taken in, to be reclothed with dignity.[75]

However, as Norman Geras points out, 'this is to commend the form, having evacuated the content. It is to give the tradition itself as a reason after rejecting the reasons of the tradition.'[76] Rorty is saying that that something is in line with the liberal tradition is in itself sufficient justification for some act or prohibition. But no argument is offered in defence of the content of that

---

[73] Richard Rorty, 'Post Modernist Bourgeois Liberalism', *The Journal of Philosophy*, 80 (1983), pp383-89.
[74] Richard Rorty, *Objectivity, Relativism and Truth*, p200.
[75] ibid., pp201-2.
[76] N. Geras, *Solidarity in the Conversation of Humankind*, p82.

tradition: '[I]t is as if we were to be told we may not, or we must act in a certain way because of *The Word*. Or it is to be offered *Our View* as a reason without any reason for *Our View*; such as to make it actually a view and not an incantation.'[77] As we saw earlier in the chapter Rorty's position here has led to comparisons with conservatism in general, and in particular with the ideas of Michael Oakeshott. Rorty actively encourages such comparisons and alleges that Oakeshott along with Rorty himself, Dewey and the later Rawls are engaged in reinterpreting liberalism on a more Hegelian and historical basis, abandoning the unencumbered self of Kantian theory for a more historical and situated conception.

How convincing is Rorty's characterisation of Oakeshott's thought as an attempt tó restate liberalism on Hegelian foundations? Oakeshott famously claims to be a conservative[78] and is widely recognised as the most important traditional, as opposed to New Right, conservative thinker of the twentieth century. Oakeshottian conservatism rests on three pillars: political scepticism; respect for established institutions and *mores*; and a pragmatic or experimental approach to the activity of politics. It is often more easily characterised in terms of what it is not, rather than what it is. For this reason conservatism is often more famous for what it opposes than for its positive prescriptions. The key to conservatism as a theory is scepticism of radical and innovative change. Conservatives take this approach because they believe society and its institutions are the achievements of centuries and it would be foolish to interfere with them recklessly and without guarantees that changed social orders would be definitely better than what has gone before. However, conservatism does not rule out all change, but argues that any change should be evolutionary; should occur only to deal with definite and recognisable social problems; and, as far as possible, should be in tune with existing patterns of social behaviour. The principle aim for any conservative is not a return to some idealised, and usually fictional, version of the past, as is the case with certain nationalist and religious fundamentalist doctrines: rather it is to maintain the stability of existing orders, not because they are as good as they possibly can be, but because people come to appreciate them and have an affection for them as they are, and because there is always the risk of replacing them with something worse. This is what Oakeshott meant when he wrote:

> [I]n political activity, then, men sail a boundless and bottomless sea; there is neither harbour for shelter nor floor for anchorage, neither starting-place nor appointed destination. The enterprise is to keep afloat

[77] ibid., p86.

[78] See Oakeshott, 'On being Conservative', in *Rationalism in Politics and Other Essays*.

on an even keel; the sea is both friend and enemy; and the seamanship consists in using the resources of a traditional manner of behaviour in order to make a friend of every hostile occasion.[79]

Oakeshott's concept of civil association clearly endorses values inherent in the English and Scottish liberal traditions. But what makes Oakeshott at best a liberal conservative, rather than a conservative liberal, is that whilst he supports limited government, he does not seek to justify it in either of the two classical liberal ways: in terms of individual rights existing prior to the formation of government or in terms of the outcomes it produces. Moreover, Oakeshott, as a noted Hobbesian, maintains a much more authoritarian position *vis à vis* the maintenance of establishment orthodoxy than does Rorty. Oakeshott is deeply ambivalent, for example, about democracy. He insists that there is absolutely no connection between the mode of association (civil association) that leads to the limited government and the liberty that he values, and the manner in which the authority of the state is constituted. For Oakeshott, civil association could thrive just as well under Hobbesian absolutism as it could under liberal democracy.[80] Rorty, following Dewey, takes a much more positive approach to democracy.[81] Nonetheless, the appeal to history, and the emphasis on form and title, are clearly representative of a conservative axiology at work within Rorty's thought. The wider implication is that he is in fact defending post-modern bourgeois *conservatism* rather than post-modern bourgeois *liberalism*, his own intentions and self-understanding notwithstanding.[82]

Rorty has recognised that liberalism cannot be a universalistic doctrine; and he is surely right to claim that liberalism depends on ethnocentricity and contingent circumstance. However, Rorty's position does not allow him to judge between states of affairs and practices which would be conducive to liberal values and those that would not. He has retained an element of liberal neutrality, at least with respect to contemporary liberal society, but only at

---

[79] Oakeshott, *Rationalism in Politics and Other Essays*, p127.

[80] Michael Oakeshott, *On Human Conduct*, pp188-93.

[81] See particularly Rorty, *Contingency, Irony and Solidarity*, Chapter 3.

[82] This is a failing in Rorty's thought which is pointed out by Norman Geras who states in *Solidarity in the Conversation of Humankind*:

> [A]ppealing to the authority of mere forms and titles, it is a style that sits ill beside either the secular or democratic habits of mind he would more generally encourage. And it sits oddly within a tradition disinclined to appeal to the authority of tradition as such, preferring the ways of deliberative reflection and reasoned advocacy. Is it not a Pyrrhic defence of the moral and intellectual legacy of humanist liberalism to fall back on such a style of exhortation? - p86.

It is a point that Steven Kautz also makes in *Liberalism and Community* (Cornell University Press, Ithaca, 1995), when he notes Rorty's positive approach to ethnocentrism, p84.

the expense of denying what makes liberalism (and for that matter conservatism) at least plausible. In the case of liberalism, by reinterpreting it as a quasi-Oakeshottian political tradition, he has evacuated it of its content as a critical theory based on reason. In fact, although he adopts the form of a conservative argument in defence of liberalism, he rejects the substance. Rorty's liberalism, therefore, is no more successful than that of Reiman, Galston or Machan in establishing a workable liberal good. As he is doubtless aware if he were to adopt the substance as well as the form of Oakeshott's conservative argument, Rorty would cease to be a liberal: but, and this he would of course deny, his adoption of its form inevitably commits him to its substance. For the form has grown, historically, out of that substance;[83] and moreover, even historicism apart, the form is inextricably linked to that substance for without it it has no logically adequate purchase. Once again, not only is liberalism not neutral (as Rorty of course admits) but in not being so it cannot but have recourse to that very tradition against which it originally defined itself.

[83] I shall develop this argument further with respect to Rorty and indeed other liberal thinkers in the concluding chapter of this book.

# 6 Conclusion

In the late 1980s and early 1990s, the decline and eventual collapse of communism, or actually existing socialism, was believed by many to confirm the ultimate triumph of liberalism. In 1989 Francis Fukuyama wrote:

> [W]hat we may be witnessing is not just the end of the cold war, or the passing of a particular period of post-war history, but the end of history as such: that is the end point of mankind's ideological evolution and the universalization of Western liberal democracy as the final form of human government.[1]

Fukuyama's belief appeared to be vindicated by the rapid collapse of 'socialist' regimes later the same year. Between June 4th 1989, the date of the first limited multi-party election in Poland, and the execution of the Ceausescus in Romania on Christmas Day 1989, single-party communist regimes fell in Poland, Hungary, the former East Germany, the former Czechoslovakia, Bulgaria and Romania. The one unifying element that could be discerned in the programmes of the revolutionaries, who ranged across the political spectrum from trotskyists and reform communists to reactionary Catholics and extreme nationalists, was that the old system of a planned economy and a one-party state had failed. What was needed was competition in the political sphere through the medium of political pluralism and a liberal democratic system, underpinned by a competitive economic free market system.

During the 'velvet revolution' in Czechoslovakia, Civic Forum (the leading revolutionary grouping in the Czech lands) were able to achieve a high degree of consensus on a document entitled, *'What we Want; The Programme and Principles of Civic Forum'*.[2] This document, describing hopes for a post-revolutionary Czechoslovakia, listed conditions that are usually regarded as liberal staples. With respect to the rule of law it stated that:

---

[1]Francis Fukuyama, 'The End of History?' in *The National Interest*, Summer 1989, pp3-10, p4.

[2] Reproduced in Bernard Wheaton and Zdenek Kavan, *The Velvet Revolution* (Westview, Oxford, 1992), Appendix B, pp206-8.

> [T]he exercise of civil freedoms will be reliably ensured by a developed system of legal guarantees. The independent judiciary will also include constitutional and administrative courts.[3]

The new political system must:

> ... remake or renew democratic institutions and mechanisms that make possible the real participation of all citizens in the administration of public affairs. ... All existing and newly emerging political parties and other social and political associations must therefore have equal conditions for participation in free elections at all levels of government.[4]

Civic Forum also wished to abandon 'the previous system of economic management' and 'create a market undeformed by bureaucratic intervention'. However, a commitment to social justice was retained:

> Czechoslovakia must become a socially just society in which the people receive help in old age, in sickness, and in times of hardship. However, a growing national economy is the essential pre-requisite for such a society.[5]

Despite the genuflection toward social justice contained in the document, this is clearly the blueprint for a liberal state complete with a market economy. It is far removed from the 1968 vision of 'socialism with a human face' or even the fabled 'third way' between socialism and capitalism. Timothy Garton Ash commented at the time:

> ... the truly remarkable thing is not the differences about the programme, but the degree of almost instant consensus.... This is a Czech phenomenon. But it is not just a Czech phenomenon, for in a different way it is repeated all over East Central Europe. Take a more or less representative sample of politically aware persons. Stir under pressure for two days. And what do you get? The same fundamental Western European model: parliamentary democracy, the rule of law, market economy. And if you made the same experiment in Warsaw or Budapest I wager you would get the same basic result. This is no Third Way. It is not 'socialism with a human face'. It is the idea of 'normality'

[3] ibid., p206.
[4] ibid., pp207-8.
[5] ibid., p207.

that seems to be sweeping triumphantly across the world. [6]

However, since the apparent triumphs of 1989 and 1990, there has been a shift. Although the pluralist political systems and market reforms have largely survived, at least in Central Europe, liberal values have been challenged by both a certain electoral resurgence of socialist parties, if not socialist systems in central Europe; and the slide toward nationalist dictatorship and clericalism in the eastern and southern areas of post-communist Europe.

Though much of this reversal is no doubt due to the economic difficulties of transition, if liberalism cannot successfully establish itself throughout post-communist Europe, where it was not only replacing discredited and repressive regimes, but also in close proximity to stable established and successful liberal democratic regimes, then the prospects for liberal success elsewhere in the world, particularly where anti-liberal sentiments are entrenched, must be questionable. One source of the current practical difficulties facing liberalism could, indeed, be its current theoretical problems, which have been examined in this book. It is at least possible that the absence of liberal traditions in some parts of Central and Eastern Europe have contributed to the comparative lack of success in the new democracies. It is also at least possible that this explains the comparative success of liberal regimes in states like the Czech Republic, Hungary and Poland: that is in those states which, in the case of the Czech Republic and Hungary, had, through the Austro-Hungarian Empire, at least some exposure to liberal, Enlightenment and proto-liberal traditions; and in the case of Poland was linked to the post-revolutionary French tradition, first through the Polish Lancer regiments in Napoleon's *Grande Armée*, and later through the Polish émigré community in France. Where, then, does this leave contemporary liberalism?

## 6.1 Liberalism's neutrality: the evolution of an illusion

Liberalism's theoretical problems have developed because liberal theorists have been unable satisfactorily to establish moral and political foundations for liberalism without resorting to the tacit assumptions of liberalism's founders such as Locke and Hobbes, and to a lesser extent Mill. The tacit moral ideal underlying Hobbes's thought was the medieval nexus of honour

[6] T. Garton Ash, *We the People* (Granta Books, Cambridge, 1990), pp103-5.

and duty, ideas which Hobbes retained from his Aristotelian roots.[7] Locke, as a Calvinist,[8] could base his moral ideal on divine law. Liberalism flourished, that is to say, because it rested on a series of tacit assumptions and values drawn from a well-established intellectual tradition in a specific geographical area.[9] The liberal quest for universalism, instead of enabling liberalism to transcend its original geographical and cultural boundaries, has had two consequences. First, it has led to a developing theoretical inconsistency within liberalism; and second and - related to the first - to the development of discrete and disparate liberal traditions.

The practical failures of liberalism in dealing with the worst aspects of industrial capitalism led to the emergence of the social liberals, influenced by Idealism, such as Green and Hobhouse. The liberal drive for universalism in societies increasingly characterised by moral pluralism led to the formulation of liberal theories by thinkers such as Weber, whose emphasis was on the development of institutions and procedures which could accommodate incommensurable ethical divisions. The result has been that liberalism today is not so much a single mode of thought but three distinct traditions. First, a tradition fundamentally informed by empiricist epistemology and ethics, and thus eschewing any substantive notion of the good, a theory represented today by deontological liberals such as Rawls and Nozick; second, a multi-faceted set of views whose common theme is the stressing of liberal political values, regardless of philosophical meta-differences, for example Bellamy and his predecessors such as Weber; and

---

[7] See for example Leo Strauss, *The Political Philosophy of Hobbes* (University of Chicago Press, Chicago,1984), Chapters 4 and 7.

[8] John Dunn has argued that Locke's views of morality and responsibility operate within a Calvinist theological world view, John Dunn, *The Political Thought of John Locke* (Cambridge University Press, Cambridge, 1982), chapter 18, pp250-2. Given Locke's famous plea for tolerance it is ironic that the Dunn should argue that the origins of Locke's political thought are Calvinist, however, it should be remembered that Locke's tolerance was extremely limited, and he did of course argue against extending toleration to Catholics and atheists. See John Locke, *A Letter Concerning Toleration*, in J.W. Gough (ed) *The Second Treatise of Government and A Letter Concerning Toleration*, Third Edition (Blackwell, Oxford, 1966), pp156-9.

[9] This point is an important theme in contemporary scholarship. For instance, Adam B. Seligman in *The Idea of Civil Society* (Princeton University Press, Princeton, 1992), points out the pre-Enlightenment origins of the staples of civil society, reason and the individual, whilst in *Whose Justice? Which Rationality?*, Alasdair MacIntyre skilfully disentangles the origins of the liberal tradition (see especially chapter 17). Enquiry into the origins of liberalism has also informed some of the debate surrounding post-modernism, in *The Ennobling of Democracy* (Johns Hopkins University Press, Baltimore, 1992), which offers a critique of post-modernist responses to contemporary political and social problems, Thomas L. Pangle looks to the sources of the liberal tradition to reinvigorate the legacy of classical republicanism.

third, social liberalism, originally formulated by thinkers like Green and Hobhouse, and which has historical and conceptual links with the contemporary communitarian-tinged attitudes of thinkers like Rorty, Walzer and Taylor, who accept, rather than advocate, liberal politics.

What links these varieties of liberalism is a set of political, rather than philosophical, values. This explains how positions as different as, for example, Mill's and Hobhouse's, are nonetheless liberal positions; and how it is that the communitarians accept liberal political - and some moral - values, despite their philosophical objections to the empiricist epistemology informing much, if not all, Anglo-American liberalism. I have argued that these values (whose putative epistemological roots the communitarians are right to criticise as inadequate) require to be rooted in a notion of the good; and, as the discussion of Rorty suggested, that the only such notion available is a conservative one.

Liberalism's orthodox history declares that it emerged as a wholly new creature in 16th and 17th century Europe. More significantly, liberalism was deemed to be a liberating force from the darkness of tradition and superstition; it is a point made trenchantly by Kenneth Minogue: '[T]he story of liberalism as liberals tell it, is rather like the legend of St George and the dragon. After many centuries of hopelessness and superstition, St George in the guise of Rationality appeared in the world somewhere about the sixteenth century.'[10] Liberalism, emerging in response to new developments in science and ethics, was formulated principally by the English writers Hobbes and Locke, but also through the ideas of other writers and movements involved in the debates surrounding the English Civil War: as John Gray puts it, 'Thomas Hobbes ... gives voice to an intransigent individualism whose consummate modernity marks a decisive breach with the social philosophy bequeathed by Plato and Aristotle to medieval Christendom'.[11]

This orthodox history is misleading. Although individuality first appeared as a relatively coherent body of ideas in the 17th century, it developed from, and was dependent upon, the assumptions inherent in the older intellectual traditions of medieval Christendom such as honour, honesty and loyalty to the state or ruler in some form.[12] However, the philosophical development of individuality is indeed the foundation of

[10] Kenneth Minogue, *The Liberal Mind*, p1.

[11] John Gray, *Liberalism* (Open University Press, Milton Keynes, 1986), p7.

[12] Ernest Gellner, for example, recognised the way in which Enlightenment rationalism corroded the foundations of stable societies. He notes: 'The Enlightenment ethic of cognition does exclude certain kinds of authority, certain ways of validating a social order, but it simply does not contain any solid, so to speak, meaty, premisses capable of engendering a concrete social alternative.' *Postmodernism, Reason and Religion* (Routledge, London, 1992), p88.

liberalism. According to Parekh it 'abstracts the person from all his or her "contingent" and "external" relations with other people and nature, and defines the person as an essentially self-contained and solitary being encapsulated in, and unambiguously marked off from the outside world by his or her body'.[13] The 'austere minimalism'[14] of this conception of individualism leads each person to define themselves in terms of their separateness from others: each person is defined not as a member of a community, nor as a participant in political society, nor even in terms of a profession or vocation; but as an entity bounded by the naked human body.

Atomism and empiricism in morality and politics, on which this conception was based, emerged from the success of the scientific method developed in 17th century Europe. Just as 17th century physics saw matter as being made up of small atoms, Hobbes took an atomistic view of human society. Society could be explained only by understanding its component parts, that is individuals. Individuals could, and indeed should, be understood as being anterior to society.[15] The nature of politics and morality could only be understood if we already understand the discrete individual units who comprise society; and people should not be understood first in the context of society, since society itself has to be explained in terms of the way people behave. Such a view makes problematic both human sociability and shared human values, however. Sociability and shared human values become things to be justified so that answers must be provided to questions such as why are we sociable? Why do we apparently share many common beliefs and prejudices?

The answer that the first exponent of individualism presented to account for this dilemma was self-interest. What Hobbes believed he was doing was presenting a mechanistic science of politics to match Newton's mechanistic account of the universe. To achieve this Hobbes had to argue that human beings were like atoms in motion, repelled by certain sensations and attracted by others. The one common fear that repelled all individuals was fear of violent death. By focusing on what he perceived as this universal element in human nature, Hobbes thought he was providing a universally applicable method which would place the foundations of government on a scientific footing. However, this is not what Hobbes achieved. The

---

[13] Bhikhu Parekh, 'The Cultural Particularity of Liberal Democracy', *Political Studies*, 1992, XL, Special Issue, 160-175, pp160-175, p161.

[14] ibid.

[15] See the Introduction to Thomas Hobbes's *Leviathan* '... by art is created that great LEVIATHAN called a COMMONWEALTH, or STATE, in Latin CIVITAS, which is but an artificial man; though of greater stature and strength than the natural for whose protection and defence it was intended;' - p5.

individual selves who contracted together to create Leviathan were clearly abstractions from 17th century English society. They entered civil society and agreed to obey a sovereign because they feared that the perils of violent death that lurked in a country riven by Civil War would spiral further out of control. Within the state, the individual selves who threatened each other could be controlled, and once the state was created fear of return to the state of nature, and with it the risk of violent death, encouraged individuals not to challenge sovereign authority or break the law.[16] However, the question then arises why individuals should keep their covenants. Why should not people trade on the gullibility of others by making but then breaking covenants? Hobbes places this objection in the mouth of a fool who would say that:

> ... there is no such thing as justice;...that every man's conservation and contentment, being committed to his own, there could be no reason, why every man might not do what he thought conduced thereunto: and therefore able to make, or not to make; keep or not keep covenants was not against reason, when it conduced to one's benefit.[17]

For Hobbes, the fool's reasoning is specious. The state exists to secure obedience to covenants. He points out that no one who breaks covenants can be received into society, except by error,[18] and he holds that no one can count on that error being made. Thrasymachus's question, though, remains; what if some person or some group of people could get away with it?

On the face of it the conclusion that this made the breaking of an agreement justifiable was a difficult one for Hobbes to avoid. Hobbesian society could exist only by virtue of the vigilance of the law and the agents of the sovereign: it could not depend on the loyalty or trustworthiness of its citizens. Why did Hobbes not address this question more explicitly? The answer is that Hobbes, despite his protestations to the contrary, was not beginning his philosophy with a blank sheet of paper after all. In his early years he had been an Aristotelian, and even included within *Leviathan* was a view of natural morality and honour. Moreover, although Hobbes initially links honour with power, '[T]o pray to another, for aid of any kind, is *to* HONOUR; because a sign we have an opinion he has power to help; and the more difficult the aid is, the more is the honour';[19] however, later Hobbes states when discussing what is or is not honourable that '*Honourable* is

[16] See C. B. MacPherson, *The Political Theory of Possessive Individualism* (Oxford University Press, Oxford, 1964), pp17-19.
[17] Thomas Hobbes, *Leviathan*, p94.
[18] ibid., p95.
[19] ibid., pp57-8.

whatsoever possession, action, or **quality** is an argument and sign of power'.[20] So although Hobbes attempts to provide a justification for human behaviour based on a social version of the laws of motion, he includes within it the idea that certain qualities are of themselves honourable.

The problem of finding a stronger foundation for sociability and obedience to a moral code, beyond self-interest was addressed both by the empiricist philosophers, Locke, Berkeley, and Hume, and later by the utilitarians. Empiricism holds that all knowledge of fact, as distinct from that of purely logical relations between concepts, has its source in experience. Empiricists maintain that all human knowledge comes from experience and that only experience can provide it with ideas, including moral ideas. Each mind must have unique experiences. No two people, not even twins, can possibly have absolutely identical experience. However, as with Hobbes, the later figures of the liberal tradition thought that everyone could agree on the desirability of pleasure and the need to avoid pain.

Yet there appears to be a contradiction between the empiricism present in Locke's *Essay Concerning Human Understanding* and the political theory presented in the *Two Treatises*. In the *Two Treatises*, Locke argued that there was a universal moral law accessible to all human beings. As the property of God, individuals had duties to their maker beyond the pursuit of pleasure and the avoidance of pain. God had made individuals free and rational so that they could order their activities in a way which would allow them to discharge their duty to God. Attempts have been made to find alternative secular, universal foundations for liberalism in terms of enlightened self-interest, psychology or human nature. Empiricist epistemology and ethics have informed all these attempts and they all face two problems.[21] First they cannot find adequate criteria for evaluating the moral worth of the choices individuals make, other than - in some cases - duty to God; and second, they cannot decide whether individuals are choosing beings because of capacities they inherently possess, or because of the capacities they have the potential to possess.

Without the underpinning of a divine law, the freedom of choice of the individual degenerates to moral subjectivism; the belief that what is right or wrong, good or bad, is simply a matter of personal preference or appetite. But in that case, this subjectivism must apply also to liberal principles like

---

[20] ibid., p59, emphasis (bold) added.

[21] Liberalism derived directly from Kant is obviously not empiricist in nature, and is beyond the remit of this book as it does not claim neutrality in the requisite sense. However, contemporary Kantians such as Rawls, at least in *A Theory of Justice*, both claim neutrality and import empiricist assumptions regarding human wants into their putative deontological liberalism.

the over-riding value of liberty. There is no moral reason why people should choose a liberal political order before a fundamentalist Islamic theocracy, for example, with all the likely repression of liberal values that such a state would entail.[22]

These historical and conceptual problems are the foundation of the current debates within liberalism. They are present because liberal theory fails to provide satisfactory answers to the question of how and why human beings are capable of making, and why they have a natural right to make, their own moral choices. Charles Taylor sums up the difficulty thus:

> [T]o ascribe the natural (not just legal right) right of X to agent A is to affirm that A commands our respect, such that we are normally bound not to interfere with A's doing or enjoying of X. This means that to ascribe the right is far more than simply to issue the injunction: don't interfere with A's doing or enjoying X. The injunction can be issued, to self or others, without grounds should we so choose. But to affirm the right is to say that a creature such as A lays a moral claim on us not to interfere. It thus also asserts something about A: A is such that this injunction is somehow inescapable.[23]

To affirm a natural right, Taylor notes, is to say both that A lays a moral claim on us not to be interfered with; and that doing or enjoying X is part of manifesting some essential human quality. But what does affirming a natural right entail? If it is rationality, then A must not only have a natural right to X but also to the unimpeded development of rationality. If it is autonomy, then A must have a right to the necessary conditions that allow personal autonomy, such as access to material resources. So, even asserting that a natural right exists has a conceptual background, in that it must include some idea of the worth of certain properties or capacities, without which they would not make sense:

> ... our position would be incomprehensible and incoherent if we ascribed rights to human beings in respect of the specifically human capacities... while at the same time denying that these capacities ought to be developed, or if we thought it a matter of indifference whether they were realised or stifled in ourselves and others.[24]

[22] See for instance Tibor Machan, 'Individualism versus Classical Liberal Political Economy', *Res Publica*, 1,1, 1995, pp3-23.
[23] Charles Taylor, 'Atomism', in S. Avineri and A. de-Shalit (eds) *Communitarianism and Individualism*, p32.
[24] ibid., p33.

The reason why natural rights are ascribed to human beings, and not to other species or objects is because human beings can be defined as creatures with, at least, the potential for rationality and autonomy, a potential that is sensed so strongly that it cannot be lost. Could this mean that human beings possess the full capacity of rationality and autonomy as a given capacity, rather than as a potential capacity that has to be developed? Liberal neutrality rests on the former assumption, that human beings possess the full capacity of rationality as a given.

If individuals are recognised as choosing beings because of the capacities they inherently possess, then it could be assumed that they will develop into rational beings whatever their condition and whatever their upbringing. However, this is nonsense. Even fictional characters like Mowgli or Tarzan required a notional society, that of wolves or apes which resembled hierarchical human societies, to allow them to develop some rationality. It is difficult to conceive of the development of any capacity regarded as human, whether it be language, rationality or sentiment, outside of some kind of society. We use language only in communicating with others; rationality is something that is taught and developed; and individuals could hardly develop the full range of human emotions if they were kept isolated from their fellows.

Rationality is especially significant in this context. It forms the basis of the idea of an individual as a chooser pursuing self-set aims. In order to show that the liberal individual requires a social context to develop their rationality it is worthwhile exploring the possibility of establishing rationality outside human society. Assuming that an individual could be given physical nourishment without human contact, what could be the choices the individual could pursue? Whether to sleep, or whether to wake; whether to eat the food when presented, or save it for later: to take exercise, or not to take exercise? These are unquestionably choices, but they are hardly the rational choices that liberal individuals would need to make in order to develop their individuality. Of issues such as the nature of a lifestyle, the type of society we desire, or our duty to our fellow citizens, the isolated individual could have no conception. Natural rights to choose can be ascribed to human beings only by asserting the worth of those human capacities which can only be developed within society. The normative consequence of this is that these uniquely human capacities to make rational and moral choices ought to be encouraged and developed within all individuals. Furthermore, the liberal individual - the individual who recognises himself or herself as a rational choosing being - far from being 'natural', is the historical product of cultures and traditions where the liberal tradition of thought originated.

Rationally choosing individuals are products of society; liberal individuals are not transcultural phenomena. The liberal individual is not representative of every human being but of a particular type of human being. The point is that if the liberal individual is to be valued, then the society that nurtures that liberal individual ought to be preserved; and so liberalism, as a matter of fact, depends on the preservation of the traditional societies which gave rise to the individualism which liberalism theorises. Is this not a recognisably conservative story, as we have seen outlined by Oakeshott? A brief examination of the thought of John Stuart Mill demonstrates this point. Mill is the crucial figure in the liberal pantheon, yet his position is fundamentally ambiguous. His thought demonstrates the tension between classical atomistic liberalism and emerging social liberalism. The main thrust of Mill's argument is fundamentally individualistic. He makes clear that the object of *On Liberty* is to delineate the area in which liberals cannot be coerced. For Mill, the only justification for coercing individuals against their will is the prevention of harm to others. Nonetheless, Mill recognises that some individuals will undertake foolish or reckless acts which may not necessarily directly harm others. Other individuals or groups are entitled to use persuasion or remonstration to induce foolish or reckless individuals away from their courses of action. What they are not entitled to is use force or compulsion.[25] This is because: '[T]he only freedom which deserves the name is that of pursuing our own good in our own way, so long as we do not attempt to deprive others of theirs or impede their efforts to obtain it. Each is the proper guardian of his own health, whether bodily, or mental and spiritual.'[26] No one, be it individual or government is entitled to interfere with the freedom of action of individuals unless it is for the protection of themselves or others. As long as an individual does not harm or threaten harm to others, they are to be free from physical, legal or moral sanction. Yet Mill introduces a caveat: '[T]hat the only purpose for which power can be rightfully exercised over any member of a *civilised* community, against their will is to prevent harm to others.'[27] What Mill turns out to be saying is that it is a certain sort of human being who must not be interfered with. The implication is that there are communities where liberty can and should be infringed, a point he makes explicit later in the same work when he asserts that despotism is a suitable mode of government for 'barbarians'.[28]

Mill here is taking an historical view of liberalism. Individuals who can benefit from liberty are the products of certain times and circumstances.

[25]John Stuart Mill, *On Liberty*, p68.
[26]ibid., p72.
[27]ibid., p68.
[28]ibid., p69.

Liberty is valuable only when people are capable of improving themselves. However, while Mill recognises the historical nature of political liberties, he misses - as we have seen - the historical nature of the liberal individual. Thus, Mill's thought reveals the central paradox in liberalism and the central theme of this book: that liberal individuality is an historical artefact, and to maintain it a certain type of society must be established. It is a paradox that is further demonstrated by Mill's view on state intervention.

In principle, Mill does not want to extend the scope of political authority without due cause, preferring to rely instead on voluntary action. Intervention is undesirable for several reasons: it involves the use of compulsory powers and so restricts the freedom of choice of individuals affected; it always involves taxation, the imposition of which offends the fundamental tenet that each person is to be rewarded according to his or her own efforts; it increases the power and influence of government and public pressure may entail the tyranny of the majority; government offices are often inefficient and their work frequently defective and badly organised as compared with private agencies; and it inhibits the habit of voluntary action by groups of individuals.[29] However, in the detailed discussion of these points in the *Considerations on Representative Government*, Mill concedes the need for a formidable agenda of public activity. Mill accepts the role of government traditionally desired by classical liberals; defence and the maintenance of internal order; the establishment of a system of courts; the enforcement of contract and the prevention of fraud; the administration of the land as a vital, limited resource; and the control of inheritance and bequest. At the same time he also gives some aspects of these matters a rather wider scope, such as when he accepts that the law might regulate contracts involving unfavourable terms for one of the parties. He deviates further from the norms of classical liberalism when he urges that, in the case of people who cannot effectively care for themselves, the *laissez-faire* principle breaks down, and government must assume responsibility.

Mill's departure from classical liberal norms was taken up by L.T. Hobhouse and T.H. Green. Whilst Green and Hobhouse adhered to certain liberal political values, their version of liberalism saw a shift in attitude toward freedom and the role of the state. While Mill's theory tacitly supports state action in support of individual self-realisation, such a vision is explicit in the thought of Hobhouse and Green. However, in these cases the justification of state action remained the ultimate well-being of individuals. Green was a Hegelian, according to whom, freedom was not confined to the

[29]John Stuart Mill, *Considerations on Representative Government*, in *Utilitarianism, On Liberty and Considerations on Representative Government*, Chapters 2 and 6.

security of life and property; it included a capacity to fulfil human potential. The liberal right to equal liberty could be achieved only when every citizen had the opportunity to lead a worthwhile life as a rational, choosing individual. The task of government was to maintain the conditions without which free exercise of human faculties was impossible. Like contemporary communitarians, he recognised that it is the potential to be rational that confers an entitlement to be treated as a rational being, and with that comes the *normative* claim that conditions should be created which will allow individuals to achieve their potential as rational beings.

Hobhouse was also in favour of more extensive government intervention. Its objective was to provide a bedrock of material comfort below which none could fall into abject poverty. The effect, Hobhouse believed, would be to enhance individual liberty, because every citizen would be able to enjoy autonomy. The aim was to guarantee the self-directing power of personality. Hobhouse recognised the ambiguity in liberalism, that it was concerned with autonomy, but that worthwhile autonomy for all could be achieved only if certain social conditions were established: hence his belief that government action was necessary to promote individual self-development. However, he failed to recognise the source of this ambiguity, namely that the liberal individual is an historical construct. Indeed Hobhouse's and Green's partial disavowal of the classical liberalism represented by Mill is an earlier version of the communitarian/deontological liberal debate. With their emphasis on the state's role in removing obstacles to self-improvement, and their idea that individuality is a quality that must be nurtured rather than something which occurs naturally, 'new' liberals like Hobhouse and Green are clearly related to contemporary communitarian liberals like Taylor. Like the communitarians, they also adhere to liberal political and moral values, but they recognise that particular conditions are necessary for the preservation of these values. As Hobhouse stated:

> … the life of the individual would be something utterly different if he could be separated from society. A great deal of him would not exist at all ... his mental and moral being would, if it existed at all, be something quite different from anything that we know. By language, by training, by simply living with others, each of us absorbs into his system the social atmosphere that surrounds us. In particular in the matter of rights and duties which is cardinal for liberal theory, the relation of the

individual to the community is everything.[30]

Furthermore, it is the potential of all humans to become rational beings that Hobhouse sees as the foundation of liberty:

> [I]t [liberty] rests not on the claim of A to be let alone by B, but on the duty of B to treat A as a rational being. It is not right to let crime alone, or to let error alone, but it is imperative to treat the criminal or the mistaken or the ignorant as beings capable of right and truth, and to lead them on instead of merely beating them down.[31]

This bears a strong resemblance to the views of Charles Taylor cited earlier in the chapter, and it demonstrates the continuity of the debate in liberalism between those who attempt to found liberalism on the metaphysical idea of the unencumbered self; and those like Hobhouse and Taylor who argue that individuality was a product of social conditions. What they both have in common, furthermore, is that they both fail to recognise the implication of this argument for the nature of liberalism. They fail to see that if it is the historical context that produces the conditions for the development of the rational liberal individual, then what we have here in terms of the *justification* of the theory is a fundamentally conservative position. This point is well illustrated by comparing two similar passages, one from a communitarian, and the other from a conservative theorist:

> [H]ow could successive generations discover what it is to be an autonomous agent, to have one's own way of feeling, of acting, of expression, which cannot be simply derived from authoritative models? This is an identity, a way of understanding themselves, which men are not born with. They have to acquire it. And they do not in every society: nor do they all successfully come to terms with it in ours. But how can they acquire it unless it is implicit in at least some of their common practices, in the ways that they recognise and treat each other in their common life... or in the manner in which they deliberate or address each other, or engage in economic exchange, or in some mode of public recognition of individuality and the worth of autonomy.[32]

> Human individuality is an historical emergence...In modern Europe this emergence was gradual, and the specific character of the individual who

[30] L.T. Hobhouse, *Liberalism* in *Liberalism and Other Writings*, p60.
[31] ibid., p59.
[32] Charles Taylor, 'Atomism', in S. Avineri and A. de-Shalit (eds) *Communitarianism and Individualism*, p44.

> emerged was determined by the character of his generation...This experience of individuality provoked a disposition to explore its own intimations, to place the highest value upon it, and to seek security in its enjoyment. To enjoy it came to be recognised as the main ingredient of 'happiness'. The experience was magnified into an ethical theory; it was reflected in manners of governing and being governed, in newly acquired rights and duties and in a whole pattern of living.[33]

Both these theorists see individuality as a product of history. Both see it as part of a whole pattern of life. Most telling of all, neither offers explicit reasons why the idea of a rational individual making moral choices should be regarded as being inherently more worthy than, say, the Aristotelian ideal of man as an integral part of nature and society, or the Hindu belief that the caste into which a person is born is not an accident, but a result of his or her actions in a previous life.

Where do these historical and conceptual comparisons lead? Let me briefly recapitulate. My argument is that liberalism misunderstands its own history, and thus, its 'own' theoretical foundations. While the philosophical development of individuality was indeed the foundation of liberalism, this was not a radical departure from the existing tradition of thought, but a development of it; and moreover, liberalism, despite its claims to the contrary, continued - tacitly at least - to adhere to a conservative version of the good. This has to be the case because the liberal individual, far from being natural, is an historical artefact, a product of time, place, culture and civilisation.

Let me illustrate the point by examining the use made by liberals and proto-liberals of the notion of an original contract, an idea devised in the 17th century to show how legitimate government was based on (implicit) consent, and taken up by, among others Rawls. He claims his principles are neutral inasmuch as he places pre-social individuals behind a 'veil of ignorance' so that they are unaware of the position they will come to occupy in society.[34]

---

[33] Michael Oakeshott, 'The Masses in Representative Democracy', in A. Hunold, (Ed) *Freedom and Serfdom: An Anthology of Western Thought*, p157.

[34] Rawls contends that his principles of justice are neutral because: '[T]he argument for the two principles of justice does not assume the parties have particular ends, but only that they desire certain primary goods. These are things that it is rational to want whatever else one wants.' *A Theory of Justice*, p253. Later Rawls is even more explicit that the principles of justice are neutral and context independent:

> ... the essential point is that despite the individualistic features of justice as fairness, the two principles of justice are not contingent upon existing desires or present social conditions. Thus we are able to derive a conception of a just basic structure, and an ideal of the person compatible with it, that can serve as a standard for appraising institutions and for guiding the direction of social change. In order to find an archimedean point it is

Once individuals are in this disinterested original position, Rawls asks what constraints on pursuing their own wants it would be rational for them to accept. But while this position may be neutral between individuals who are 'wanting' beings of liberalism,[35] it cannot be neutral between those recognise themselves as individuals, and those who reject the 'austere minimalism' of that liberal concept of the individual, and who hence, do indeed, recognise themselves as specific and variously encumbered people, as many critics have pointed out.[36] Rawls's claim to neutrality therefore falls: his conception of individuality - that very 'austere minimalism' which makes the 'neutrality' of the original position theoretically available - is not a neutral one, but rather reflects the historical and conceptual circumstances that gave it birth.

## 6.2 A viable liberalism?

If liberalism's attempts at self-defence have failed, is some other form of defence of liberalism possible? Let us begin from the idea that liberalism is in fact no more than the product of the political traditions which existed in Britain, parts of Western Europe and North America during the seventeenth and eighteenth centuries. These traditions, conveniently abridged and entitled 'liberalism', were seen to offer modes of government that were less repressive than existing types of government, and also to offer better opportunities for the security and fulfilment of intellectually and politically

---

> not necessary to appeal to a priori or perfectionist principles. By assuming certain general desires, such as the desire for primary social goods, and by taking as a basis the agreements that would be made in a suitably defined initial situation, we can achieve the requisite independence from existing circumstances. - p263.

The origin of Rawls's 'original position' then is unequivocally the notion that moral agreement can be founded on something internal to each individual that is not arbitrary by determining that there are some things individuals' must want, whatever else they want. Philippa Foot in *Vices and Virtues* (Oxford, Blackwell, 1978) offers a convincing account of the origins of just such an argument. See *Vices and Virtues*, p122.

[35] Bob Brecher in *Getting What You Want?*, chapter 3 sees Rawls's attempt to establish a compelling theory justice as based upon the a claim about human nature, i.e. our good consists in getting as much of what we want as is reasonably possible. See particularly, pp66-7.

[36] For example, communitarians such as Charles Taylor, *Sources of the Self* (Cambridge University Press, Cambridge, 1992), Part I; and Michael Sandel in 'The Procedural Republic and the Unencumbered Self', *Political Theory*, 12 (February 1984), pp81-96; and even specifically liberal writers such as Kymlicka in *Multicultural Citizenship* and Galston in 'Value Pluralism and Political Liberalism', *Report from the Institute for Philosophy and Public Policy*, Volume 16, No. 2, Spring 1996. http://www.puaf.umd.edu/ippp/galston.htm 30/11/97 who are concerned with group and minority rights. It is a critique that Alasdair MacIntyre also makes from a neo-Aristotelian standpoint in *After Virtue*, Second Edition, chapter 17.

aware classes than in other societies then extant. In societies that adjoined those of Britain, Western Europe and North America, or were transplanted from them, and as a result shared at least some of the traditions from which liberalism emerged, states eventually evolved that could be recognised as operating within the liberal tradition, but with national and regional variations.

Now, the liberal states and societies that evolved in this way can indeed be seen as less repressive, and more materially successful than other forms of political organisation, especially in those areas that had political, social and religious traditions closely related to those in the areas where liberalism originated. However, recognising the truth of this statement is not the same as proving, once and for all, that liberalism is the sole model of the optimal political and social arrangement for all mankind. Moreover, such recognition does not lead to the brand of liberalism without foundations advocated by Rorty whose anti-essentialist view of the liberal tradition, although using some of the same arguments as conservatism, is necessarily fissiparous: he offers no way of uniting the various and competing elements within liberalism. What he offers is not one view of what liberalism is, one that we must accept because it is *Our View*, but rather several competing statements of *Our Liberal View* that we must accept because they are ours. Rorty invokes Oakeshott's notion of conversation to describe political activity, he, like Oakeshott, sees it as a 'conversation not an argument'.[37] However, given the diversity of the liberal tradition that Rorty holds to be *Our View*, it seems much more likely that it will indeed be an argument, or even just a noise, rather than a conversation. Recognition that the liberal states and societies that emerged in, or were transplanted from, Britain, Western Europe and North America can be seen as less repressive and more materially successful than other forms of political organisation, does allow the defence of liberal values on the basis of their being part of a holistic tradition of political activity that has developed at specific times and in specific parts of the world. In areas where it has been firmly established, it has been a generally successful tradition in terms of both political stability, and material prosperity for most of the population, most of the time. Moreover, people who live in societies governed by the liberal tradition of politics have found much to enjoy in liberal ways of life. They therefore deem that it is worth retaining, defending where necessary, and indeed, where possible, improving. Nonetheless, members of such societies realise that these arrangements are not perfect, but that they need both to be maintained and to

[37] Richard Rorty, *Philosophy and the Mirror of Nature*, pp389-94; Oakeshott, *Rationalism in Politics*, pp124-5.

evolve. This raises an important question about the nature of political and social change within liberal societies. As citizens who enjoy the way of life provided by liberal societies, and who recognise that they might lose much by radical change, they tend to favour continuity, but at the same time they understand that as circumstances change so political arrangements must adapt. Therefore, there needs to be some understanding of how change can occur whilst minimising loss and the risk of loss. The only reliable guide in these circumstances is not the political theory of liberalism, which as we have seen is not antecedent to practice, but practice itself - practice, which is, of course, the product of existing traditions of behaviour within liberal states. But such a way of understanding the activity of politics, at least with respect to liberalism, must be restricted to the times and places which have an extant liberal tradition that has been legitimated both by circumstances of comparative prosperity, and the enjoyment of the ways of life facilitated by the establishment of liberal values. Such a defence is stronger than Rorty's 'minimalism' because not only does it recognise that liberalism is valuable because it eschews cruelty, but because it offers ways of life which people find congenial and, more importantly, it offers prudential reasons for rejecting policies, practices and ways of life which threaten the well-being of the liberal tradition.

The justification I have just described for the maintenance and retention of liberal values is not, however, itself a liberal one. It cannot be so, because it is based on two factors foundationalist liberals of any type would unequivocally reject: first the subjective preference that liberal societies are ours and that we value them for that reason alone; and second because they are ours and we have found much to enjoy in them we will defend them against perceived and actual challenges from within and from without. In fact this is exactly what the defence of liberalism mounted by writers such as Galston and Reiman in fact amounts to, even though they are not prepared to cede as much. They could hardly do so. For it is also precisely the position of a conservative theorist like Michael Oakeshott:

> [T]he political theory of individualism should ... be understood as the elucidation of a view of the office of government appropriate to certain circumstances. And the chief feature of these circumstances is the appearance of subjects who desire to make choices for themselves, who find happiness in doing so and who are frustrated in having choices imposed upon them. In order to begin to think about the manner of governing appropriate in these circumstances we do not need to demonstrate that a disposition of this sort has eternal validity, that it represents the fundamental structure of human nature, or that no other

disposition is conceivable; all we need do is to recognise the appearance of such subjects - namely, subjects intent on the enjoyment of individuality - in sufficient numbers to make it appropriate to consider the corresponding office of government. What has to be elucidated is not an eternally valid notion of government, but a notion of government appropriate to subjects of this sort.[38]

For Oakeshott, the problem with many liberal theorists is that they have attempted to do too much. The best liberal writers are those who 'have not lost sight of the fact that what they were doing is no more than exploring a theory of government appropriate to certain historical circumstances'[39] (even though such recognition ought to preclude their remaining liberals at least as hitherto understood). Complex normative foundations for liberal government are unnecessary. All that is required as a normative justification for liberal values, if not of liberalism, as a complete political philosophy, is the recognition of the existence of individuals who recognise themselves as such:

> ... we require for our starting-place nothing more than the recognition of the existence of subjects of this sort [individuals]. We know well enough that this is an acquired disposition, we know that there have been communities of men from which it has been absent or in which it was relatively insignificant; and we know that such communities may re-emerge. But all this offers no hindrance to the elucidation of the political theory of individualism. All that could make such a political theory unintelligible would be the demonstration that subjects of this disposition have never existed; and all that could make such a political theory of merely historic interest would be the demonstration that subjects of this sort do not now exist. And neither of these propositions is capable of being convincing or even plausible.[40]

Such a justification of liberal values is both sensible and coherent. The problem is that no liberal, apart from someone like Rorty who entirely rejects any attempt to offer foundations, could accept such a limited defence of the liberal order as a starting point. First, it is based on prejudice in favour of existing institutions and rejects the search for universalist foundations. Second, it also openly recognises that the illiberal groups within liberal states can be tolerated only insofar as they do not transgress the norms laid

---

[38] Michael Oakeshott, *Morality and Politics in Modern Europe*, p84.
[39] ibid., p85.
[40] ibid., p84.

down by liberal values.[41] But liberal theorists have never been able to present coherent universal moral foundations for liberal values; and we have seen why the liberal quest for foundations must prove futile. Liberalism cannot be sustained on its own basis. Rather, liberalism must be founded on the pre- and proto-liberal traditions which gave birth to its founding texts (such as Locke's *Two Treatises*, Paine's *Rights of Man*, the *Constitution of the United States* and the *Declaration of the Rights of Man and the Citizen*) rather than from the texts themselves: for these were *in fact* abstractions from extant political behaviour and arrangements, and not, their authors' views to the contrary notwithstanding, universal truths accessible to disinterested reason.

Liberalism is the product of certain times and certain places. It is not a universally applicable coherent system of thought based on eternally valid precepts discovered by reason. It is not neutral between competing conceptions of the good; it is at best only neutral between the competing wants of individuals. It is simply something abstracted from the political traditions of the lands that gave it birth. Does this fatally weaken liberalism? I venture to suggest not. Political activity whether it is in terms of practice or theory seldom if ever begins from a blank piece of paper. It is almost always, in Oakeshott's conservative terms, 'attending to the arrangements' of already existing societies.[42] This is surely what liberal theorists do, although they rarely admit it. But consider Oakeshott's definition of politics:

> [P]olitics is the activity of attending to the general arrangements of a collection of people who, in respect of their common recognition of a manner of attending to its arrangements, compose a single community. To suppose a collection of people without recognized traditions of behaviour, or one which enjoyed arrangements which intimated no direction for change and needed no attention, is to suppose a people incapable of politics. This activity, then springs neither from instant desires, nor from general principles, but from the existing traditions of behaviour themselves. And the form it takes, because it can take no other, is the amendment of existing arrangements by exploring and pursuing what is intimated in them.[43]

Now, if we think back to the concerns examined throughout this book

[41] This position also explains why Kymlicka, whilst ostensibly defending diversity, is in fact defending diversity only within the liberal paradigm and only for those people who actually recognise themselves as individuals on the liberal model of the individual. Yet this is precisely the only task liberal theorists can perform.

[42] Oakeshott, *Rationalism in Politics*, p123.

[43] ibid., pp123-4.

we discover that pursuing the intimations of the liberal tradition is exactly what they have been doing. Galston and Kymlicka, for example, are concerned to establish the maximum level of tolerance for groups within liberal societies. This attempt is intimated by liberal preoccupations with tolerance and equality. Their failure is occasioned by their (understandable) inability to transcend the tradition of which they were a part, so that they were unable to extend toleration to groups who did not accept the premises of the liberal tradition. This is the basis of the relationship between liberalism and conservatism. It is only through reversion to conservative ideas of the priority of practice over theory and the defence of existing orders that liberalism can defend its core values. It is only by utilising these arguments, which were developed by conservatives to defend the remnants of the older tradition on which liberalism was founded, that liberal values ultimately can be defended.

# Bibliography


Ancient Order of Foresters, *Ceremony of Initiation*, 1879.

Arnold Matthew, *Culture and Anarchy and other Writings*, Cambridge University Press, Cambridge, 1993.

Avineri Shlomo and de-Shalit Avner (eds) *Communitarianism and Individualism*, Oxford University Press, Oxford, 1992.

Bellamy Richard, *Liberalism and Modern Society*, Polity Press, Cambridge, 1992.

Berlin Isaiah, *Four Essays on Liberty*, Oxford University Press, Oxford, 1969.

Bliss W.P.D. (ed) *The Encyclopaedia of Social Reform*, London, 1898.

Bosanquet Helen, *The Strength of the People: A Study in Social Economics*, London, 1902.

Boucher D. and Kelly P. (eds) *Social Justice*, Routledge, London, 1997.

Brecher Bob, *Getting What You Want? A Critique of Liberal Morality*, Routledge, London, 1998.

Burke Edmund, *Reflections on the Revolution in France*, Penguin, Harmondsworth, 1969.

Collini Stefan, *Public Moralists: Political Thought and Intellectual Life in Britain 1850-1930*, Oxford University Press, Oxford, 1991.

Conway David, *Classical Liberalism: The Unvanquished Ideal*, Macmillan, Basingstoke, 1995.

Cowling Maurice, *Mill and Liberalism*, Second Edition, Cambridge University Press, Cambridge, 1990.

Crisp Roger, *Mill on Utilitarianism*, Routledge, London, 1997.

Donner Wendy, 'Mill's utilitarianism', in John Skorupski (ed) *The Cambridge Companion to Mill*, Cambridge University Press, Cambridge, 1998.

Douglas R. Bruce, Mara Gerald R. and Richardson Henry S. (eds) *Liberalism and the Good*, Routledge, London, 1990.

Dunn John, *The Political Thought of John Locke*, Cambridge University Press, Cambridge, 1982.

Festenstein Matthew, *Pragmatism and Political Theory*, Polity Press, Cambridge, 1997.

Foot Philippa (ed) *Theories of Ethics*, Oxford University Press, Oxford, 1967.

Foot Philippa, *Vices and Virtues*, Blackwell, Oxford, 1978.

Franco Paul, *The Political Philosophy of Michael Oakeshott*, Yale University Press, New Haven, 1990.
Franco Paul, 'Michael Oakeshott as Liberal Theorist', *Political Theory*, Vol. 18, No. 3, August 1990, pp411-36.
Friedman R.B., 'A New Exploration of Mill's Essay On Liberty', *Political Studies*, Vol. 14, 1966, pp281-304.
Frowen Stephen F. (ed) *Hayek: Economist and Social Philosopher*, Macmillan, Basingstoke, 1997.
Fukuyama Francis, 'The End of History?', *The National Interest*, Summer 1989, pp3-10.
Fukuyama Francis, *The End of History and the Last Man*, Penguin, Harmondsworth, 1992.
Galston William, *Liberal Purposes*, Cambridge University Press, Cambridge, 1991.
Galston William, 'Value Pluralism and Political Liberalism', *Report from the Institute for Philosophy and Public Policy*, Volume 16, No. 2, Spring 1996, http://www.puaf.umd.edu/ippp/galston.htm 30/11/97.
Gamble Andrew, *Hayek: The Iron Cage of Liberty*, Polity, Cambridge, 1996.
Garton Ash Timothy, *We the People*, Granta Books, Cambridge, 1990.
Gellner Ernest, *Postmodernism, Reason and Religion,* Routledge, London 1992.
Geras Norman, *Solidarity in the Conversation of Human Kind*, Verso, London, 1995.
Grand United Order of Oddfellows, *Initiation Ceremony*, 1864.
Grand United Order of Oddfellows, *Ritual of the Grand United Independent Order of Oddfellows*, 1865.
Gray John, *Hayek on Liberty*, Second Edition, Blackwell, Oxford, 1986.
Gray John, *Liberalism*, Open University Press, Milton Keynes, 1986.
Gray John, *Liberalisms: Essays in Political Philosophy*, Routledge, London, 1989.
Gray John, *Post-Liberalism*, Routledge, London,1993.
Gray John, *Berlin*, Fontana Press, London, 1995.
Gray John, *Mill on Liberty: A Defence*, Second Edition, Routledge, London, 1996.
Gray John and Smith G. W. (eds) *J. S. Mill: On Liberty in Focus*, Routledge, London, 1991.
Green David, *Reinventing Civil Society*, IEA Health and Welfare Unit, London,1993.
Green T.H., *The Works of T.H. Green* (ed) R.L. Nettleship, 3 vols. London 1885-8.
Green T.H., *Prolegomena to Ethics*, Fourth Edition, Clarendon Press,

Oxford, 1899.
Greenleaf W. H., *The British Political Tradition, Vol. I The Rise of Collectivism*, Routledge, London, 1988.
Greenleaf W. H., *The British Political Tradition, Vol. II The Ideological Heritage*, Routledge, London, 1988.
Hamowy Ronald, 'Law and the Liberal Society: F.A. Hayek's *Constitution of Liberty*', *Journal of Libertarian Studies*, 2, 1978, pp287-97.
Hayek F. A., *The Road to Serfdom*, Routledge, London, 1944.
Hayek F. A., *The Sensory Order*, University of Chicago Press, Chicago, 1952.
Hayek F. A., *The Constitution of Liberty*, Routledge & Kegan Paul, London, 1960.
Hayek F.A., *Studies in Philosophy, Politics and Economics*, Routledge & Kegan Paul, London, 1967.
Hayek F.A., *Individualism and the Economic Order*, Routledge, London, 1976.
Hayek F.A., *New Studies in Philosophy, Politics, Economics and the History of Ideas*, Routledge & Kegan Paul, London, 1978.
Hayek F. A., *Law, Legislation and Liberty*, Vol. I-III, Routledge & Kegan Paul, London, 1982.
Hayek F.A., *Knowledge, Evolution and Science*, Routledge & Kegan Paul, London, 1983.
Hayek F. A., *The Fatal Conceit: The Errors of Socialism*, Routledge & Kegan Paul, London, 1988.
Himmelfarb Gertude, *On Liberty and Liberalism: The Case of John Stuart Mill*, Alfred A. Knopf, New York, 1974.
Himmelfarb Gertude, *The De-moralization of Society*, IEA Health and Welfare Unit, London, 1995.
Hobbes Thomas, *Leviathan*, Blackwell, Oxford, 1957.
Hobhouse L.T., 'The Ethical Basis of Collectivism', *International Journal of Ethics*, VIII, 1897-8, pp137-56.
Hobhouse L.T., *Development and Purpose: An Essay towards a Philosophy of Evolution*, London, 1913.
Hobhouse L.T., *Liberalism and Other Writings*, Cambridge University Press, Cambridge, 1994.
Horton John and Mendus Susan (eds) *After MacIntyre*, Polity Press, Cambridge, 1994.
Hunold A. (ed) *Freedom and Serfdom: An Anthology of Western Thought*, Reidel, Dordrecht, Holland, 1961.
Kant Immanuel, *Critique of Pure Reason*, Macmillan, London, 1929.
Kant Immanuel, *Groundwork of the Metaphysic of Morals*, trans. H.J. Paton,

Harper and Row, New York, 1964.
Kant Immanuel, 'The Metaphysics of Morals', in Hans Reiss (ed) *Kant's Political Thought*, Cambridge University Press, Cambridge, 1977.
Kautz Steven, *Liberalism & Community*, Cornell University Press, Ithaca, 1997.
Kley Roland, *Hayek's Social and Political Thought*, Clarendon Press, Oxford, 1994.
Kristol Irving, *Two Cheers for Capitalism*, Basic Books, New York, 1978.
Kukathas Chandran, *Hayek and Modern Liberalism*, Clarendon Press, Oxford, 1990.
Kukathas Chandran, 'Are there any Cultural Rights?' in Kymlicka, (ed) *The Rights of Minority Cultures*, Oxford University Press, Oxford, 1995.
Kukathas Chandran and Pettit Philip, *Rawls: A Theory of Justice and its Critics*, Polity Press, Cambridge, 1990.
Kymlicka Will, *Liberalism and Community and Culture*, Oxford University Press, Oxford, 1989.
Kymlicka Will (ed) *The Rights of Minority Cultures*, Oxford University Press, Oxford, 1995.
Kymlicka Will, *Multicultural Citizenship*, Clarendon Press, Oxford, 1995.
Locke John, *Two Treatises on Civil Government*, Mentor, Cambridge, 1963.
Locke John, *A Letter Concerning Toleration*, in J.W. Gough (ed) *The Second Treatise of Government and A Letter Concerning Toleration*, Third Edition, Blackwell, Oxford, 1966.
Mabbott J.D., 'Interpretations of Mill's Utilitarianism', in Philippa Foot (ed) *Theories of Ethics*, Oxford University Press, Oxford, 1967.
Machan Tibor, *Capitalism and Individualism*, St. Martin's Press, New York, 1990.
Machan Tibor, 'Individualism versus Classical Liberal Political Economy', *Res Publica*, 1,1, 1995.
Machan Tibor, 'Does Libertarianism Imply the Welfare State?' *Res Publica*, Vol. III, Number 2, 1997, pp131-48.
MacIntyre Alasdair, *After Virtue*, Second Edition, Duckworth, London, 1985.
MacIntyre Alasdair, *Whose Justice? Which Rationality?* University of Notre Dame Press, Notre Dame, 1988.
MacIntyre Alasdair, 'The spectre of communitarianism', *Radical Philosophy*, 70, 1995, pp34-7.
MacPherson C. B., *The Political Theory of Possessive Individualism*, Oxford University Press, Oxford, 1964.
McCloskey H.J., *John Stuart Mill: A Critical Study*, Macmillan, London, 1971.

Meadowcroft J. (ed) *Hobhouse; Liberalism and other Writings*, Cambridge University Press, Cambridge, 1994.

Mendus Susan, *Toleration and the Limits of Liberalism*, Macmillan, Basingstoke, 1989.

Mill John Stuart, *Principles of Political Economy*, First Edition, London, 1848.

Mill John Stuart, *A System of Logic*, Longman's, Green and Co., London, 1900.

Mill John Stuart, *Utilitarianism, On Liberty and Essay on Bentham*, edited and introduced by Mary Warnock, Fontana, London, 1962.

Mill John Stuart, *Collected Works*, J.M. Robson (ed) University of Toronto Press, Routledge, Toronto and London, 1963-91.

Mill John Stuart, *On Liberty*, Penguin, Harmondsworth, 1974.

Mill John Stuart, 'M. de Tocqueville on Democracy in America', in Geraint L. Williams (ed) *John Stuart Mill on Politics and Society*, Fontana/Collins, Glasgow, 1976.

Mill John Stuart, *Utilitarianism, On Liberty and Considerations on Representative Government*, Everyman, London, 1984.

Mill John Stuart, *On Socialism*, Prometheus Books, Buffalo, 1987.

Mill John Stuart, *Autobiography*, Penguin, Harmondsworth, 1989.

Mill, John Stuart, *Three Essays on Religion*, Prometheus Books, Buffalo, 1998.

Minogue Kenneth, *The Liberal Mind*, Methuen, London, 1963.

Morales Helen, *Perfect Equality: John Stuart Mill on Well-constituted Communities*, Rowman and Littlefield, London, 1996.

Morley John, *On Compromise*, London, 1886.

Mulhall Stephen and Swift Adam, *Liberals and Communitarians*, Second Edition, Blackwell, Oxford, 1997.

Nozick Robert, *Anarchy, State, and Utopia*, Blackwell, Oxford, 1974.

Oakeshott Michael, 'The Claims of Politics', *Scrutiny* 8, 1939-1940, pp146-51.

Oakeshott Michael, 'The Masses in Representative Democracy', in A.Hunold (ed) *Freedom and Serfdom: An Anthology of Western Thought*, Reidel, Dordrecht, Holland, 1961.

Oakeshott Michael, *Rationalism in Politics and Other Essays*, Methuen, London, 1962.

Oakeshott Michael, 'Talking Politics', *The National Review* 27, Dec 5, 1975, pp1426-27.

Oakeshott Michael, *On Human Conduct*, Clarendon Press, Oxford, 1975.

Oakeshott Michael, *Morality and Politics in Modern Europe*, Yale University Press, New Haven and London, 1993.

Pangle Thomas L., *The Ennobling of Democracy*, Johns Hopkins University Press, Baltimore, 1992.

Parekh Bhikhu, 'The Cultural Particularity of Liberal Democracy', *Political Studies*, 1992, XL, Special Issue, pp160-75.

Parekh Bhikhu, 'The Rushdie Affair: A Research Agenda for Political Philosophy', in Kymlicka (ed) *The Rights of Minority Cultures*, Oxford University Press, Oxford, 1995.

Pelczynski Zbigniew and Gray John (eds) *Conceptions of Liberty in Political Philosophy*, The Athlone Press, London 1984.

Rawls John, *A Theory of Justice*, Oxford University Press, Oxford, 1972.

Rawls John, *Political Liberalism*, Columbia University Press, 1996.

Rayner Jeremy, 'The Legend of Oakeshott's Conservatism: Sceptical Philosophy and Limited Politics', *Canadian Journal of Political Science*, XVIII:2, June 1985, pp313-38.

Raz Joseph, 'Multiculturalism: A Liberal Perspective', *Dissent*, Winter 1994, pp67-79.

Reiman Jeffrey, *Critical Moral Liberalism: Theory and Practice*, Rowman and Littlefield Publishers Inc., Lanham, Maryland, USA, 1997.

Richter Melvin, *The Politics of Conscience: T. H. Green and his Age*, Thoemmes Press, Bristol, 1996.

Riley Jonathan, 'J.S. Mill's Liberal Utilitarian Assessment of Capitalism Versus Socialism', *Utilitas* 8, pp39-71.

Riley Jonathan, 'Mill on Justice', in D. Boucher and P. Kelly (eds) *Social Justice*, Routledge, London, 1997.

Riley Jonathan, *Mill on Liberty*, Routledge, London, 1998.

Robson John (ed) *The Collected Works of John Stuart Mill*, University of Toronto Press, Routledge, Toronto and London, 1963-91.

Robson John, *The Improvement of Mankind: The Social and Political Thought of John Stuart Mill*, The University of Toronto Press, Toronto, 1968.

Robson John, 'Civilization and Culture as Moral Concepts', in John Skorupski (ed) *The Cambridge Companion to Mill*, Cambridge University Press, Cambridge, 1998.

Rorty Richard, *Philosophy and the Mirror of Nature*, Princeton University Press, Princeton, 1980.

Rorty Richard, 'Post Modernist Bourgeois Liberalism', *The Journal of Philosophy* 80, 1983, pp383-9.

Rorty Richard, *Contingency, Irony and Solidarity*, Cambridge University Press, Cambridge, 1989.

Rorty Richard, *Objectivity, Relativism and Truth*, Cambridge University Press, Cambridge, 1991.

Rorty Richard, *Achieving Our Country: Leftist Thought in Twentieth-Century America*, Harvard University Press, Cambridge, Massachusetts, 1998.

Ryan Alan, *John Stuart Mill*, Second Edition, Macmillan, London,1987.

Ryan Alan, 'Mill in a liberal landscape', in John Skorupski (ed) *The Cambridge Companion to Mill*, Cambridge University Press, Cambridge, 1998.

Sandel Michael, *Liberalism and the Limits of Justice*, Cambridge University Press, Cambridge, 1982.

Sandel Michael, 'The Procedural Republic and the Unencumbered Self', *Political Theory*, 12, February 1984

Scruton Roger, *The Meaning of Conservatism*, Second Edition, Macmillan, Basingstoke, 1984.

Scruton Roger (ed) *Conservative Thinkers: Essays from the Salisbury Review*, The Claridge Press, London 1988.

Selbourne David, *The Principle of Duty*, Sinclair-Stevenson, London,1994.

Seligman Adam B., *The Idea of Civil Society*, Princeton University Press, Princeton, 1992.

Shearmur Jeremy, *Hayekian Liberalism as a Research Programme*, Routledge, London, 1996.

Shklar Judith N., *Ordinary Vices*, Harvard/Belknap, Cambridge, Massachusetts, 1984.

Skorupski John (ed) *The Cambridge Companion to Mill*, Cambridge University Press, Cambridge, 1998.

Smart J. J. C. and Williams Bernard, *Utilitarianism For & Against*, Cambridge University Press, Cambridge, 1973.

Smiles Samuel, *Self Help*, London, 1859.

Smiles Samuel, *Character*, London, 1871.

Smiles Samuel, *Thrift*, London, 1876.

Smiles Samuel, *Duty*, London, 1880.

Strauss Leo, *The Political Philosophy of Hobbes*, University of Chicago Press, Chicago,1984.

Taylor Charles, *Sources of the Self*, Cambridge University Press, Cambridge, 1992.

Taylor Charles, 'Atomism', in S. Avineri and A. de-Shalit (eds) *Communitarianism and Individualism*, Oxford University Press, Oxford, 1992.

Ten C.L., *Mill on Liberty*, Clarendon Press, Oxford, 1980.

Ten C.L., 'Mill's Place in Liberalism', *The Political Science Reviewer* 24, 1995, pp179-204.

Ten C.L., 'Democracy, socialism and the working classes', in John Skorupski (ed) *The Cambridge Companion to Mill*, Cambridge University Press, Cambridge, 1998.

Thomas William, *Mill*, Oxford University Press, Oxford, 1985.

Urmson J.O., 'The Interpretation of the Moral Philosophy of John Stuart Mill', in Philippa Foot (ed) *Theories of Ethics*, Oxford University Press, Oxford, 1967.

Walzer Michael, 'Philosophy and Democracy' *Political Theory* 9, 1981, pp379-99.

Walzer Michael, *Spheres of Justice*, Blackwell, Oxford, 1983.

Warnock Mary (ed) John Stuart Mill, *Utilitarianism, On Liberty and Essay on Bentham*, Fontana, London, 1962.

Wheaton Bernard and Kavan Zdenek, *The Velvet Revolution*, Westview, Oxford, 1992.

Williams Geraint L. (ed) *John Stuart Mill on Politics and Society*, Fontana/Collins, Glasgow, 1976.

Williams Howard, *Kant's Political Philosophy*, Blackwell, Oxford, 1983.

Wolff Jonathan, *Robert Nozick: Property, Justice and the Minimal State*, Polity Press, Cambridge, 1991.